T5-ANW-013

CANADA AND THE UNITED NATIONS

RETHINKING CANADA IN THE WORLD

Series editors: Ian McKay and Sean Mills

Supported by the Wilson Institute for Canadian History at McMaster University, this series is committed to books that rethink Canadian history from transnational and global perspectives. It enlarges approaches to the study of Canada in the world by exploring how Canadian history has long been a dynamic product of global currents and forces. The series will also reinvigorate understanding of Canada's role as an international actor and how Canadians have contributed to intellectual, political, cultural, social, and material exchanges around the world.

Volumes included in the series explore the ideas, movements, people, and institutions that have transcended political boundaries and territories to shape Canadian society and the state. These include both state and non-state actors, and phenomena such as international migration, diaspora politics, religious movements, evolving conceptions of human rights and civil society, popular culture, technology, epidemics, wars, and global finance and trade.

The series charts a new direction by exploring networks of transmission and exchange from a standpoint that is not solely national or international, expanding the history of Canada's engagement with the world.

http://wilson.humanities.mcmaster.ca

1 Canada and the United Nations
Legacies, Limits, Prospects
Edited by Colin McCullough and Robert Teigrob

Canada and the United Nations

Legacies, Limits, Prospects

Edited by

COLIN McCULLOUGH AND ROBERT TEIGROB

Foreword by Lloyd Axworthy

McGill-Queen's University Press
Montreal & Kingston • London • Chicago

BRESCIA UNIVERSITY
COLLEGE LIBRARY

© McGill-Queen's University Press 2016

ISBN 978-0-7735-4824-4 (cloth)
ISBN 978-0-7735-4825-1 (paper)
ISBN 978-0-7735-9998-7 (ePDF)
ISBN 978-0-7735-9999-4 (ePUB)

Legal deposit fourth quarter 2016
Bibliothèque nationale du Québec

Printed in Canada on acid-free paper that is 100% ancient forest free
(100% post-consumer recycled), processed chlorine free

McGill-Queen's University Press acknowledges the support of the Canada
Council for the Arts for our publishing program. We also acknowledge the
financial support of the Government of Canada through the Canada Book
Fund for our publishing activities.

Library and Archives Canada Cataloguing in Publication

Canada and the United Nations (Montréal, Québec)
  Canada and the United Nations: legacies, limits, prospects/
  edited by Colin McCullough and Robert Teigrob.

(Rethinking Canada in the world; 1)
Includes bibliographical references and index.
Issued in print and electronic formats.
ISBN 978-0-7735-4824-4 (cloth). – ISBN 978-0-7735-4825-1 (paper). –
ISBN 978-0-7735-9998-7 (ePDF). – ISBN 978-0-7735-9999-4 (ePUB)

  1. United Nations – Canada. 2. Internationalism. 3. Canada – Foreign
relations. I. McCullough, Colin, 1982–, author, editor II. Teigrob, Robert,
1966–, editor III. Title. IV. Series: Rethinking Canada in the world; 1

JZ4997.5.C3C35 2017   341.23'71   C2016-905368-7
                                            C2016-905369-5

This book was typeset by Marquis Interscript in 10.5/13 Sabon.

Contents

Figures

Acknowledgments

COLIN McCULLOUGH

I am grateful, first and foremost, for the love and support that Lee Slinger offers me on a daily basis. She believed in this project and encouraged me to see what would happen if I reached out to a group of scholars and civil servants across the country who I respected and who I hoped would be interested in talking about Canada's relationship to the UN. Robert Teigrob has been a wonderful colleague and coeditor, and his passion for scholarship has made this a far superior collection than it could have been otherwise. Our contributors were also attentive, engaged, and encouraging throughout this process. I would especially like to thank Kim Nossal for his sage advice and his belief in this project.

McGill-Queen's University Press has given us a great deal of care as this project crystallized. Jonathan Crago reached out to us and believed that what we had was a project with a great deal of potential. Shelagh Plunkett has steered the collection through the last stages of production and made sure that everything looked great. Everyone else who helped this book become a reality has my thanks as well.

This project also would not have been possible without the support of the Wilson Institute for Canadian History at McMaster University. Its former chair, Viv Nelles, felt that Canada's relationship to the UN was a valuable topic that could bring scholarly, civil servant, and civil society voices together, and we hope this volume is a proud part of his legacy there. The current chair, Ian McKay, has been a valued ally of this project from before his appointment onward.

ROBERT TEIGROB

Foremost thanks to my friend and colleague Colin McCullough, who conceived of the June 2015 "UN at 70" conference that led to this collection, invited me along for the ride, and performed the bulk of the organizational work that made our gathering such a resounding success. The members of the United Nations Association in Canada who attended the conference enriched both our discussions and the book chapters that follow. The people at the Wilson Centre for Canadian History were generous with their time and funding, and Ian McKay deserves special thanks for initiating the Rethinking Canada in the World series and making this compilation its inaugural volume. I second Colin's commendation of Jonathan Crago and all of the delightful and capable folks at McGill-Queen's, and of Shelagh Plunkett, who delivered timely and expert copy editing. Ryerson University's Faculty of Arts awarded a grant for indexing, and Stefan Fergus provided that service with characteristic professionalism. Finally, ominous warnings that one should never volunteer to herd a multiauthor compilation to print proved groundless, at least among this collection of writers: each delivered first-rate and speedy contributions and responses at every stage of the process, and it was an unalloyed pleasure to collaborate with and get to know them. Cheers to you all.

Foreword

Lloyd Axworthy

I was recently asked by an interviewer about a turning point in my early life that led to my involvement in global matters. I thought back to when I was a senior in high school in the North End of Winnipeg. Our history teacher had assigned a class project visiting the downtown Civic Auditorium to listen to a Canadian who had just won the Nobel Peace Prize for having invented the notion of UN peacekeeping, an initiative that greatly helped in the settlement of the Suez Canal conflict in 1956.

While I didn't understand it at the time, it was a defining moment. The man on the stage with the polka dot bow tie was Lester Pearson setting out a new framework of international cooperation based on the United Nations, an idea inspiring to this student at the time and far reaching for the determination of Canada's role in the world.

As the previous world war had shown, issues even then had become global in scope and impact. The risk to people had become horrendous, as the Holocaust bore witness. There was an overpowering need to build war-torn economies, rid the shackles of colonialism, and begin shaping a system of human rights. This would require extraordinary commitment from the members of the newly formed United Nations, and it was Pearson's belief that Canadians had a special role to play in providing leadership in shaping the UN as a peacemaking, global agency. It became a foundation for Canadian foreign policy over the intervening decades, until the early years of the new millennium, the post-9/11 years.

The Conservative government that came to power in 2006 clearly signalled their indifference if not outright disdain towards the UN. They took little interest in its proceedings, and downgraded peacekeeping to the point that our armed forces were no longer trained in the practice of peacekeeping. Our foreign assistance to Africa was virtually eliminated. There was pushback on the issue of international indigenous rights. This detachment was widely noticed and Canada paid a price. Our comeuppance was the failure to win a coveted seat on the Security Council.

That is now about to change. The new government of Justin Trudeau has signalled that they are ready to reengage.

It comes at a propitious time. The UN is in a political uptick. In the past several months the world institution has sponsored and hosted international initiatives that have resulted in agreement on a new set of international sustainable development goals, major reforms in transparency and governance leading to an open process for choosing the next Secretary General, peacekeeping overhauls and interventions in several countries to deter acts of genocide and ethnic conflicts, tough new Security Council financial sanctions against ISIS and North Korea, and the climate change summit in Paris that brought together 183 countries agreeing on a new platform to tackle perhaps the most significant global risk, and is now playing a useful and enabling role in negotiating a Syrian ceasefire.

Inherent in these UN initiatives and events has been the willingness of countries and leaders to find consensus on crucial issues that span the globe. It didn't need major restructuring of international architecture. It's been an interesting process of reform of existing institutions and practices and a renewed realization that sovereignty of states is not an immutable, rigid principle but one where nation-states can accommodate and can live by tenets of rights and the rule of law. Here are the optimistic words of Achim Steiner, head of UNEP, in speaking to the board of CUSO: "Collective, multilateral action is being rebooted, foreshadowing the beginning of a new era." Giving substance to his words, he set out his plans for a new UN Assembly of Environmental Governance.

This is not to suggest that all is well with the world or the UN. Conflicts and war still victimize hundreds of thousands of the most vulnerable of people. The inequality gap widens. Natural disasters and pandemics call for resources far beyond the present financial capacity. There will have to be significant action on controlling emissions and insuring adaptation to the negative impacts of climate change already underway. The growing reality of the broad scale global migration of people from homelands beset by violence, drought, and oppression calls for an extensive global, collaborative effort. The threat of terrorism must be met with a full court press. No one would underestimate the scope and magnitude of the problems.

In counterpoint, however, there is the growing recognition of the need to meet the issues and to do so together. This will demand the reform of the institution and its practices. A new UN narrative is called for.

And that is what is significant about the meeting at McMaster University that provided the place and platform for these papers to be presented. It's a signpost in setting out a pathway that has been little travelled by scholars in recent years but now needs heavy traffic. There are a host of serious issues needing good research and academic attention. What to do about the veto on UN actions to protect people. The unrepresentative nature of the Security Council institution. How the technology of information can be employed to increase participation. The yet-undetermined ways and means of enforcing the SDGs and carbon emissions. The ever-growing demand, often unmet for humanitarian assistance (a recent estimate for 2016 indicates $20 billion US to support eighty-seven million people spread over thirty-seven countries).

Peacekeeping is an increasingly more complicated task than it was in Pearson's day. In fact the UN is in one of its most active peacekeeping periods with more than 120,000 troops and a budget of eight and one-half billion dollars. The UN peacekeepers are helping to stop or reduce the level of violence in a number of areas, often calling on robust use of arms. There are currently sixteen UN peacekeeping operations being conducted across four continents.

One of the real issues in mounting effective peacekeeping missions is finding sufficient, well-trained militaries. Western democracies are the most reluctant participants. It is generally true that democratic Western governments are leery of putting "boots on the ground" in fear of a public backlash. It's time for a new peacekeeping formula – a UN-specific standby force must be one of the next major areas of reform to be debated. It's an exceedingly difficult political issue to tackle and needs serious inquiry and invention, setting out a new direction for the UN.

One would think this is an area where Canada in its commitment to return to UN duty would excel, but, as professor Walter Dorn of the Canadian Military College has pointed out in a recent report:

The loss of CAF experience in the field since 2005 carries a high price. The Canadian Forces, which once deployed in large numbers, now has little peacekeeping experience on which to base its contributions to UN PKOs. The methods, standards, numbers and doctrines of the United Nations have all evolved considerably over the past decade as the UN experienced the surge of the new century but Canada has not kept up.

This is true in a number of fields important to the UN; Canada will have to play a catch-up game. All the more reason why this symposium and the papers arising from its work should be the forerunner of a much more energetic and comprehensive treatment of the role Canada should play in the politics, operation, and reform of the UN.

CANADA AND THE UNITED NATIONS

The Politics of Getting Along

Canada's First Seventy Years in the United Nations

Robert Teigrob and Colin McCullough

By the fall of 2012, most observers of Canada's rapport with the United Nations had developed a fairly accurate estimate of the ruling Conservative Party's regard for the international body. To the few who harboured any haziness on the matter in the wake of seven years of Tory rule, Canadian minister of foreign affairs John Baird offered a helpful primer in the form of a 1 October address to the UN General Assembly. Less a typical diplomatic address than a paternalistic lashing, Baird's speech accused the globe's paramount organization of "spend[ing] too much time on itself," of "endless, fruitless, inward-looking exercises," of coasting on "best efforts" and "good intentions." The from-the-mountaintop aura of the rebuke was only enhanced by the Canadian minister's Jeremiah-worthy forewarnings to those who would defy his message: Baird insisted that the UN must impose immediate economic sanctions against the Syrian regime of Bashar al-Assad – at that moment engaged in a bitter civil conflict against a confusing array of little-known rebel groups – in order to "stem the crimson tide of this bloody assault. Until the last syllable of recorded time," Baird intoned balefully, "the world will remember and history will judge Member States that are allowing atrocities to continue."[1]

A relatively short span of temporal syllables after Baird unleashed his verbal bombs, the Royal Canadian Air Force was dropping real bombs on some of those same anti-Assad rebels, by now internationally renowned and reviled as the sadistic warriors of the "Islamic

State" and its various aliases; the Canadian sorties served to effectively, though unofficially, shore up the fortunes of the hated al-Assad government. The affair is illustrative of a number of important truths, perhaps chief among them the notions that successful mediation of conflicts between and within states is often unfathomably complex, and that pious prognostications about faraway and evolving events should thus be leavened with a measure of humility. Accordingly, deliberations marked by caution, patience, bridge-building, and oratorical deescalation – what in other contexts Baird scorned as "gabfests" held before the "altar of compromise and consensus" – might represent a surer path to progress.[2] "Going along to get along," another of Baird's straw man caricatures of multilateralist praxis, at least carries the prospect of "getting along"; the Canadian minister's lone wolf routine, conversely, yielded few tangible results save for landing foreign affairs Canada in the unfamiliar role of ambassadorial *persona non grata*.[3]

Those interested in Canada's place in the world would also find in Baird's 1 October dressing down a distillation of some of the core elements of the past decade of UN-Canadian affairs. While the Harperites' disposition toward global governance and Canada's legacy of international mediation counted both fervent backers and detractors, analysts sat in accord on the basic elements of that temperament: a penchant for drawing stark distinctions between the virtuous and the iniquitous (for instance, Ukrainians and Israelis blameless, their antagonists the Russians and Palestinians wholly culpable); by extension, a desire to line up opinion and policy against the designated offender rather than broker a mutually suitable and potentially face-saving bargain (e.g., in the case of Iran and its nuclear ambitions); a habit of bolting from committees, conferences, and even countries overseen by ideological foes (Iran again; the UN Conference on Disarmament after North Korea assumed the rotating presidency; the 2013 Commonwealth Summit, hosted in autocratic Sri Lanka); an effort to constrain those members of Canadian civil society who might frustrate the Conservative's foreign aims (through defunding, the rescinding of charitable status, and targeted Canada Revenue Agency audits); an emphasis on tightly controlling the government's message by giving its diplomats scripts rather than the freedom to exercise personal discretion.[4] The censored foreign service bureaucrats summed up the new directives thusly: "Do nothing without instructions. Do not expect instructions."[5]

On some matters, as even supporters must concede, the Harper regime's posture appeared more than a little contradictory: despite frequent assurances that a "principled foreign policy" served as the unstinting watchword for Canada's global dealings, the Conservatives issued a concurrent directive that economic self-interest govern the allocation of foreign aid. They then informed the UN that the Canadian government's duty to safeguard human rights did not extend to monitoring the nation's corporations overseas. (The sigh of relief from Canadian mining interests, in particular, was tangible.) Likewise, Harper exhibited few scruples in conducting trade with such human rights-phobic regimes as China and Saudi Arabia, brokering a deal with the latter to sell $15 billion worth of military equipment that may well be deployed to burnish the House of Saud's reputation for brutalizing its own people.[6] And alongside the Conservatives' insistence that the UN act immediately and decisively to punish violators of the organization's edicts and principles (Assad, e.g.), the same government relied upon the sheltering moat of Westphalian sovereignty when it found itself at odds with the strictures of international law. The delivery of real and perceived enemies to the notorious torture chambers of the Afghan judicial system provided one instance, while bombing campaigns conducted on Libyan and Syrian territory without UN authorization offered another. A third involved the utter disregard, from day one of the Conservative Party's mandate, for the legally binding Kyoto Protocol. Canada subsequently withdrew from the pact altogether, a move that placed the nation in league with Andorra, South Sudan, and the United States as the only nonsignatories of the agreement; the extraordinary and unprecedented withdrawal itself placed Canada, on that score at least, in a league of its own.[7]

The wisdom and efficacy of this constellation of acts and attitudes will be assessed for years to come, although the Canadian government's failure in 2010 to gain a seat on the Security Council, a first after six successful campaigns for the post, provided some indication of the rest of the world's verdict on the approach. What the contributors to this collection of essays on the history of the Canada-UN relationship can say without equivocation, on the other hand, is that the style and substance of the Harper government's international agenda represented a sharp pivot from previous federal policy and from past *and* contemporary Canadians' attitudes toward internationalism and the UN. In other words, Baird's avowal in a 2014 interview that his government stood firmly within the tradition of Canadian internationalism and that it faithfully "promote[d] Canadian values," does not stand up to basic standards of evidence.[8]

This volume emerged from a conference entitled *The UN at 70: A Canadian Perspective* held at the Wilson Institute for Canadian History at Hamilton's McMaster University in June 2015. As the conference's organizers, we hoped that this anniversary would inspire a broad range of Canadians to consider their nation's past, current, and future standing in the postwar system of global governance. Happily, our call for presenters and attendees yielded a sizeable and enthusiastic gathering. Presenters included influential members of the academy, civil society, and Canada's Department of Foreign Affairs and International Trade; their papers examined the legacies and prospects surrounding this country's interactions with multilateralism, global governance, and international law. Audience members provided informed and engaging queries and commentary; in addition to the academics, students, and members of the public in attendance, we were pleased to welcome guests from the United Nations Association in Canada, who timed their annual meeting to coincide with our conference.

Although our panellists gave varying grades to Canada's historic contributions to UN-related initiatives and to the effectiveness of the UN as a whole, their presentations were united in viewing the Harper government's policy toward internationalism and the world body as something new, as a wilful dismantling of Canada's legacy of peacekeeping, multilateralist internationalism, and UN leadership. As these essays make clear, Canadians within and beyond government of virtually every political alignment, region, and ethnocultural identity have for generations comprised some of the UN's most committed champions. They have demonstrated a relatively consistent faith in the ideas of global governance, mediation, constructive engagement, and consensus building. They have looked to the UN as a bulwark against undue US dominance and as a means of enhancing Canada's international status, and have pointed to their multilingual and multicultural nation as a working model for productive international collaboration. Many Canadians have anointed the organization as the world's best hope to redress a range of dilemmas including poverty, inequality, environmental degradation, hunger, disease, racism, and imperialism. Accusations that the UN is inert and ineffective, in other words, represent only a fraction of the range of Canadians' views about the organization; moreover, the bulk of these accusations have been directed at the UN's inability to broker and maintain peace as opposed to its wider humanitarian agenda. At the same time, detractors habitually undervalued the undeniable contributions the organization *has* made to curbing international violence. British historian and essayist Tony Judt is surely correct to observe that "the world would be a decidedly nastier place" without it.[9]

Of course, Canadians' identification with the UN and liberal internationalism had distinct limits and was never static or monolithic. Canada was decidedly *un*neutral during the Cold War, even as the country strove, with some success, to carve out a role as an intermediary. And while the Harper government exhibited an unprecedented apathy toward the conciliatory activities of the UN, Canada's standing as the globe's peacekeeping luminary had been tempered by post-Cold War contributions to military operations in Iraq (1991), Kosovo (1999), and Afghanistan (2001–11), along with a coincident decrease in troop commitments to peacekeeping missions. Fondness for the UN has ebbed and flowed according to the perceptions of the organization's effectiveness, transparency, and financial prudence, as well as calculations of how its collective international initiatives might influence Canada's economy, unity, and sovereignty. Doubts have arisen, too, regarding the influence that a small nation like Canada could exercise in the world at large and as part of an organization that represented powerful interests not necessarily in accord those of the nation. At the same time, most Canadians were never naïve enough to expect that the UN would usher in a millennium entirely free from want and fear and recognized that the world body, like all organizations, reflected flaws inherent to humanity as a whole. In his address to "UN at 70" conference attendees, Canadian historian and former diplomat John English summed up this pragmatic sensibility by invoking former Secretary General Dag Hammarskjöld's famous maxim: "The United Nations was not created to bring us to heaven, but in order to save us from hell."

We organized our conference panels around broad themes: 1) Canada's historic – and generally productive and progressive – relationship with the world body; 2) civil society, "ordinary Canadians" and the UN; and 3) Canada's present and future with the organization. Taken as a whole, the panellists painted the UN as an imperfect yet indispensable agent of global governance and an

agency that both reflected and shaped high-minded Canadian attitudes to the world beyond its borders. As such, the essays that grew
out of our meeting serve as a log for the nature and evolution of
Canadian internationalism and a counterpoint to the Harper government's combination of indifference and hostility to an international regime that Canada had done so much to shape. Our hope is
that readers will be reminded that the nation has made an immense
contribution to the evolution of global governance, justice, and rec-
onciliation and that Canadians have habitually identified closely
with the world body and held it in high regard. As a corollary, these
essays indicate that the more recent emphasis on Canada's identity as
a "warrior nation" represents a distortion of history, not to mention
a blind alley for a minor military power like Canada.

This volume fills a void in academic and popular assessments of
Canada's relationship with the UN. While Adam Chapnick's *The
Middle Power Project* (2005) told the story of the founding of the
world body and a handful of authors have tackled Canada's contributions to specific peacekeeping missions and UN agencies, there has
been no general, comprehensive look at this relationship since
1956.[10] In the 1960s, a number of works by political scientists such
as James Eayrs and Donald Gordon and historians such as J.L.
Granatstein evaluated Canada's association with the UN in light of
its failures to find permanent peaceful solutions to the world's problems.[11] Most of these works were published by or emerged out of
conferences held by the Canadian Institute of International Affairs.
Such works tended to focus on more "traditional" subjects of
Canadian foreign policy, namely who made policy and how it was
implemented. Government reports and diplomatic records formed
the bulk of the sources used in these works, and, while excellent
accounts of official policy, they provided little discussion of nongovernmental interactions with the UN.

The Department of External Affairs published its own account of
the Canadian involvement with the UN in 1966; this was a history of
the work being done by the government in the areas of peace, security, and disarmament; equal rights and the self-determination of
peoples; economic, social and humanitarian cooperation; and how
the UN was a "centre for harmonizing the actions of nations."[12]
While it covered many topics, this book was designed to be a com-
pact survey of Canada's participation in UN activities and to moti-
vate future engagement with that organization. As governmental

interest in peacekeeping declined during the Pierre Trudeau years, so did the work of political scientists and military historians.[13]

Renewed scholarly work on Canadian internationalism has appeared since the waning years of the Cold War, when Canadian governmental interest in the UN was rekindled. These studies continued to focus primarily on peacekeeping, but the Canadian association with the UN was considered, by that time, to be a "traditional" part of the country's international policy.[14] Colin McCullough, a coeditor of and contributor to this collection, examines Canadian attitudes towards peacekeeping in *Creating Canada's Peacekeeping Past* (2016), and many of his conclusions are borne out in the chapters that follow. However, he takes his province to be the Canadian affinity for peacekeeping, which omits the multitude of other manners in which Canadians participated at the UN. Granatstein, surely Canada's most prolific foreign policy scholar, has written extensively about Canada's dealings with the UN, though normally under the larger umbrella of discussing its foreign policies since 1945 or, more recently, in describing "who killed the Canadian military?"[15]

This compilation is also marked by considerable methodological breadth: some contributors focus on the "high politics" of UN-nation-state interactions; others look at the role of nongovernmental actors; several employ cultural and postcolonial analyses to wrestle with such issues as gender, class, and race, approaches that have moved very slowly into assessments of Canadian international relations. Such attention to the social positioning of various citizens and groups broadens our understanding of what internationalism meant to a wider range of Canadians, even as it reinforces the fact that – owing to factors like education levels, social connections, resources, and leisure time – the majority of those who interacted formally with the world body remained Anglo elites, male and female.

This collection begins with David MacKenzie's history of Canadian internationalism in the years before the creation of the world body. The author considers enthusiasm for the UN a logical outgrowth of the country's longstanding inclination to seek out a range of international partners rather than struggle for parity in relations with their far more powerful American and British counterparts. Somewhat paradoxically, then, sacrificing a measure of autonomy to international organizations served to enhance Canadian sovereignty and international recognition; the embrace of internationalism also reflected a growing worldwide inclination towards rules-based integration that continues to this day. Canadians of the interwar era sometimes cooled their enthusiasm for a project that could embroil them in foreign conflicts and undercut national unity and over which they often had little control. Nevertheless, the author maintains that the realities of a world "increasingly expressed through the UN system and international organizations in general" mean that "[n]ow is not the time to withdraw; indeed, it is more important than ever to embrace Canada's long history of involvement in international organizations."

In her essay on the use of propaganda films by the United Nations Relief and Rehabilitation Administration (1943–47), Suzanne Langlois confirms the growing enthusiasm for liberal internationalism among Canadians even before the official founding of the UN. Recognizing the role film had played in moulding public opinion in totalitarian states and lacking the resources to assemble their own film section, UNRRA relied instead on productions from existing companies in Britain, the United States, and Canada. The latter's National Film Board assumed a leading role, distributing thousands of prints of UNRRA-approved productions to Canadian cinemas and nearly every corner of the world. The NFB works in particular took pains to rise above partisanship and moralizing, insisting that communists, too, deserved both respect and provisions. As a whole, the film project sought to broadcast three basic messages: to North Americans, the unfathomable destitution facing populations in war zones; to the war's victims, the benefits of liberal democracy; and to both, the urgent need for world amity, cooperation, and governance. Langlois writes that the UNRRA effort "created an unusual long-distance visual dialogue between local audiences and the diverse people receiving aid," positioning both the UN and postwar Canada as champions of internationalism and trusted agents of humanitarian aid.

While the new world body's social and political initiatives drew applause, its political (in)actions often did not. The ink was barely dry on the UN Charter before Cold War bipolarity effectively thwarted the Security Council's ability to punish aggressor states. But as David Webster writes, Canadians of the era continued to focus on the organization's strengths rather than bemoan its limitations, pouring themselves into UN efforts to lessen global economic disparities. Drawing on models developed to assist their own country's underprivileged, Canadians played central roles in technical assistance and development efforts; here, the nation's bilingualism, absence of colonial holdings, and reputation for impartiality made Canadian operatives among the most trusted liaisons between the industrialized world and the Global South. Many of these development efforts were welcomed, but Western representatives also displayed vestiges of the paternalism endemic to traditional imperialism and sought to implement a one-size-fits-all model of liberal internationalism irrespective of local variables. And while magnanimity surely motivated these efforts, so too did economic self-interest and the desire to preempt any Third World gains by the Soviets. The latter, however, points to a recurring theme: Canadian understandings of internationalism habitually linked the nation's security with the well-being of those abroad.

Tarah Brookfield's study of the Canadian branch of the United Nations Association reveals how deeply this dedication to liberal internationalism ran among many average Canadians. Traumatized by two global conflicts and the prospect of nuclear war, Canada's UNA members held that a dedication to internationalism formed the basis of any sane expression of Canadian nationalism. The organization sought to encourage global fealties by hosting events celebrating Canada's many ethnocultural groups – long before the advent of official multiculturalism – and by anticipating Lester Pearson's call for an international peacekeeping force by nearly a decade. The UNA also provided a rare and mostly welcoming outlet for women concerned about international matters, and owing to the group's nonconfrontational approach and "respectable" middle- and upper-class membership, a platform for promoting peace and internationalism largely immune to the era's reflexive "fifth-column" smears. While official membership rolls remained small, Brookfield argues that the media's warm treatment of the branch, along with the general public's generous contributions to programs like UNICEF, provide a fuller measure of the country's attachments to both the UN and foreign peoples.

Colin McCullough's chapter reaffirms this general Canadian disposition, demonstrating the broad, nonpartisan consensus in support of UN peacekeeping that marked the latter half of the twentieth century. In political speeches, high-school textbooks, letters-to-the-editor, and opinion polls, a plurality of citizens viewed participation in peace operations as a balm for a range of concerns: their own nation's global stature, the historic foreign policy rift between the nation's "two solitudes," the human suffering bred by warfare – even as a practical model for diffusing day-to-day schoolyard rows. Here again, citizens linked mediation efforts with the defence of their own country's borders and reputation, reckoning that traditional combat missions would create foreign enemies and harm future peace brokering. Citizens could also employ peacekeeping as alleged confirmation of their moral superiority and sometimes demonstrated an inflated view of their nation's UN role and achievements; the near-beatification of Lester Pearson speaks to both of these inclinations. Neither of these less flattering tendencies, on the other hand, undermines McCullough's core thesis that peacekeeping served as a fundamental lodestone of postwar Canadian unity and identity, as a kind of shorthand for definitions of the nation's internationalist ethos.

UN member states are often accused of using the international forum to advance narrow national interests, and Canada is certainly not immune from this charge. At the same time, as Kim Nossal argues in this volume, Canadian leaders frequently used speeches at UN plenary sessions to pursue what former diplomat Allan Gotlieb called the "romantic," or idealistic, side of Canadian foreign policy. Nossal borrows the American term "bully pulpit" to characterize Canadian officials' homilies before the General Assembly, but as employed here, the term carries its more venerable and positive connotation as a "superb platform" from which to raise vital issues. For decades, as Nossal explains, Canada's prime ministers and foreign affairs personnel alike have conducted this manner of "pulpit diplomacy" before the General Assembly, be they UN champions (i.e., governments from 1945–2006), or UN cynics (no great mystery, we trust, by this point). And while the champions, too, could use pointed words to demand more of the institution, the country's reputation for international cooperation and principled "honest brokerage" meant that those words translated into to real progress on significant issues. South African apartheid, land mines abolition, "Responsibility to Protect," the International Criminal Court, and environmental protection stand out as files on which significant progress was made and on which Canada gained increasing international regard.

Greg Donaghy's case study of one "romantic" project, the Trudeau government's attempt to broker an ambitious New International Economic Order (NIEO) agreement, outlines that administration's version of a principled foreign policy: namely, one aimed at bridging the vast political and economic disparities inherent to the global

North-South relationship. The prime minister's careful, pragmatic, and consistent engagement with any willing international partners revealed ample measures of realism and idealism, rendering Trudeau what Donaghy terms a "romantic realist." And on key issues the Liberals adopted a stand that was both ethical and decidedly unpopular, shaming others into abandoning their self-interest and uniting behind Canada. To wit, here was consensus building that was roughly the opposite of "going along to get along." However, success on the NIEO file was thwarted by a range of international and domestic complications. Perhaps most frustrating for Trudeau was the mulishness of Canada's own political and bureaucratic elite, who sought to diffuse the prime minister's initiatives through watered down counterproposals and protracted jawing. UN deliberations, disparaged by later critics as mere "gabfests," appeared among the lowest of Trudeau's hurdles and Canadian officials among the keenest gabbers. (Here, it must be admitted that Harper's muzzling of government bureaucrats would have served Trudeau well!) Despite the failure of the NIEO negotiations, Canada's consistent moral leadership on the matter enriched both its reputation and the North-South dialogue, providing the basis for less dramatic, yet important, future gains within and beyond the strictures of the UN.

It was during this same era that some Canadians began raising doubts about the wisdom of their country's substantial commitment to UN peace operations, as Kevin Spooner's chapter explains. The competing, and to some military officials more vital, role in NATO stretched Canadian resources, and as critics like J.L. Granatstein observed, peacekeeping was "a dirty, thankless job" (a statement that, while true enough, does not necessarily invalidate the effort and indeed points to a degree of laudable altruism inherent to the practice). Over the next decades, opposition to "blue-helmet" operations expanded, fuelled by a combination of economic uncertainty, the 1990s resurgence of NATO, and ineffective and/or botched UN operations – most infamously, the sickening behaviour of Canadian peacekeepers in Somalia. To a certain extent, then, Harper simply applied the *coup de grâce* to a waning tradition, and as Spooner observes, the prime minister was at the very least more forthright than his two Liberal predecessors in squaring the rhetoric and practice of Canadian peacekeeping. As the author points out, however, the Chrétien- and Martin-era disengagement from peace operations was not accompanied by a generalized withdrawal from the obligations of global governance. Instead, as Kim Nossal also made clear, Canadian officials of the era took the lead on a host of other pressing, and largely fruitful, UN initiatives. Moreover, Canadians as a whole continue to revel in their reputation as UN peacekeepers. Clearly, this self-image has become increasingly divorced from fact, but it also suggests that future governments invested in a more irenic international bearing need not fear that infuriated mobs will storm Centre Block over any perceived violence deficit in Canadian foreign affairs.

Those who would pan the UN as a failed experiment in dreamy idealism might ask themselves a simple question: what path would the postwar order have taken without it? It is virtually impossible to imagine meaningful and celebrated international initiatives like a worldwide human rights proclamation, a land mines treaty, an international court, a global refugee agency, and a strategy for safeguarding human security without the fulcrum of a supranational organization. (The more immodest of Canadians might also add, with some justification, that their nation was also indispensable in these matters.) In her afterword, Kathryn White argues that it is likewise difficult to imagine that state actors weaned before the altar of power politics and national interests would, on key matters, move so far from political realisms' precepts without pressure from nongovernmental actors. Using the current activities of UNA-Canada as an example, she points to civil society's role as the eyes, ears, and conscience for international policymakers, a job that continues to expand as the result of globalization's facilitation of knowledge gathering and dissemination.

In sum, there exists a distinctive and relatively consistent Canadian bearing toward the UN, one that has evolved and matured since that organization came into being in 1945 and one that allows us to stake out some of the parameters of Canadian internationalism as a whole. Among the country's politicians and diplomats, this bearing has manifested as a readiness to facilitate dialogue between antagonistic parties, to assume the lead on key files, and to remind the world that interests must also accommodate ideals – objectives that various governments pursued for a range of aims, both domestic and international, realistic and "romantic." Among average citizens, the fondness for the international body and liberal internationalism as a whole can be measured by the fact that definitions of prototypical "Canadian-ness" correlate strongly with core UN ideals and activities: namely, an internationalist ethos predicated on inclusivity, mediation, and fair-mindedness, along with an affirmation of the considerable role Canadians have played in the organization's governance and peacekeeping operations. Of course, Canadians' self-image has not always aligned with reality, any more than the UN has always lived up to the lofty expectations articulated by its founders. But in an era whose most prevalent security concerns – international terrorism, an exponential rise in refugees, the upheavals wrought by climate change – are not constrained by borders, to "go it alone" is to willingly embark upon the path of most resistance. Canada's newly elected Liberal government has pledged to restore the more idealistic tenor of Canadian foreign relations (their reluctance to cancel the inherited Saudi arms deal notwithstanding) and to seek a warmer relationship with the world; the degree to which the world will reciprocate after nearly a decade of Canadian disengagement, hostility, and missed opportunities is more difficult to forecast.[16]

NOTES

1 "Address by Minister Baird to United Nations General Assembly, October 1, 2012," Foreign Affairs, Trade and Development Canada, http://www. international.gc.ca/media/aff/speeches-discours/2012/10/01a.aspx?lang= eng, accessed 6 August 2015.

2 First Baird quote cited in Brooke Jeffrey, *Dismantling Canada: Stephen Harper's New Conservative Agenda* (Montreal and Kingston: McGill-Queen's University Press, 2015), 241; second cited in Jeremy Kinsman, "The Legacy of the Honest Broker," *Policy Magazine*, January/February 2014, 14.

3 Baird cited in Campbell Clark, "John Baird's Canada: No Longer Content to 'Go Along Just to Get Along,'" *Globe and Mail*, 10 August 2012. For a small sampling of the vast literature on Canada's diminished status, see Kinsman, "The Legacy"; Jeffrey, *Dismantling Canada*, 366; Fen Hampson and Paul Heinbecker, *Canada Among Nations, 2009–2010: As Others See Us* (Montreal-Kingston: McGill-Queen's University Press, 2009), 378; and Joe Clark, *How We Lead: Canada in a Century of Change* (Toronto: Random House, 2013), chapter 6.

4 For a summary of the contours of Harper's international posture from both supporters and detractors, see *Policy Magazine*'s special issue on the

topic entitled "No More Honest Broker," January/February 2014, http://
policymagazine.ca/january_february_2014.html, accessed 6 August 2015.

5 John Ibbitson, "Stephen Harper: The Making of a Prime Minister," *Globe
and Mail*, 31 July 2015.

6 Mark MacKinnon, "How Harper's Foreign Policy Focus Evolved from
Human Rights to the 'Almighty Dollar,'" *Globe and Mail*, 27 November
2013; Marie-Danielle Smith, "Scathing UN Report a Rallying Cry for Civil
Society, Opposition," *Embassy*, 23 July 2015, http://www.embassynews.
ca/news/2015/07/23/scathing-un-report-a-rallying-cry-for-civil-society-
opposition-parties/47425, accessed 6 August 2015; Steven Zhou,
"Canada's Foreign Policy: Business before Human Rights," *Al Jezeera*,
18 March 2014, http://www.aljazeera.com/indepth/opinion/2014/03/
canada-foreign-policy-business--20143114585 5179629.html, accessed
6 August 2015; Mike Blanchfield, "Ottawa Clashes with UN Human
Rights Panel over Mining Complaints," *Globe and Mail*, 8 July 2014.

7 Damian Carrington and Adam Vaughan, "Canada Condemned at Home
and Abroad for Pulling out of Kyoto Treaty," *The Guardian*, 13 December
2011.

8 "Q&A: A Conversation with John Baird –'We Promote Canadian
Values,'" *Policy Magazine*, January/February 2014, 4, http://policymaga-
zine.ca/pdf/5/articles/PolicyMagazineJanuary-February-BairdQ&A.pdf,
accessed 7 August 2015.

9 Tony Judt, *When the Facts Change: Essays 1995–2010* (New York:
Penguin, 2015), 253.

10 Adam Chapnick, *The Middle Power Project: Canada and the Founding of
the United Nations* (Vancouver: UBC Press, 2005); F.H. Soward and Edgar
McInnis, *Canada and the United Nations* (prepared for the Canadian Insti-
tute of International Affairs and the Carnegie Endowment for International
Peace, New York, 1956). For a sample of works that look at Canada's con-
tribution to various UN agencies and missions, see Department of External
Affairs, *Canadians and the United Nations, 1945–1975* (Ottawa: Minister
of Supply and Services, 1977); Fred Gaffen, *In the Eye of the Storm: A
History of Canadian Peacekeeping* (Toronto: Denau and Wayne, 1987);
Clyde Sanger, ed., *Canadians and the United Nations* (Ottawa: Department
of External Affairs, 1988); Kevin Spooner, *Canada, the Congo Crisis, and
UN Peacekeeping, 1960–64* (Vancouver: UBC Press, 2009); Andrew F.
Cooper, *Tests of Global Governance: Canadian Diplomacy and the United
Nations World Conferences* (Tokyo: UNU Press, 2004); Susan Armstrong-
Reid and David Murray, *Armies of Peace: Canada and the UNRRA Years*
(Toronto: University of Toronto Press, 2008).

11 J.L. Granatstein, ed., *Canadian Foreign Policy since 1945: Middle Power or Satellite?* (Toronto: Copp Clark, 1969); James Eayrs, *Future Roles for the Armed Forces of Canada* (Toronto: Canadian Institute of International Affairs, 1969); A.M. Taylor, David Cox, and J.L. Granatstein, eds., *Peacekeeping: International Challenge and Canadian Response* (Toronto: Canadian Institute of International Affairs, 1968); Stephen Clarkson, ed., *An Independent Foreign Policy for Canada?* (Toronto: McClelland and Stewart, 1968); J. King Gordon, ed., *Canada's Role as a Middle Power* (Toronto: the Canadian Institute of International Affairs, 1966).

12 The Department of External Affairs, *We the Peoples... Canada and the United Nations, 1945–1965* (Ottawa: Queen's Printer, 1966).

13 Eayrs's seminal series *In Defence of Canada*, published in five volumes between 1964 and 1983, contains virtually no mention of peacekeeping. The first three volumes deal with the time period before the inception of peacekeeping in 1956. The final two volumes, *Growing Up Allied* and *Indochina: Roots of Complicity* also fail to mention UN service, a notable oversight that says much about how little stock Eayrs put into peacekeeping as an aspect of Canadian foreign policy. See James Eayrs, *In Defence of Canada*, vol. 1–5 (Toronto: University of Toronto Press, 1964–1983).

14 Some of the best examples are Costas Melakopides, *Pragmatic Idealism: Canadian Foreign Policy, 1945–1995* (Montreal and Kingston: McGill-Queen's University Press, 1998); Joseph T. Jockel, *Canada and International Peacekeeping* (Washington, DC: The Center for Strategic and International Studies, 1994); Tom Keating, *Canada and World Order: The Multilateralist Tradition in Canadian Foreign Policy* (Toronto: Oxford University Press, 2002); Andrew F. Cooper, *Canadian Foreign Policy: Old Habits and New Directions* (Scarborough: Prentice-Hall, 1997); Peter Gellman, "Lester Pearson, Collective Security, and the World Order Tradition of Canadian Foreign Policy," *International Journal* vol. 44, no.1 (1988): 68–101; Robert Bothwell, *Alliance and Illusion: Canada and the World, 1945–1984* (Vancouver: UBC Press, 2007); Mark Neufeld, "Hegemony and Foreign Policy Analysis: The Case of Canada as Middle Power," *Studies in Political Economy* 48 (1995): 7–29.

15 Two examples of Granatstein's work are J.L. Granatstein, ed., *Canadian Foreign Policy since 1945* and J.L. Granatstein, *Who Killed the Canadian Military?* (Toronto: Harper Collins, 2004).

16 Stephen Chase, "Canada's Arms Deal with Saudi Arabia Shrouded in Secrecy," *Globe and Mail*, 21 January 2016.

1

Before the UN

Early Canadian Involvement with International Organizations

David MacKenzie

Canadians and their governments have long been supporters of international organizations. From the United Nations and its realm of specialized agencies, offices, and commissions to a wide array of security, economic, regional, and cultural organizations and on to multiple NGOs dealing with disarmament, environmentalism and human development, international organizations became a central part of the Canadian world view in the years following the Second World War. International organizations offered security in numbers and provided an international stage on which to perform and further world order, peace, stability, multilateral cooperation, and trade; they served as vehicles to achieve and enhance national unity, international recognition and prestige and were used both as a way to pursue security under an American defence umbrella and, at the same time, a shield against the pull or domination of the United States.

For reasons of history, geography, and politics, Canada was a natural supporter of international organizations, and the roots of this support are normally traced back to the Second World War and characterized as an expression of Canadian liberal internationalism. It was the experience of that war and the Cold War that led Canadians to seek security in international organizations. But were there lessons learned about international organizations *before* the United Nations that Canadians brought to this new postwar world? Canadian diplomat John Holmes, who had been present at the creation of the UN system, suggested that "Canada's more enthusiastic participation in the details of international life during and after the Second World War marked a notable change of direction, but it was conditioned by what had been learned and felt before." Holmes added that "the long experience of empire and commonwealth, of the North Atlantic triangle in which Canada had sought shelter, and the efforts to come to grips with the League were embedded in the subconsciousness of Canadians as they arrived at 'the middle way.'"[1] Canadians began thinking about international organizations before the United Nations, but this "long experience" that was gained in the pursuit of the national interest was uneven, unplanned, and, more often than not, unexpected. The other essays in this volume look specifically at the United Nations; this essay examines Canadian involvement in international organizations before the UN.

International organizations are usually regarded as a European creation, from the Catholic Church to the early antislavery societies to the creation of the International Red Cross in the nineteenth century. International governmental organizations are seen to have evolved from the arrangements that followed the defeat of Napoleon and the 1815 Congress of Vienna when the great powers came together to settle mutual problems of borders, territory, and the reintegration of France into the European system. Recognizing the need for more formal and permanent consultation, what began as a conference evolved into an alliance and then a more permanent arrangement – the Concert of Europe. The Concert of Europe, or the Congress System, was a series of great power conferences, held over the nineteenth century, set up to maintain the balance of power in Europe. Conferences were held to deal with a broad assortment of issues, from immigration and colonial possessions to trade and communications, and more formal arrangements concerning dispute settlement and arbitration were discussed at two international conferences at The Hague, in 1899 and 1907. At the same time, industrialization and technological advancements increased the need for international cooperation, from postal services and telegraph communications to the use of rivers that crossed international boundaries, and sparked the creation of several European specialized technical agencies such as the Universal Postal Union.[2] With great power leadership and responsibility, regular international conferences, and specialized institutions with a permanent structure and existence, the foundations of modern international organizations were in place by the outbreak of the First World War.

International organizations in the Western Hemisphere have as long a history as those in Europe, dating back to the 1826 Congress of Panama and early efforts to foster inter-American cooperation. These early efforts to achieve an alliance and even a confederation of South American states were the focus of several conferences during the nineteenth century, but they were largely unsuccessful. More success was achieved at the First International Conference of American States held in Washington, DC, in 1889–90. Attended by most of the independent American republics, the Washington Conference discussed trade liberalization, arbitration, and dispute settlement, and it issued a number of nonbinding recommendations on issues dealing with customs regulations, extradition, and consular fees.[3] More important, the conference created the Commercial Bureau of the American Republics, a secretariat that gave a permanent and ongoing existence to a new international organization. Second and third conferences were held, respectively, in Mexico City in 1901–02 and Rio de Janeiro in 1906, and these conferences set the pattern for a fairly regular series of hemispheric summits over the following decades. At the fourth conference, in Buenos Aires in 1910, the Commercial Bureau of the American Republics was renamed the Pan American Union (PAU), and it came to play a central role in the emerging "Inter-American system" which comprised a series of conferences, several inter-American organizations, and an array of treaties and agreements.[4] The PAU evolved into a standard international governmental organization, with the secretariat establishing a library and publishing a bulletin and performing its main function of collecting and disseminating commercial statistics and other information in an effort to stimulate trade. It was, at first, primarily a commercial and cultural organization established to enhance trade and promote closer relations within the Western Hemisphere.

By the outbreak of the First World War multiple conventions and treaties had been produced, dealing with arbitration, patent and copyright, extradition, and various legal and commercial issues. And, although mutual defence was not seriously discussed before the outbreak of the Second World War, concerns over American interventions in Latin America had become the topic of debate at the various conferences. In addition, in a fashion similar to the League of Nations (and, later, the United Nations) a number of technical specialized organizations or institutes, with their headquarters situated in various member-states, were created for specific tasks, including the Pan

American Sanitary Bureau (1902) and, later, the Pan American
Institute of Geography and History (1929), the Pan American Child
Institute (1927), and the Inter-American Commission of Women
(1928).[5]

Canadian membership or participation in the activities of the PAU
was rarely discussed before the First World War. Canadians did not
attend the conferences and the activities of the PAU received little
public interest in Canada, and, for those newspapers that did show
interest, the view on membership was often negative.[6] Moreover,
there was little chance that Canada could have successfully joined the
organization had it wanted to. First, the PAU was open to all independent American republics and Canada was neither fully independent nor a republic.[7] Second, given that the PAU members were
represented by their ministers in Washington, until Canada had diplomatic relations with the United States it would have been impossible to attend the meetings (unless Canada was represented by the
British ambassador in the US, an unlikely event) or to be accepted as
a member by the United States. Third, as a member of the British
Empire, Canadian membership in the PAU would have been a cause
for concern over the potential infiltration of British views into the
organization. The United States government, while acknowledging
the eventual membership of Canada, was especially concerned
through the interwar period over the possibility of British influence
seeping into the chambers of the PAU surreptitiously via Canadian
attendance.[8]

Nevertheless, the possibility of Canadian membership was raised
on a number of occasions and for some observers it was inevitable.
Andrew Carnegie's original support for Canadian membership was
widely known, and it was demonstrated through the engraving of the
Canadian coat of arms on the PAU's Washington headquarters – the
building that Carnegie's money had paid for. Another story circulated widely that in 1910 US Secretary of State Elihu Root had placed
a vacant chair with "Canada" inscribed on the back in the PAU governing council chamber, and there it sat through every meeting, wait-
ing to be filled.[9] There were also Canadian voices raised in favour of
membership. Much of the PAU's focus was on commercial issues and
it was argued that membership could benefit both Canada's hemispheric trade beyond the United States and its banks, insurance companies, and other businesses operating in Latin America. For others
it was a logical extension of Canada's growing independence to

embrace its American heritage and join the "neighbourhood"; it just made sense that through membership Canada would enhance its position in the hemisphere, at relatively low cost or risk. But before 1914 trade with Latin America was low, and, as one author explained, Canadians then and later "realized that it was not necessary to be a member of the Pan American Union to do business with the United States and the Latin American Republics."[10]

More important was Canada's relationship with the United States, and, in the latter half of the nineteenth century, this relationship, at least with respect to multilateral institutions, developed in a fashion not dissimilar to that of Europe and the rest of the Western Hemisphere. The late nineteenth-century trilateral relations of Canada, the United States, and Great Britain – the North Atlantic triangle – is not a subject of much interest among historians today, with the focus on fishing rights, pelagic sealing, border disputes, and failed trade negotiations, but, as in Europe, the movement toward international organization can be traced from the ending of a major conflict (in this case the American Civil War), it was directed by great powers seeking peaceful means of dispute settlement, and it evolved from informal negotiation and conference to more formal Joint High Commissions to a permanent intergovernmental institution.

From Confederation to the early twentieth century, Canadians became involved in a series of Joint High Commissions, arranged – like those of the Concert of Europe – to settle problems of mutual concern, in this case between Britain and the United States. Canada was very much a junior participant, but the issues discussed were of great importance to Canadians and with each succeeding commission the role played by Canadians increased. Equally important, given the great military, economic, and geographical advantages held by the United States in North America, it was increasingly clear to the Canadians as well as the British that negotiating with the United States via international arbitration and a series of Joint High Commissions – where the two sides were represented by equal numbers – was a far better process than any kind of military confrontation which they knew they could not win. For Canadians, however wary they might have been of engaging in any sort of institution that could be dominated by the United States, the goal of bringing the Americans in and getting them to the negotiating table where numerous issues could be discussed simultaneously was always better than a direct confrontation; even if many of the immediate decisions or international arbitration decisions went against Canada, its long-term interests were better served.[11]

The first Joint High Commission, held in 1870, dealt with Anglo-American problems left over from the Civil War and produced the landmark Washington Treaty of 1871. Prime Minister Sir John A. Macdonald wore two hats, first as a member of the British team and, second, as the spokesperson for Canadian concerns. It was an awkward position, and Macdonald was unsuccessful in either reviving reciprocity or gaining American compensation for the destruction caused by the Fenian raids, but Canadians benefited from the improvement in Anglo-American relations that followed. In addition, Canadians benefited by the subsequent generous compensation awarded by international arbitration for American access to the fisheries and from the British loan guarantees for railway and canal construction that Macdonald received in return for his support for the Washington Treaty.[12] Further Joint High Commissions were held in 1887–88 and in 1898–99, and at these meetings various issues of trade, fisheries, and pelagic sealing were discussed. Agreement was also reached at the latter Commission to send the dispute over the Alaska Boundary to international arbitration. The tribunal decision of 1903, which favoured the American position, was met with considerable outrage by the Canadians, but even here that outrage was directed more at the actions of the British government than at the process of Joint High Commissions.[13]

Two things regarding Canadian-American border issues had become apparent by the turn of the century; first, the British government increasingly viewed these issues as solely North American and of little concern to broader British strategic interests; second, the Canadians and Americans recognized that such cross-border issues would be a permanent element of the Canadian-American relationship. As a result of the British wish to remove themselves from such "local" issues and the joint Anglo-American desire to settle the remaining issues in North America, the two countries embarked on a round of negotiations that produced a series of treaties and agreements that effectively resolved most outstanding problems and helped solidify the Anglo-American *rapprochement*. The most important outcome of this "cleaning of the slate," at least for our purposes here, was the 1909 Boundary Waters Treaty, which, in addition to dealing with water issues concerning the Milk and Niagara Rivers, created the International Joint Commission (IJC).

Building on the informal process of earlier Joint High Commissions, the IJC was created as a permanent organization with equal representation of three commissioners from each side and a number of appointed secretaries and other officials as needed. Its mandate was primarily to deal with issues arising from shared boundary waters, but the treaty itself gave considerable latitude for the IJC to discuss and report on virtually any issue agreed to by the two governments. The IJC suited the Canadians fairly well; for Prime Minister Sir Wilfrid Laurier it made sense to have a permanent organization to handle multiple issues because the chances for Canadian success were much higher there than the alternative of fighting each and every dispute on its own merits with a far more powerful neighbour.[14] In this way, the IJC became the first Canadian-American intergovernmental institution that, as John Holmes wrote, "sought successfully to provide Canada with protection in dealing with a giant neighbor which cannot avoid being overwhelming no matter how good its intentions."[15] By the outbreak of the First World War international organization had become an important part of the Canadian-American relationship, and the IJC is still in operation today, and its structure and methods served as a model for other Canadian-American institutions from the Permanent Joint Board on Defence to the St Lawrence Seaway Commission.

The end of the First World War formally introduced Canadians into the world of international organizations, even if in a somewhat backdoor fashion. Thanks to Prime Minister Sir Robert Borden's desire to have separate representation for Canada at the 1919 Paris Peace Conference and then to register an independent Canadian signature on the Treaty of Versailles, he also gained membership for Canada in the League of Nations. There was some question at the time whether or not Canada *should* be in the league: Canada was not a fully sovereign state, it had increasing trade connections with the outside world but relatively little to do in the way of foreign affairs, Canada had no international diplomatic representation and was not recognized by other countries, and it had only a small department of external affairs for studying international issues or devising policy. And yet, Canadians wanted to be in the League of Nations and believed they had earned the right to be there thanks to their contribution to the war effort. As historian G.P. de T. Glazebrook wrote, "they sought recognition of the right of representation not because they wanted the opportunity of securing territory or other objectives – not even because they were deeply concerned with the form of world order – but because they wanted acceptance of Canadian status as a principle."[16]

It would not be the last time that Canada sought to join an international organization because of the status or international prestige that membership would confer. But it is not completely fair to suggest that status was the only thing that the Canadian government sought through membership in either the new league or in the International Labour Organization (ILO), which was also under discussion at Paris. Borden and the rest of the Canadian delegation clearly viewed the proposed league and labour organizations as important institutions that would help settle the numerous problems left over from the war, contribute to solving international disputes, and, more generally, help to prevent another war and promote good political and economic relations. The Canadians played only a modest role in Paris and no Canadian participated in any significant way in the drafting of the league covenant or the labour convention,[17] but interest in both organizations was strong, and Canada's possible role within them received considerable attention.

One of the major concerns of the Canadians in Paris – again relating to status – was whether Canada could be a member of the league council or the ILO's governing body. Both bodies had places reserved for representation by smaller powers, but early draft proposals appeared to exclude the Dominions. In the league, the "British Empire" was listed as a permanent council member – did that rule out independent membership of a single member of the Empire? In the ILO, early drafts limited membership of the governing body to "states" and specifically excluded "dominions and colonies," which directly disqualified Canada. Borden and the others were outraged – to the point of threatening to withdraw from the league itself – and the Canadian team (in conjunction with other Dominion governments) complained and launched a vigorous campaign to amend the offensive wording. With American support, the objections of the Italians, Japanese, and others were overcome and the "obnoxious clause" was removed from the ILO convention.[18] Regarding the league covenant no words were changed but Borden successfully extracted an extraordinary signed statement from the "big three" leaders – President Woodrow Wilson, Prime Minister David Lloyd George, and President Georges Clémenceau – acknowledging the

Canadian position that "representatives of the self-governing Dominions of the British Empire may be selected or named as members of the Council."[19] Without question it was a victory for Canada and a testament to Borden's determination to further Canadian autonomy; it also illustrated another aspect of Canada's relations with international organizations in that much of Canada's attention and efforts were focused on issues that had little to do with the actual goals, role, or function of the organization itself.

As participants at the Paris Conference, Canadians were also drawn into the creation of another international organization: the International Commission on Aerial Navigation (ICAN). The negotiation of a convention to regulate international civil aviation and for the establishment of an organization to oversee its implementation was the idea of the French government, and it arose from the recognition of the need for cooperation between states in international flying. All the allied governments represented at Paris were invited to join and most did. For Borden and the Canadians it was a familiar story – they were not involved in the early discussions, and in the original British and French draft conventions separate membership for the Dominions was not clearly conceded. More important, the proposed convention gave ICAN considerable influence in regulating international commercial aviation in areas such as transit rights and customs, and it granted more voting power to the great powers, including the United States. There were great concerns that these elements would place Canada at a disadvantage with its American neighbour when it came to cross-border aviation relations. Borden spoke out immediately regarding the "the importance which international flying might assume in the Western Hemisphere and the difficulties that would ensue if this traffic were in any way regulated by a Body on which Canada did not have a voice equal to that of the United States." There was no way that Canada could accept such an arrangement, he continued, "which empowered a body of people sitting in Europe to make regulations governing traffic between Canada and the United States."[20]

The Americans were cool to the whole idea and were sceptical even of the need for an international aviation organization at that time. Ultimately, of course, it didn't matter in that although the United States signed the convention, like the Treaty of Versailles and the league covenant, it was never ratified by the Senate, and the United States did not join ICAN. But during the conference when it still appeared that the Americans would participate, the Canadians worked hard to have Canadian-American aviation relations removed from the convention, or at least to not have it apply to North America. After much debate the best the Canadians could do was the addition of an amendment to the convention that permitted the signing of bilateral protocols between states to regulate matters of common interest. This was enough to satisfy the Canadians, and by 1922 ICAN was in operation from its headquarters in Paris.[21]

ICAN was not a specialized agency of the League of Nations, but there were distinct parallels between the two. Like the league, the membership of ICAN fluctuated as new members arrived and others left, it was dominated by the European states, the absence of great powers such as the United States was a serious problem from the beginning, and it did not survive the Second World War. From a Canadian perspective, the great concerns over the Paris Convention and their efforts to isolate Canadian-American aviation relations became a nonissue. With the United States remaining outside the organization and with trans-Atlantic commercial aviation decades away, ICAN had little impact on the development of international civil aviation in Canada. The organization itself disbanded and was replaced, in 1944, by the International Civil Aviation Organization, but the experience of ICAN serves as another example of, first, the importance that Canadian officials and diplomats put on ensuring that in any international organization all bilateral dealings with the United States should be conducted on an equal basis and, second, the great reluctance on behalf of Ottawa to agree to anything that might limit, encroach on, or interfere with Canadian sovereignty.

The other major Canadian concern about the League of Nations was aimed directly at the heart of the league covenant and the establishment of collective security. Article 10 called on all members "to respect and preserve as against external aggression the territorial integrity and existing political independence of all Members of the League," and for Canadian governments – both Liberal and Conservative – this was an intolerable burden for Canadians. For President Wilson and the Europeans, especially the French and several smaller states, Article 10 was central to the whole concept of collective security and of the league itself. For the Canadians, having just come through a devastating war which they had not started but had torn the country apart, the thought of having to do it over and over again to protect the Europeans from themselves seemed unreasonable. The league could provide the machinery for international conciliation and mediation, and there was support for its function as a place to negotiate and debate important issues, but its potential to bring Canadians into global conflicts was unacceptable for Ottawa. Canada was far from the world's trouble spots and unlikely to require the support of the league; it was asking too much of a small nation to commit to Article 10. As Prime Minister Borden put it, "let the mighty, if they will, guarantee the security of the weak."[22]

Borden and the delegation at Paris launched a campaign to remove Article 10 from the covenant and when that failed, to amend the article into meaninglessness. These efforts were continued by the Mackenzie King Liberals well into the 1920s and maintained until it was clear that Article 10 would never be applied against the wishes of any member, including Canada.[23] At the same time, there was widespread support for the league at home during both the 1920s, when the league seemed to work well, and the 1930s, when the league appeared unable to stop the drift to war. Groups such as the League of Nations Society, the Canadian Institute of International Affairs, Rotary clubs, academics, peace activists, and others put faith in international organization as the best way to maintain the peace. Canadian governments recognized that there were political benefits from league membership and Canada was a regular and full participant in league sessions throughout the interwar period and a member of the league council in 1927. The ambivalence toward the league was clear, but when push came to shove the political benefits from the domestic popularity and the international recognition that came with membership outweighed the potential risks associated with Article 10.

The Canadian role in the fall of the league and the descent into war in 1939 was modest and has been much criticized. Canadian policy, according to two historians, was "cautious rather than cowardly, but certainly undistinguished," even if it "commanded the support of most Canadians."[24] The response to the Manchurian crisis, the Italian-Ethiopian conflict, and the various other crises differed depending on the unique circumstances of each, but Ottawa was consistent throughout the decade in its reluctance to support any policy that might provoke a war that involved Canada. It might have been ignoble and contrary to the essence of the league, but the policy was understandable. Nobody wanted to go to war again; the memories of the first war were all bad and another war might be far worse, but it was equally clear that if Britain went to war Canada would follow. So, if the league worked as it was designed it could drag Britain and Canada into a conflict; if it didn't work then its weakness could make the international situation more dangerous and still drag Britain and Canada into a conflict; either way it seemed incapable of preventing another war. Mackenzie King, who often spoke of the league in favourable terms, wrote in his diary in 1944 that he "did not believe there would have been a war if the League of Nations had never existed."[25] Only a few would have gone so far as to blame the league for the war, but by 1944 most Canadians had turned away from the league and shifted their hopes and attention onto its successor.

In many ways the most important international organization for Canadians before the United Nations was the British Empire/ Commonwealth. Although an empire – by definition – cannot be considered a true international organization, as the Empire evolved into the Commonwealth between 1917 and 1931 it took on the trappings of one. This evolution also followed that informal process from occasional conference to regular meetings to more formal organization. Many early supporters of closer relations within the Empire called for imperial federation, with Canada and the other Dominions contributing to and directly participating in imperial affairs. For such individuals this new arrangement might include an imperial parliament with strong legislative powers and with membership elected from around the empire. The idea of a larger imperial state based on shared language, traditions, and history can seem today as either quaintly old fashioned or breathtakingly futuristic, but the movement towards the creation of some kind of imperial suprastate was stillborn. Instead the process evolved in a different direction toward an association of states with no legislative powers or ability to force its will upon its members – in other words, an international organization.

Turning the Empire into something bigger or different was an early goal of many individuals in Britain and the Dominions from the creation of the Imperial Federation League in 1884 through the First World War. Colonial conferences to discuss mutual problems within the Empire were held in London in 1887, 1897, and 1902 and in Ottawa (to discuss Pacific trade) in 1894.[26] Trade and tariffs, imperial relations, defence, and migration were all topics of discussion and the failure to resolve imperial differences only underlined the need for further – and more regular – gatherings. These colonial conferences took on a more formal nature early in the new century, and there was considerable discussion in 1907 over the Colonial Office's suggestion of renaming the semiformal but irregular conferences as an "Imperial Council" and by creating a permanent commission to prepare subjects for discussion and to report on how best to carry out the council resolutions. Such a proposal would necessitate a permanent secretarial staff, to perform the functions of a secretariat, within the Colonial Office.

The Canadian government was cool to the proposal and the concerns it raised were similar to those seen earlier in Canadian-American institutions – the desire not to be locked into a lopsided arrangement with the mother country in which the stronger power could influence or commit the weaker into action against its will. The proposed council, responded Laurier's government, indicated "a more formal assemblage, possessing an advisory and deliberative character, and in conjunction with the word 'Imperial', suggesting a permanent institution which, endowed with a continuous life, might eventually come to be regarded as an encroachment upon the full measure of autonomous legislative and administrative power, now enjoyed by all the self-governing Colonies."[27] Thanks to this Canadian opposition, the suggestion was dismissed; in its place the Canadian suggestion to use the term "Imperial Conference" at future meetings was accepted. Henceforth the imperial conference would be, in the words of Sir Wilfrid Laurier, "a conference between governments and governments."[28]

The Laurier government, while often professing an openness to change within the Empire, did little to renegotiate the imperial relationship, but forces unleashed by the First World War led to a redefinition of the British Empire, turning a colonial relationship into one of equal governments. Canadians played a leading role in this transformation, including prime ministers from both political parties: Sir Robert Borden and Mackenzie King. Beginning with the negotiation of Resolution IX of the 1917 Imperial War Conference, which recognized the Dominions as freely associated and autonomous nations within an "Imperial Commonwealth," to the Balfour Report from the 1926 Imperial Conference to the 1929 Operation of Dominion Legislation and Merchant Shipping Conference to the 1931 Statute of Westminster, which gave legal sanction to the earlier conference recommendations, full Dominion autonomy was acknowledged, and all the colonial connections with the British government were removed (except for those connections specifically reserved by the Dominions themselves).[29]

This new Commonwealth was an international organization in all but name. It was an international intergovernmental body, created by its members, with agreed rules, set up to undertake tasks and solve problems of mutual interest. It was comprised of sovereign governments freely choosing to be members; it held regular governmental meetings, with an increasing number of joint activities and bodies; and it provided a forum for debate and study of various issues of importance. The lack of a permanent secretariat (the Commonwealth Secretariat was not created until 1965) was not a significant drawback in that this role was largely performed by the Dominions Office and, later, the Commonwealth Relations Office in London. Even the dominance of Great Britain in the early years of the Commonwealth was mitigated by the fact that it could no longer force its will on the different members as it might have been able to do in the years before the First World War; indeed, British authority in the Commonwealth was no different than what was found in other international organizations with great powers, such as the Pan American Union.

Canadians played a significant role in the constitutional evolution of the Empire into the Commonwealth, but once that had been achieved they were much more cautious in participating in the new organization's activities. Foreign affairs, defence, trade, transportation, and communications issues dominated in the interwar years and on each topic Canadian governments were reluctant participants at best. The South Africans and Irish continued to worry about the constitutional relationship between the Dominions and the mother country, but from the 1932 Imperial Economic Conference in Ottawa to the 1937 Imperial Conference in London the Canadians strove to limit their actions and commitments. There was some limited cooperation within the Commonwealth, including imperial trading agreements, plans for an Empire Air Mail scheme, and for the creation of a joint operating company to establish a transatlantic air service, but behind every promise, suggestion, and proposal lurked the question of Canadian national unity.

English and French-speaking Canadians had always viewed the Empire differently and the experience of the First World War served only to highlight and exacerbate these differences. The legacy of conscription – the political divisions, the bitter wartime election, and the isolation of Quebec – cast a long shadow over all imperial dealings in the interwar period. That the Empire had evolved into something new was probably lost on most Canadians for there was little evidence, on the surface at least, that anything had changed. As a result, as the threat of a second European war increased in the 1930s all aspects of the Commonwealth relationship fell under scrutiny, and the Mackenzie King government surrendered to a policy of "no commitments" and "Parliament will decide." Much has been written about Canadian foreign policy in this "low dishonest decade," but the point here is that the policy of limited action and no commitments in the name of preserving national unity was applied to international organizations as it was everywhere else.

Canadians viewed the approach to the Second World War through their memberships in the Commonwealth and the League of Nations. In both organizations they were reluctant participants; they fretted about status and tended to avoid commitments. From Ottawa's perspective, membership in these organizations was more likely to bring Canada into a war than keep Canada out. There may have been a question of which organization offered the best chance to provide for Canadian security – the league or the Commonwealth – but there was little question that when Canadians went to war in 1939 it had more to do with their membership in the British Commonwealth than in the League of Nations. As John Holmes put it, Canada could not "escape from the dilemma that the avoidance of formal commitments had left it still deeply committed to the United Kingdom."[30] In an odd way the Empire/Commonwealth worked better as a defence and collective security organization than did the League of Nations.

The politics of national unity loomed large whenever Canadians were involved in international organizations before the UN even, in some cases, those organizations in which they were not members, such as the Pan American Union. And in the PAU, as was so often the case when it came to international organizations, the Canadian debate over participation had less to do with what the organization stood for (commercial and cultural cooperation) and more about Canada's relationship with the United States and Great Britain. In advance of the 1928 Havana Conference, for example, Canadian membership was once again raised, this time by the Mexican government. When Canada's newly appointed minister in Washington,

Vincent Massey, learned of Mexico's intentions he warned Ottawa against any rash moves: membership "would not be in the interests of the Dominion, [it] would lower her prestige in this country [i.e. the United States], and, generally, would, almost inevitably, lead to unfortunate consequences."[31] O.D. Skelton, the under-secretary of state for external affairs, responded with the government's position that, while Canada might have interests in the dealings of the Pan American Union, "in view of the rivalries between the United States and the Latin-American countries, and of the fact that our entrance into the Union is desired by our Latin-American friends in order that we may serve as a counterpoise to the United States, we are of the opinion that, for the present at least, it would not be desirable to join if invited."[32]

Interest in Canadian membership rose during the 1930s as the political situation in Europe deteriorated. By this time there were fewer roadblocks to membership – Canada now had diplomatic representation in Washington, and, thanks to the 1931 Statute of Westminster, questions over Canadian independence were largely muted. The issue of Canadian membership usually arose in advance of the ministerial inter-American conferences that were held in 1933, 1936, and 1938. Canadians did participate in a variety of technical conferences and, in 1937, signed the Inter-American Radio Communications Convention, but these actions did not lead to increased support for PAU membership.[33] Expressions of direct American opposition were rare, and Washington may have acquiesced had the states of Latin America insisted on seeking Canadian membership, but American concerns over the possible infiltration of British influence lingered behind the scenes and probably precluded any direct invitation to Ottawa.[34] As late as 1938, American Secretary of State Cordell Hull informed his delegation that Washington "has always maintained the position that the periodic inter-American conferences ... have been held to discuss matters of special interest to the *Republics* of the Western Hemisphere."[35]

The approach of war, however, sparked increased interest and, for the first time, serious debate in Canada over PAU membership, but again the discussion appeared to concentrate more on the looming international crisis than on the Pan American Union itself. In a general way, pro-British sentiment, primarily in English Canada, tended to remain opposed to PAU membership and expressed more concern over the entrenchment of American neutrality; more isolationist (or anti-British) Canadians tended to advocate closer inter-American relations as a counter balance to the imperial connection which seemed to be dragging Canada into another war. The Co-operative Commonwealth Federation (CCF), for example, urged the government to send delegates to the 1938 conference in Lima, and its members, including J.S. Woodsworth and Agnes Macphail, spoke warmly about the PAU in the House of Commons.[36]

Support for the PAU was always greater in French Canada, although before the war even in Quebec there was relatively little interest or enthusiasm for close relations or membership in the PAU. Observers regularly referred to the "Latin" and Catholic connections between French Canadians and Latin Americans but rarely did they explain how these would translate into closer relations beyond a general sense of mutual support vis-à-vis the "Anglo-Saxons."[37] More often, "embracing our American heritage" was discussed as another way to diminish Canada's close relationship with Great Britain and to move Canada towards greater independence. For example, Henri Bourassa, who had long espoused a broader sense of Canadian nationalism free from the imperial connection, was a longtime supporter of Canada joining the PAU. Back in the House of Commons in the late 1930s, he regularly urged participation in the PAU conferences and he saw in Latin America people who shared with Canadians a view of the United States. "Why not join the Pan American union, in which we would be far more at home than we are in the League of Nations?" he asked in the House in 1935. "There we would meet the representatives of all those states of South America which, in some respects, are in close understanding with the United States, but in others have the same feelings of diffidence that we have and which are natural in small or weak nations toward a very large one, dominating the continent?"[38]

Canada's relationship to the PAU remained in this suspended status until the outbreak of the Second World War. Hugh Keenleyside, a first secretary in the Department of External Affairs, summed up the state of affairs early in 1937: "A fair summary of the Canadian attitude would probably be the statement that *general opinion* is apathetic, that *informed opinion* is predominantly favourable, and that *editorial opinion* is hesitant but in general tends to be favourable."[39] What was also clear was that Ottawa held the key to membership: it was unlikely that if Canada made a clear expression of interest in joining the PAU that either the Latin American states or the United

States would oppose. Equally it was unlikely that either the Latin American states or the United States would make an official request for Canada to join unless Ottawa made it clear that it would welcome such a request. And Ottawa never made the request: the geographic and cultural distances were vast; concerns over American domination of the organization were too serious; there were always better ways to manage the Canadian-American relationship bilaterally; and general Canadian indifference was ubiquitous. No state north or south of the Rio Grande seemed adamantly opposed; none appeared all that interested in forcing the issue. The refrain became one of "Don't ask; don't oppose."

The war raised new security issues and, with the closing of some European markets, concerns over the impact of the war on Canadian trade. Within a few years diplomatic relations had been exchanged with several states in the hemisphere (Brazil and Argentina in 1941, Chile in 1942, and Peru and Mexico in 1944) and new trade initiatives begun.[40] Ottawa equally became more open to participating in Pan American affairs by joining the Inter-American Statistical Institute in 1943 and by attending two conferences in 1942, the Pan American Sanitary Conference in Rio and the Inter-American Conference on Social Security in Santiago.[41] More public interest appeared as well, as evidenced in the wartime creation of the various groups that promoted the study of Spanish and Portuguese, including the Pan American League of Canada, the Canadian Inter-American Association, and L'Union des Latines d'Amérique.[42] In addition, several authors at the time and shortly thereafter pointed to the 1940 Ogdensburg Agreement between Canada and the United States, which established the Permanent Joint Board on Defence to examine common defence issues, as a harbinger of future hemispheric cooperation. Because it dealt with the defence of the "north half of the western hemisphere" Ogdensburg was taken by some as referring to anything north of the equator and therefore Canada was now inevitably involved in hemispheric defence. As McGill law professor John Humphrey argued in 1942, "Canada entered the Pan American system through the back door at Ogdensburg on August 18, 1940."[43] It is hard to see such statements as anything more than wishful thinking, given the nature of the agreement and the subsequent role of the PJBD, but for many observers it did suggest a Canadian shift away from Britain towards the Americas.

Nevertheless, the war did not spark a great rush to inter-Americanism or membership in the PAU. A public opinion poll undertaken by the Institute of Public Opinion in 1944 revealed that 72 per cent of adult Canadians knew little or had never heard of the PAU.[44] In terms of trade, in 1939 South America accounted for only 1.8 per cent of Canada's total exports and 2.8 per cent of total imports, compared to the United States, which in 1940 sent more than 18 per cent of its exports to Latin America.[45] And, despite Ogdensburg's supposed delegation of hemispheric responsibilities to Canada, no invitation arrived to two important meetings of American foreign ministers held in Havana (1940) and Rio (1942). If anything, being the only autonomous state in the hemisphere to declare war in September 1939 only highlighted Canada's unique position outside the PAU; conversely, by following Britain's lead into the war Canada's actions likely only confirmed Washington's sense that Canada remained too "British" and committed to the Empire/Commonwealth, actions which justified continued American opposition to Canadian membership in the PAU.[46]

Whatever limited support there was for moving ahead with membership in the PAU evaporated, somewhat ironically, in the midst of the great wartime burst of enthusiasm for international organizations. As a result, in the lead up to the 1945 United Nations Conference in San Francisco, Canadian support very much swung behind the global UN over the regionalism of the PAU. Indeed, many Canadians were disheartened by the activities of the "Latin American bloc" at the civil aviation conference in Chicago in November 1944 and further by the Pan American common front that emerged from the Chapultepec Conference held in Mexico City early in 1945. For the Canadian government, regionalism was to be avoided everywhere in favour of multilateralism. Even the CCF, which had earlier supported closer relations with the PAU, backed away from this position to focus more attention on the United Nations.[47] It took many years before Canadian interest revived. In the postwar years Canadians continued to fill their defence and security needs through the United Nations and the western alliance and not the regional Organization of American States. It is a telling point that, from 1949–54, no questions were raised in the House of Commons about membership in the OAS.[48] Canada did not join the organization until 1989.

By the middle of the Second World War the characteristics that defined postwar Canadian involvement in international organizations were clearly on display, first, with the establishment of the United Nations Relief and Rehabilitation Administration and second, with the conferences that created a host of other organizations that would be subsumed into the UN system after 1945, including the Food and Agriculture Organization, ICAO, and the Bretton Woods organizations.[49] Canada's substantial role in the war effort, coupled with growing security concerns for the future and the understanding that the demands on Canada to contribute to the postwar world in both military and nonmilitary ways would only increase, helped spark a new perspective on international organizations. New words would soon be used to describe Canadian foreign policy and its relations with international organizations, from the functional principle, multilateralism, and liberal internationalism to helpful fixer, middle power, soft power, and quiet diplomacy. Things changed dramatically and within a decade of the war. Edgar McInnis, the president of the Canadian Institute of International Affairs, would write that "there are few countries that have more reason than Canada to appreciate the inescapable connection between international organization and the national interest."[50] But the truth of those words was rooted far more in the experience of the Second World War than in the lessons learned from the early Canadian involvement in international organizations.

There are several trends that emerge in an examination of Canadian involvement with international organizations before the UN. First, Canadian interest in and the role played by Canadians in these early organizations often had little to do with what the organization itself was established to do – Canadians usually had other goals in mind in addition to imperial defence, cultural exchanges, hemispheric trade promotion, or collective security. As a result, the Canadian interest in these organizations was often considerable but focused on side issues of recognition and status, which most other states took for granted; their approach was, in many cases, essentially negative in their efforts to limit the power and influence of these organizations, and their contribution to the functioning of these organizations was usually minor in importance.

Second, there was a general hesitation about Canada's involvement in any organization that either the United States or Great Britain dominated and, conversely, the desire to use these international organizations, under the right circumstances, for the pursuit of better relations with both these great powers. It was a delicate balancing act to use international organizations to achieve the goals of status, security, trade, etc. without surrendering too much freedom of action. Canadians became involved in international organizations because of their relationships with the United States and Great Britain; their support for these organizations rose and fell to the extent that they helped or hindered those relationships.

Third, the pursuit and defence of national sovereignty became one of the prime goals for Canadian governments with respect to international organizations, and no government was willing to enter into any organization that seemed to threaten or deny that sovereignty. Unlike a country like the United States which could shape or bend international organizations to its will or threaten to withhold dues and make other unilateral demands to reduce its share or burden, Canadians used these same organizations for the boost to sovereignty that membership offered while at the same time ensuring that participation did not put undue limits on Canada's autonomy of action. Americans then and now used international organizations to do what they wanted in the pursuit of American interests; Canadians tried to prevent international organizations from forcing them to do things they didn't want to do.

Fourth, Canadians viewed virtually any participation in international organizations before the Second World War through the lens of national unity. It was one of the great ironies that, while international organizations offered an opportunity to enhance Canadian autonomy and international recognition, when they actually took action they threatened the delicate balance of Canadian national unity. On one hand, Canadians were spared the divisions and partisan bickering over international organizations seen in the United States, between Republicans and Democrats (over league membership and, more recently, the UN), and both major federal parties turned to international organizations to pursue their own interests, but on the other, membership in these same international organizations posed a potential threat to national unity when they took the actions that they were designed for. Because English and French Canadians viewed membership in international organizations in different ways, interwar Canadian governments, especially the King Liberals, went to great lengths to reduce or limit automatic commitments or any commitments made that involved Canada without Canadian consent. National unity became one of the central goals of international organization: as Mackenzie King said in the House of Commons in 1936, "I believe that Canada's first duty to the League and to the British Empire, with respect to all the great issues that come up, is, if possible, to keep this country united."[51]

After the Second World War, while the Canadian emphasis on status, recognition, and protection of sovereignty diminished, in many ways the politics of national unity remained at the heart of Canadian foreign policy and Canada's relations with international organizations. In 1977 Prime Minister Pierre Trudeau echoed Mackenzie King when he said that the end of Canada "would create shock waves of disbelief among those all over the world who are committed to the proposition that among man's noblest endeavors are those communities in which persons of diverse origins live, love, work and find mutual benefit."[52] A case could be made that participation in international organizations after the Second World War was a force for national unity – from peacekeeping to the struggle against international communism – but participation in international organizations before the United Nations was, for the most part, a source of national *dis*unity.

In the end we are left with ambivalence in the pursuit of Canadian interests. Canadians participated in international organizations before the UN for several different reasons, but for the most part they had relatively little ability to control these organizations or the issues that they addressed. As members they pursued their own goals of independence, friendly relations with the United States and Great Britain, international status and recognition, and a range of economic, cultural, and national interests. Canadians wanted to be in international organizations for the status and prestige that came with membership (coupled with the anxiety that arose if they felt they might be excluded), but as members they were often reluctant participants within these same organizations. Equally, they were wary of membership in organizations in which the United States chose not to be a member, while at the same time concerned about being in an organization in which the United States *was* a member. And underneath all the interests, goals, and actions remained the politics of national unity.

Modern international organizations have broadened in number and scope to include other issues – human rights, health, the environment, crime, trade, international development, etc. – and Canadian international activity is increasingly expressed through the UN system and other international organizations. Today, as the other essays in this book demonstrate, the United Nations and international organizations in general have a greater influence than ever in Canadian political and economic life, from subsidies, trade, and security to the seal hunt, the environment and climate change, and international terrorism. With the UN, NATO, the G8, the Commonwealth, La Francophonie, the OAS, etc., and, with the rise of the BRICS and other regional actors, Canada is increasingly insignificant in global terms. Now is not the time to withdraw; indeed, it is more important than ever to embrace Canada's long history of involvement in international organizations.

NOTES

1 John Holmes, *The Shaping of Peace: Canada and the Search for World Order, 1943–1957*, volume I (Toronto: University of Toronto Press, 1979), 4.
2 See Inis L. Claude, *Swords into Plowshares: The Problems and Progress of International Organization* (London: University of London Press, 3rd edition, 1964), 17–35; Stephen S. Goodspeed, *The Nature and Function of International Organization* (New York: Oxford University Press, 2nd edition, 1967), 23–9; David MacKenzie, *A World beyond Borders: An Introduction to the History of International Organizations* (Toronto: University of Toronto Press, 2010), 4–7.
3 John P. Humphrey, *The Inter-American System: A Canadian View* (Toronto: Macmillan Co., 1942), 49.
4 Humphrey, *The Inter-American System*, 19.
5 Margaret Ball, *The OAS in Transition* (Durham, NC: 1969), 13–15; and Carlos Stoetzer, *The Organization of American States: An Introduction* (New York, 1965), 6–8.
6 Eugene H. Miller, "Canada and the Pan American Union," *International Journal* 3, no. 1 (Winter 1947/1948): 29.
7 It should be noted that both Brazil and Hawaii had been invited to earlier conferences when neither was technically a republic. See Humphrey, *The Inter-American System*, 283.
8 Douglas Anglin, "United States Opposition to Canadian Membership in the Pan American Union: A Canadian View," *International Organization* 15 (1961): 3.
9 Anglin, "United States Opposition," 2.

10 Marcel Roussin, "Evolution of the Canadian Attitude towards the Inter-American System," *The American Journal of International Law*, 47, no. 2 (April 1953): 298.

11 The standard works on late nineteenth-century Canadian-American diplomacy are C.P. Stacey, *Canada and the Age of Conflict:Volume 1: 1867–1921* (Toronto: University of Toronto Press, reprinted 1984), 17–121; Robert Craig Brown, *Canada's National Policy 1883–1900: A Study in Canadian-American Relations* (Princeton: Princeton University Press, 1964); Charles Callan Tansill, *Canadian-American Relations, 1875–1911* (Gloucester, MA: Peter Smith, 1964); James Morton Callahan, *American Foreign Policy in Canadian Relations* (New York: Macmillan Co., 1937), 326–492.

12 See Stacey, *Canada and the Age of Conflict*, 25–30 and, more generally, Goldwin Smith, *The Treaty of Washington 1871: A Study in Imperial History* (Ithaca, NY: Cornell University Press, 1941).

13 In addition to those books mentioned in note 11, see Norman Penlington, *The Alaska Boundary Dispute: A Critical Reappraisal* (Toronto: McGraw Hill, 1972).

14 N.F. Dreisziger, "Dreams and Disappointments," in Robert Spencer, John Kirton, and Kim Richard Nossal, eds., *The International Joint Commission Seventy Years On* (Toronto: Centre for International Studies, 1981), 19.

15 John W. Holmes, "Introduction: The IJC and Canada-United States Relations," in ibid., 6.

16 G.P. de T. Glazebrook, *A History of Canadian External Relations* (Toronto: Oxford University Press, 1950), 307–8.

17 See Margaret Macmillan, "Canada and the Peace Settlements," in David MacKenzie, ed., *Canada and the First World War: Essays in Honour of Robert Craig Brown* (Toronto: University of Toronto Press, 2005), 383.

18 Robert Borden quoted in Richard Veatch, *Canada and the League of Nations* (Toronto: University of Toronto Press, 1975), 7–8.

19 Macmillan, "Canada and the Peace Settlements," 390–1; "Declaration on the Status of the Self-Governing Dominions under the Covenant of the League of Nations, May 6, 1919," *Documents on Canadian External Relations* (*DCER* Hereafter), vol. 2, *The Paris Peace Conference of 1919* (Ottawa 1969), doc. 134, 150–1.

20 Borden quoted in "Extracts from Minutes of Twenty-First Meeting of British Empire Delegation, April 14, 1919," *DCER* vol. 2, doc. 106, 113–14.

21 See David MacKenzie, *Canada and International Civil Aviation: 1932–1948* (Toronto: University of Toronto Press, 1989), 12–13.

22 Borden quoted in Glazebrook, *History of Canadian External Relations*, 312.

23 For the campaign against Article 10 see Veatch, *Canada and the League*, 72–90.

24 F.H. Soward and Edgar McInnis, *Canada and the United Nations* (New York: Manhattan Publishing Company, 1956), 2.

25 King quoted in Veatch, *Canada and the League of Nations*, 16.

26 Stacey, *Canada and the Age of Conflict*, 46; for the standard works on this topic see: John Edward Kendle, *The Colonial and Imperial Conferences, 1887–1911* (London: Longmans, 1967); Donald C. Gordon, *The Dominion Partnership in Imperial Defense, 1870–1914* (Baltimore: The Johns Hopkins Press, 1965); Carl Berger, *The Sense of Power: Studies in the Ideas of Canadian Imperialism, 1867–1914* (Toronto: University of Toronto Press, 1969).

27 Dispatch to the Colonial Office, 20 April 1905, quoted in Maurice Pope, *Public Servant: The Memoirs of Sir Joseph Pope* (Toronto: Oxford University Press, 1960), 170.

28 Quoted in Stacey, *Canada and the Age of Conflict*, 80.

29 See Robert Craig Brown and Robert Bothwell, "The 'Canadian Resolution,'" in Michael Cross and Robert Bothwell, eds., *Policy by Other Means: Essays in Honour of C.P. Stacey* (Toronto: Clarke, Irwin, 1972), 163–78; Philip G. Wigley, *Canada and the Transition to Commonwealth: British-Canadian Relations 1917–1926* (Cambridge: Cambridge University Press, 1977); Robert F. Holland, *Britain and the Commonwealth Alliance, 1918–39* (London: Macmillan, 1981).

30 Holmes, *The Shaping of Peace*, 17.

31 Vincent Massey to under-secretary of state for external affairs, 9 January 1928, DCER, vol. 4: 1926–1930 (Ottawa 1971), doc. 551, 673–4.

32 O.D. Skelton to Massey, 13 January 1928, DCER, volume 4: 1926–1930, doc. 552, 674.

33 Humphrey, *The Inter-American System*, 260.

34 Anglin, "United States Opposition," 3–5.

35 My emphasis, quoted in ibid., 6.

36 Miller, "Canada and the Pan American Union," 29–30.

37 Iris S. Podea, "Pan American Sentiment in French Canada," *International Journal* 3, no. 4 (Autumn 1948): 348.

38 Podea, "Pan American Sentiment in French Canada," 335.

39 Hugh Keenleyside, "Memorandum" 8 January 1937, in *DCER*, vol. 6: 1936–1939, doc. 498, 668.

40 D.R. Murray, "Canada's First Diplomatic Missions in Latin America," *Journal of Interamerican Studies and World Affairs* 16, no. 2 (May 1974): 153–72.

41 Anglin, "United States Opposition," 13; see also Marcel Roussin, "Canada: The Case of the Empty Chair," *World Affairs* 116, no. 1 (Spring 1953): 15–16.

42 Miller, "Canada and the Pan American Union," 31.

43 Humphrey, *The Inter-American System*, 16–17. See also Miller, "Canada and the Pan American Union," 26; and P.E. Corbett, "Canada in the Western Hemisphere," *Foreign Affairs* 19, no. 4 (July 1941): 780.

44 Miller, "Canada and the Pan American Union," 34.

45 Corbett, "Canada in the Western Hemisphere," 779; Humphrey, *The Inter-American System*, 9.

46 Anglin, "United States Opposition," 7–8.

47 Miller, "Canada and the Pan American Union," 33–4; Anglin, "United States Opposition," 15; Adam Chapnick, *The Middle Power Project: Canada and the Founding of the United Nations* (Vancouver: UBC Press, 2005), 97–8; David MacKenzie, *ICAO: A History of the International Civil Aviation Organization* (Toronto: University of Toronto Press, 2010), 36–7; Manuel S. Canyes, "The Inter-American System and the Conference of Chapultepec," *The American Journal of International Law* 39, no. 3 (July 1945): 504–17.

48 J.C.M. Ogelsby, "Canada and the Pan American Union: Twenty Years On," *International Journal* 24 (1968–69): 572.

49 See Holmes, *The Shaping of Peace*, 22–104; A.F.W. Plumptre, *Three Decades of Decision: Canada and the World Monetary System, 1944–75* (Toronto: McClelland and Stewart, 1977), 17–60; Susan Armstrong-Reid and David Murray, *Armies of Peace: Canada and the UNRRA Years* (Toronto: University of Toronto Press, 2008), 17–75; MacKenzie, *Canada and International Civil Aviation*, 144–200.

50 Soward and McInnis, *Canada and the United Nations*, vii.

51 Mackenzie King quoted in Soward and McInnis, *Canada and the United Nations*, 3.

52 Trudeau quoted in Harald Van Riekhoff, "The Impact of Prime Minister Trudeau on Foreign Policy," *International Journal* 33, no. 2 (Spring 1978): 269.

BRESCIA UNIVERSITY COLLEGE LIBRARY

2

"Neighbours Half the World Away"

The National Film Board of Canada at Work for UNRRA (1944–47)

Suzanne Langlois[1]

INTRODUCTION

The United Nations Relief and Rehabilitation Administration (UNRRA) was founded in November 1943 to help the destitute populations of war-ravaged areas upon the conclusion of military operations. It was created to provide initial delivery of material, medical, sanitary, and food supplies in the liberated zones of Europe and Asia and to displaced persons from several countries who remained present in German territory. From 1944 onwards, film agencies produced material to explain and promote these large-scale international humanitarian interventions, and the National Film Board of Canada (NFB) was among the most active production units helping to structure such campaigns. This chapter examines the cinematographic contribution of the National Film Board of Canada during the last years of the Second World War and its immediate aftermath, first to introduce UNRRA to national and world audiences, then in creating, supporting, and maintaining the commitment of ordinary citizens, far removed from the theatres of war, to assisting distressed civilians in war-torn lands. I discovered the significance of this particular series of NFB films through my research on the early films of the UN as neglected sources to document the history of international organizations during the twentieth century. This material can deepen our understanding of the uses of cinema and shed light on the complexities and difficulties of propagandizing functional internationalism during historic periods of transition while imagining a cooperative postwar world. These films question our methods and concepts when thinking beyond the national context of film production and distribution and when studying how both UNRRA and the National Film Board of Canada tried to problematize the transition to peacetime.

The political catchwords of the Allies were "to win the peace," and time was believed to be of the essence during this dangerous phase of transition. UNRRA's internationalist film propaganda project was intended to mobilize citizens and foster collective solidarity for victims of war; to open a space for a renewed attempt at long-term international cooperation; to interpret the support mission as fulfilling a fundamental commitment, a moral obligation that would also bring mutual advantages. To do so, the NFB used various narrative strategies and visual support techniques, in film and still photographs, to expose viewers to the plight of individual civilian victims and to introduce the donors and suppliers to those benefiting from relief: providers who were not anonymous governments and organizations only, but ordinary people, civilians like them, working to help them. This may be the most innovative aspect of these films because it created an unusual long-distance visual dialogue between local audiences and the diverse people receiving aid. Like other contributors to this collection, including Tarah Brookfield and David Webster, who research the multiple ways the UN undertaking can be assisted, and, like Colin McCullough, try to explain how perceptions are constructed, and document the uses and meaning of cultural productions in supporting missions, I use film as a mediating agent between the international organization and its diverse audiences in Canada and abroad. I try to understand what role a public institution such as the National Film Board of Canada could play in that mission, at that precise time and, more specifically, what visual material such as documentary films can contribute to our knowledge of history.

Besides identifying narrative and visual strategies, a full appreciation of the films produced by the National Film Board of Canada for this postliberation cinematographic experiment requires examining them as a series and connecting national and international archives: the NFB archives are located in Montreal (Quebec) and the UNRRA archives are held at the United Nations in New York; taken together, these sources document and corroborate the planning, production, dissemination, and reception of this film series.[2] There is still much research to be done to examine the entire UNRRA film propaganda campaign to which other production units, mostly from the United States, Britain, and smaller European allies, also contributed. There were about a dozen edited UNRRA films, although the *Union List of U.N.R.R.A. Film* compiled in 1949 indicates twenty-nine such films.[3] This total number included the classification "Newsreel," which indicated an item in an edited, released newsreel as well as some unedited material, part of which may have been used in edited films and newsreel. This last format circulated widely. UNRRA's documents indicate that newsreels depicting various phases of its work were shown in the US, Canada, the UK, Latin America, Denmark, Germany, Austria, Hungary, Italy, France, Belgium, and Czechoslovakia.[4] The NFB, however, was the organizing partner of UNRRA's endeavour to plan a film service while the war had not yet ended and to provide a coherent set of short films and documentary materials until UNRRA's mission ended in June 1947. International archives were essential to the full understanding of the role of the NFB as the linchpin of UNRRA's film propaganda campaign: the NFB provided technical expertise in personnel and production capacity, a dedicated internationalist and civilian point of view, access to formidable stock shots collections, and the commitment to get up-to-date raw footage and photographic documentation as events unfolded following military operations in distant locations. In the case of the films produced by the NFB for UNRRA, significant findings therefore came from the UNRRA's archives in New York and the Office of War Information (OWI) in Washington, which documented a broader institutional and international dissemination and complemented our understanding of the NFB as an international actor.

This chapter will situate the NFB as a production unit during and after the Second World War, examine the series of films related to UNRRA, and analyze them in the postliberation transitional phase as mediating agents between ordinary Canadians and civilian victims of war. The periodization of this historical phase uses the perspective of the *transition* from war to peace (*sortie de guerre*), a timeframe that begins in 1944 and ends in 1947, subsuming the traditional fixed dates of the end of the war, 8–9 May 1945 for Europe and 2 September 1945 for the surrender of Japan. This periodization signals a social and cultural approach to the history of the war; the methodology used to analyze artefacts such as moving pictures requires the combination of qualitative and quantitative sources to document not only the production and distribution but, whenever possible, to provide the assessment of reception of the films in various contexts. It also requires examining how a film that is a combination of images in movement and sound (including voice-over) can produce meaning when brought together, this without neglecting the resonance of each individual component, which can in turn dominate, blend with, or overwhelm the others.

The historiography of UNRRA has developed significantly in the last ten years but its film program remains in the shadows. Studies on wartime documentary output have also been expanding but most often with a focus on national and/or military perspectives, the war years structuring the whole approach of documentary films. The most interesting research connecting with the topic of this chapter is work on the international movement of documentary film and how it informed production beyond the national construct and over a longer timeframe.[5]

UNRRA was a topic widely discussed during its brief existence (1943–47), and became the subject of an enormous three-volume history in 1950,[6] but was soon relegated to being viewed as an outdated and much criticized internationalist and utopic experiment of the immediate postwar, further discredited by the bitter polarization of world politics that dominated from then on. Internationalist films followed the same path: often commented upon while UNRRA was active[7] but quickly disappearing as the Cold War set in and the United States embarked upon its own plan for relief and development of Western Europe, the Marshall Plan. The UNRRA film program was nevertheless a novelty. As Patricia J. Torson stressed in the preface to her 1947 study, it was the first film program carried out by an international agency of the United Nations.[8] The Edinburgh International Film Festival, established in 1947 as the International Festival of Documentary Films, was dedicated to such productions during the early years of its existence, and most of the subsequent UN film production has been shown there.[9] In cultural and educational circles, this production was highly visible.

The end of the Cold War has redirected and renewed interest in understanding the crucial ten years that followed the Second World War, the decade 1945–55 remaining a field largely open to new historical research.[10] The changes that occurred within the discipline of history during the last thirty years have also facilitated the opening of new chapters in the scholarly examination of UNRRA. It now benefits from more integrated perspectives on political, social, and cultural history of internationalist experiments that go beyond traditional institutional histories of international organizations or agencies.[11] It must also be understood that international organizations were literally in the process of inventing themselves, and their areas of intervention were not entirely delineated; researchers must always explore overlapping webs.[12] Technological change – especially digitization – and cultural interest combined in the last decade to revisit the war and postwar years, yet the archival material – both images and paper – on this early film production remain difficult to access; it is not surprising that historical research has been limited. Like the George Woodbridge history of 1950, this cinematographic material has been forgotten, if not dismissed as equally uninteresting. This is what British historian and television producer Ben Shepard had to say about the NFB films for UNRRA:

> How, in our modern culture – where evil is sexy, goodness is dull, and organized goodness is dullest of all – can we find a way to make organized altruism interesting? The roots of this go back many years. The selling of Hitler was in the hands of Joseph Goebbels, Albert Speer, and Leni Riefenstahl, who created an iconography which still pervades popular mass culture; whereas the selling of the United Nations Relief and Rehabilitation Administration (and of the humanitarian ideal it stood for) was entrusted to the National Film Board of Canada, whose feeble efforts to create an imagery of international brotherhood and cooperation are long forgotten.[13]

One could discuss if the production was forgotten because of its style, content, lack of strength, or for other reasons, including how the UN alliance was presenting the films dedicated to civilian relief. One thing seems certain though – no other organization had the means and resources to do what UNRRA, even imperfectly, accomplished during the urgent transition of liberation. The very word *propaganda*, however, had become problematic towards the end of the war, as there was an understanding that audiences were fragmented by different experiences and wary of the highly emotional propaganda, the kind they had been submitted to during the conflict. There was reluctance in using the term for material produced for the civilian mission of the Allies and later by the United Nations Organization[14] and its specialized agencies such as UNESCO. Nevertheless, the objectives were clearly propagandist: to inform and educate certainly but also to convince and change attitudes and to achieve their goals. If the Nazis ambitioned to found a grandiose Thousand-Year Reich for the master race, UNRRA was concerned with "decent human ends" as John Grierson presented it.

I THE NATIONAL FILM BOARD OF CANADA: BE CONCERNED WITH THE "HERE AND NOW"

The National Film Board of Canada was founded in May 1939 by the federal government of Canada to further unify the country by familiarizing Canadian audiences with modern ways of understanding their own country and the world. The first film commissioner and creative mind of the NFB was Scottish documentary filmmaker, producer, and film theoretician John Grierson (1898–1972) who led the institution from May 1939 to August 1945. Grierson had started his career in Britain during the 1920s and became one of the leaders of the British documentary film movement and head of Britain's General Post Office Film Unit, an exceptionally dynamic film production unit during the 1930s.[15] The interwar period was a time of profound turmoil in European life and social conditions, which was a consequence of years of war and revolution. It was also a time when new technologies were becoming facts of everyday life for the increasing urban masses. Despite this, old social problems and barriers persisted, aggravated by economic uncertainties. This short period of European cinema from 1927 to 1933, sometimes referred to as the *Nouvelle Vague documentaire*,[16] effected the transition between silent and sound film – years when some *avant-garde* cinematographers explored the medium's formal and social potential.

John Grierson believed the techniques of mass communications played an essential role, within this context, in building a socially and politically responsible society. He forcefully repeated that film must be at the service of a democracy that was in the midst of total war. In 1942 he wrote:

The Germans believed that democracy had no genuine convictions for which people would be willing to stake their lives. They proceeded cynically on that assumption. [...] It behoves us to match conviction with greater conviction and make the psychological strength of the fighting democracies shine before the world.[17]

For Gary Evans, Grierson succeeded in making the World War "urgent, immediate, and personal" for Canadian audiences; on them he imposed a sense "of collective responsibility to act selflessly, and pointed to the great rewards to accrue in the postwar world of peace."[18]

Enjoying broad freedom of action, John Grierson applied to the wartime production of the NFB his principle that documentary filmmakers should be concerned with the "here and now of our own society," searching to "find the patterns of the social processes."[19] Grierson believed that they had in their hands the only aesthetic instrument that could bring the complexities of a cooperative world into relationship and order. The war did not change this fundamental approach. The vast majority of filmmakers involved in documentary production were working with governments. This had already been the case since the 1930s, but Grierson, looking around himself in late 1945, was speaking about the filmmakers of the English and Canadian schools of documentary filmmaking and the creative workers in the United States. This group included several exiled European filmmakers. As Grierson stated, "We are all of us, first and foremost, observers of our time; students of the political and social realities, and artists only in that regard."[20] As the war ended, he was convinced that, for the ordinary man, film had become the "seeing eye of his active and creative citizenship,"[21] a searchlight, a key to understanding the social structure. He noted that hundreds of creative workers had created thousands of films according to this very line of thinking – films that amounted to instruments of progressive understanding and progressive citizenship. When he reflected on the films made during the war, he concluded:

> [... A]ll the best documentary work has been done on the deeper, more lasting levels of human effort. What remains, now that the war is over, is what we have done to describe the nature and the aspirations of the United Nations to each other, what has been done to describe the new spirit of unity at home and of international cooperation abroad.[22]

It was under his supervision that the NFB produced two documentary-compilation film series: *Canada Carries On*, introduced in early 1940 as a monthly issue, and *The World in Action*, added in 1942 and issued every six weeks throughout the Allied Nations. Both series are considered critical and commercial successes.[23] The projected Canadian and international audiences were not mutually exclusive and several titles from the two series circulated both in Canada and abroad. The experience of total war did not preclude a vision for the future – quite the contrary – and channelling vast forces for "decent human ends" was very much on the mind of the film commissioner. He used film as an instrument of public education with an internationalist point of view. These were the objectives and spirit that informed the NFB productions created for the United Nations' relief efforts. The whole *World in Action* series deliberately adopted the United Nations' viewpoint, an argument well appreciated by a *New York Times* commentator: "[T]he editorial sights of the *World in Action* subjects are raised high above the level of nationalism."[24]

2 THE NATIONAL FILM BOARD OF CANADA AT WORK FOR UNRRA

The NFB was immediately involved with wartime propaganda and gathered a strong team of filmmakers and technicians who would generate a message of international cooperation during the transitional period between war and peace. Two experts from the NFB were lent to UNRRA in early 1944 to help organize its film section. Technicians were in short supply at the end of the Second World War, and the experts recommended that UNRRA should make the best use of existing agencies to develop its film program rather than attempt to duplicate a whole film section that would be difficult to put into place.[25] National agencies from Canada, the United Kingdom, and the United States became involved in the production of films that explained and described UNRRA and its operations.[26]

In newly liberated zones of Europe, film projections were scheduled within days, if not hours, following the end of war operations. Enemy films were seized in cities and villages, and Allied productions took over immediately in movie theatres or in improvised settings if no electric power was available.[27] Such mobile projectors were later used by UNRRA to show films in its refugee camps in Italy.[28] London was the hub for Allied film planning operations in Western Europe and North Africa. The NFB had an office in the city, where the European regional office of UNRRA was also located. In addition, the NFB distributed its films through its own circuits; the NFB estimated that by 1948 its community showings attracted nine million viewers

annually.[29] In 1944–45 alone, 2,155 prints of NFB productions
circulated worldwide for foreign nontheatrical distribution, including prints sent to Egypt and to North Africa[30] where UNRRA was
administering refugee camps. The list of recommended 16mm films
on UNRRA and world relief problems that was issued by UNRRA's
Visual Media Branch in March 1946 included nine titles, three of
them NFB productions.[31] A small number of films were specifically
made for UNRRA, and as a contributor to the administration's film
program, copies of NFB films circulated in numerous locations
in Europe.

The NFB contributed a visual education program to foster the ideals of a large scale and necessary humanitarian intervention for civilians, a principle that came to life in the aftermath of the First World
War;[32] the ideals of democracy and international cooperation were
also included in the outlook. In addition, the NFB produced many
films and newsreels that could be used by UNRRA as part of its public
information program; the list of UNRRA's archival material indicates
even more footage shot by NFB cameramen abroad in devastated
areas of Europe and China.[33] UNRRA worked hard to gain access for
filming teams to all newly liberated theaters of war. It was not easy,
neither in Europe nor in Asia, but the situation in Western Europe
was more readily documented than the one in Central and Eastern
Europe. In Asia, the visual material was mostly about China and
Formosa, despite the fact that urgent relief evaluations had reached
UNRRA already in 1944 about the Dutch East Indies, Burma,
Malaysia, the British zone of Borneo, Hong Kong, Indochina, and
the Philippines. It was understood that China had unique needs and
that the relief operations there would be unparalleled. China had a
UNRRA office (United China Relief) in Chungking and worked
closely with the UNRRA office in Sydney, Australia, in particular for
the control of contagious diseases.[34] During the summer of 1944,
UNRRA estimated that there were twelve million displaced persons in
Europe – nine million in Germany alone, not including POWs – and
forty million displaced persons in China.[35] These anticipated numbers were below those revealed at the end of war. In any case, UNRRA
was very much aware that the challenges would be extraordinary
and that relief missions had to be planned on an unprecedented scale.
In this chapter, however, my focus will remain on Europe.

The National Film Board of Canada worked with film material
collected during the Second World War by different agencies and

Allied military film corps, as well as with visual evidence gathered by its own cameramen and photographers, who were sent to different areas of Europe, from Holland to the Balkans. The films produced not only emphasized the need for immediate help and urgent physical reconstruction but also the necessity of reaffirming the political and moral values of democracy, respect for human rights, and international cooperation. For its productions, the NFB had access to exceptional film material because Ottawa had been chosen as the British Commonwealth's depository for captured enemy footage.[36] There were, therefore, plenty of stock shots and clips, but they required expert editing and integration of visual material, sound, and narration to achieve coherent productions.

The Canadian government set a precedent among the Allies by allocating $50,000 of its UNRRA administrative contribution to film services to be supplied by the NFB.[37] The short documentary film *In the Wake of the Armies: UNRRA*[38] was the first to serve these objectives. The archival documentation concerning the making, the content, and distribution of this film indicates a prototype for later productions.[39] The UNRRA's archives in New York provide essential information on the extensive distribution of this short documentary. It came out even before UNRRA's Public Information Division was formally organized in April 1944. Footage was selected as early as December 1943, the editing and scripting took place in February 1944, and the film was released in March 1944; it preceded by one year any other documentary film released on UNRRA.[40] It was widely distributed in North America and abroad despite being part of the *Canada Carries On* series. Patricia J. Torson, who had privileged access to everyone involved with UNRRA film production at the time of her research (1947), mentions that an American version of that prototype film was produced in April 1944 and paid for by Canada.[41]

In the Wake of the Armies: UNRRA was shown at a preview in Washington on 20 June, 1944. The remarks by the Director General of UNRRA, Herbert H. Lehman, point to the successful link established by the film between North American audiences and the populations of devastated areas. The task of relief for the liberated areas was presented using pictures of destroyed cities, hungry victims of Nazi persecution, and homeless refugees. I insist on the terms *liberated* areas and civilian *victims* of war and occupation, as UNRRA had rules about those who were to receive immediate help; the films, however, were less specific even if the visual connotations appear to be immediately understood by viewers: the polysemy of images opened a space beyond these restrictions. The film also explained the situation in terms of Canada's own national life. This appeared as a welcome point of view for Lehman who wrote:

> [The task of relief] has also been shown to us as something related to the daily lives of the people of Canada – indeed, of North America as a whole. It has been shown as the object of salvage schemes, as something dependent on the continued management of food in the more fortunate lands, as something to which all citizens are making personal contributions. I think it is immensely valuable to have these two aspects related so closely.[42]

According to Lehman, this understanding would help UNRRA in many other ways, such as attracting recruits and obtaining the aid of voluntary agencies and other similar organizations that were concerned with effectively accomplishing this relief work.

Two months later, making use of the solemn words of President Roosevelt in his famous "Four Freedoms Speech" of 6 January 1941, the Information Sheet issued by the National Film Board insisted on this broader understanding of the relief effort: "Our future lies in our answer to the destruction and poverty in Europe – in UNRRA we have taken a first step toward bringing the people of Europe a freedom from fear and want upon which our own freedom depend."[43] Canadians were able to appreciate what their participation in UNRRA's relief work could bring to the war-stricken populations and what it would mean for themselves in terms of work and security. It also presented another angle to the rescue efforts – that of the added audience in Europe that Lehman could not foresee. By the end of June 1944, however, unfolding events on all European fronts, the Eastern front, as well as in Italy and Normandy, were indicating the level of destruction and misery UNRRA would face. The organization was already taking care of 45,000 refugees: Yugoslavs, Greeks, and Poles in its camps in the Middle East and Southern Europe;[44] by November 1944, the six refugee camps of the Middle East were helping 54,000 persons, and UNRRA established a seventh camp at Philippeville in Algeria.[45] The Second Session of UNRRA was held in Montreal, at the Windsor Hotel, on 16 September 1944; Lester B. Pearson was elected chairman of that session; UNRRA had arrived at its period of action.[46]

In the Wake of the Armies: UNRRA was in line with the two distinct tasks of UNRRA's Public Information Programme:

[...] to provide the contributing countries with reports of the diverse and world-wide activities of the organization which they were supporting; and to make sure that the receiving countries understood and appreciated the nature of UNRRA and the sources of the relief supplies which it was providing.[47]

The *Union List of U.N.R.R.A. Film* compiled in 1949 presents the film in similar terms of "problems of relief and rehabilitation in liberated countries with relationship to world supplies, peace and security."[48]

In the Wake of the Armies: UNRRA enjoyed the wide distribution of the *Canada Carries On* series, which was released throughout Canada to almost 1,000 cinemas by Columbia Pictures of Canada.[49] Home audiences for *Canada Carries On* numbered 2.25 million viewers per month; *The World in Action* drew two million in Canada and ten million per month in the United States, and one million saw the French translations; the worldwide audience for NFB newsreel material was estimated at forty to fifty million a week.[50] From 1942 on, NFB productions were also seen in Britain and forwarded from there throughout the British Empire. The NFB had offices in New York, Chicago, and London. In addition, nontheatrical distribution reached several million viewers in North America and Britain. In fact, as underlined by Patricia Torson, the UNRRA documentary film program "was built up for the most part for the very large audience outside of the cinema theatres."[51] In his report of February 1945 the director of UNRRA's Visual Media Branch, Williams H. Wells, provided distribution and screening details for one such nontheatrical institutional example: the United States Office of War Information had informed his office that "[...] six out of the nineteen nontheatrical distributors of IN THE WAKE OF THE ARMIES reported twenty-four showings during the month. (15 reports not yet in.) Ten additional showings were booked direct through UNRRA, one of them for the War Production Board where 2000 employees saw the picture."[52] Such precise information is not common but helps to contextualize the dissemination of the visual material for information and training purposes.

By February 1945, the National Film Board of Canada was adding new footage and edited material: cameraman Nicholas Read
shot images of UNRRA relief at the Cine-Citta camp in Rome[53] and
the NFB produced the discussion trailer *Getting the most out of a
film: UNRRA – In the Wake of the Armies*. The three-minute discussion film (trailer) was made for noncommercial showings such as
those of the Trade Union Circuits. It introduced the questions raised
by the film through a discussion led by a representative of the
Workers' Education Association. The points brought up included
the "Canadian representation in UNRRA, how the organization
obtains its funds, how support of UNRRA will react on the jobs of
Canadian workers, and whether supplies sent by the organization
will be used as a political weapon."[54] Noncommercial distribution,
especially for series such as *Canada Carries On*, part of which was
the short documentary *In the Wake of the Armies: UNRRA*, was
accompanied by documentation prepared by the NFB in collaboration with the Canadian Council of Education for Citizenship.[55]

Films were also distributed in the Americas, through theatrical
and nontheatrical networks, in the appropriate formats (35mm and
16mm) and in various languages to reach the widest audience possible. The US Office of War Information allocated 90,000 feet of its
own 16mm film stock to supply 150 additional prints of *In the Wake
of the Armies: UNRRA*.[56] The OWI also ordered twenty-five prints
for its own use because its twenty prints were booked solid for a
month or more and could not meet demand.[57] The United States
Army Signal Corps had requested permission to use parts or all of the
film for its armed forces' newsreel, the *Army-Navy Screen Magazine*.[58]
William H. Wells was very pleased with the Latin-American version
of the film, each version bringing in a South American and Brazilian
angle to the film through the script and some visual material.[59]

To follow up on the objectives, a filmstrip of forty-eight frames,
UNRRA goes into action, was made in May 1945.[60] The reading
commentary emphasized the same problems facing relief work to be
performed by UNRRA, except that, by that time, the sheer magnitude of the problems was better known. The filmstrip and the commentary begin with a symbol, a photograph of the first full shipment
of UNRRA relief supplies sailing for war-stricken Europe. Then, the
familiar narrative pattern of the devastation and of the urgent
needs in clothing, medicine, food, and water supplies is followed by
cautionary frames explaining the limitations of UNRRA. A chart

showing the six-month relief needs in dollars for Europe and Asia brings the estimate to more than $200 billion. The next frame shows the actual funds available to UNRRA alongside the total need. The organization could count on less than $2 billion worth of supplies and services contributed by the members of the United Nations that had not been invaded. Obviously this could meet only a fraction of the needs – sadly, the lament is still true for today's relief operations. The filmstrip indicates UNRRA's priorities, the first one being the welfare of children who, incidentally, were very present in postwar documentary and fiction cinematography; they ideally served the urgency of relief action and focused the perception of viewers on the coming generation. All children were considered victims of the war. Furthermore, the care and repatriation of millions of displaced persons amounted to a gigantic task that could not succeed without the cooperation of the military. Despite the immense satisfaction of seeing this first ship set sail for Europe, a sombre mood pervades the message.

Other films were made by the National Film Board of Canada in support of UNRRA and its work: *Now – the Peace* (May 1945), *Food – Secret of the Peace* (July 1945), *Friends in Need* (September 1945), *Suffer Little Children* (December 1945), *Out of the Ruins* (August 1946). Production files provide information on the distribution details of both film formats. *Now – the Peace*, commissioned by the US State Department, presented the United Nations peace plans. It was started in February and completed in May of 1945. The film director, Stuart Legg, made use of visual material from diverse sources: Fox, Pathé, NFB, the War Office, the Signal Corps, the Canadian Army Film Unit, *Triumph of the Will*. The *World in Action* series, which included the films *Now – the Peace* (May 1945) and *Food – Secret of the Peace* (July 1945), benefited from the distribution network of United Artists and its 6,000 cinemas throughout the United States and Latin America.[61] It is clear that the very structure of commercial film programming (newsreel to short film to feature film) contributed to the distribution of such material. A similar structure had become common in Europe during occupation and after liberation.

The 16mm version of *Now – the Peace* was accompanied by a discussion guide and was released in the United States by Brandon Films, Inc. from New York. The order leaflet stated: "Movies helped win the war – Use 16mm movies to build the peace!"[62] Posters identify target audiences: all youth and adult groups in and out of school,

and "of specific interest for world friendship assemblies." The NFB
collected evaluation reports sent by the Educational Film Library
Association (New York) to public institutions. In February 1946, one
such evaluation came from the Cleveland Public Library where *Now
– the Peace* was rated as having a high value for film forums, high
schools and college classes, and adult education. As a special strength
of the film, the evaluators noted: "Film gives a fuller and more complete picture of UNO than do any of the other films on the same
subject."[63] *Now – the Peace* introduced the failures of the League of
Nations between the wars; the underlying issue was collective security and the capacity of the new organization to intervene in a time of
international crisis. At the time, there was indeed a real will by the
UNO to distance itself from the League of Nations; nevertheless, it
owed much to its predecessor.[64]

The 16mm copies which circulated in the nontheatrical rural and
industrial circuits of the NFB reached millions of people each week,
the rural circuits alone reaching a yearly audience of four million,
while 1,000 industrial plants throughout Canada screened the
UNRRA documentaries.[65] The films were accompanied by extensive
relevant documentation – information sheets, booklets, commentar-
ies, factual data, and brief discussion films – as well as focus questions to engage the audiences of those screenings. Short questionnaires
were distributed to viewers and I use them in my research as small-
scale, selective, public opinion polls. Ordinary topics were explained
in their larger context, and their significance in political and socio-
logical terms was always demonstrated.

Food – Secret of the Peace (July 1945) was produced by Stuart
Legg, who had also directed and produced the 1941 film *Food –
Weapon of Conquest* explaining how Nazi-occupied countries were
forced to hand over their farm produce to Germany and consequently
suffered from hunger. In 1941, Legg's film had already explained,
"the Western world must now not only feed its own overseas armies,
but must also meet the challenge of feeding hundreds of millions in
continental Europe and Asia during the postwar years." The require-
ment for such provisions had been made clear early on in the war,
even by Winston Churchill in August 1940 during one of his historic
speeches, but it had to be carefully explained again after victory over
Nazi Germany. The voice-over for *The World in Action* series men-
tions that in normal times, Europe almost feeds itself, but now no

part of the continent can do so. "The Soviet Union and her neighbour nations in the East," states the narrator, "require every pound of food that they can grow. And so, upon the Allies who seek the friendship of the West, there falls the task of providing for its needs as best they can."[66] The American version opens with pressing questions about employment for the 600,000 men who are demobilized every month: "What price in unemployment must the nation pay for peace? How long to reconvert?" and then it addresses the issue of hunger and food riots in Europe that should be of concern to US citizens.[67] This version does not mention the Soviet Union and Eastern Europe. It closes with the statement that "food no less than freedom is the secret of our peace." The Canadian version ends with the narrator stating: "This new Europe of tomorrow is part of our world today." In this particular case, the archival material provides versions of the wording adapted to national markets and audiences. It seems that the attitude of Canada, a smaller ally despite its significant material contribution to the war effort, was less indifferent regarding the great alliance than the attitude of the United States towards the Soviet Union would indicate. Anticommunism was equally present in Canada, but Canadians were also aware that the Soviet Union was in a difficult position despite its victory over Germany and that it could not participate in the urgent relief mission for Western Europe. Already in the summer of 1943, Canadians were sending building material for the reconstruction of Stalingrad; images of this assistance were included in the film *In the Wake of the Armies: UNRRA*.

The production file of *Food – Secret of the Peace* contains valuable information on nontheatrical circulation in Canada and audience reception, an insight into the immediate reaction to a film and, possibly, to a changed attitude towards world issues. In November and December 1945, the NFB released ninety copies of the film to its field representatives for industrial and rural promotion and an additional sixty to film councils, film libraries, and the volunteer projection service for community promotion. There were also screenings for civil servants. Promotional kits were sent along with the copies, and, following the screenings, the field representatives would collect reactions and forward their reports back to the NFB. The most frequent remark was, "the audiences who saw the film had never before realized just how severe the hunger situation was in Europe." More precise information of the film's impact appears in the following report:

[...] the film did a fine job in offsetting the unwarranted griping
about necessary Government controls and rationing from the
people covered by his circuit. He went on to say that this principle could apply to all imminent controls while, if the films were
shown well in advance of the actual enactment of controls, it
would prevent much antagonism and misunderstanding such
as strikes, etc.[68]

Another commentary explained that the Drumheller Valley Miners
(in Alberta), who were recently on strike over meat rationing, had a
great deal to say about the film in conjunction with their strike:
"Many miners said that they should never have gone on strike for
such a cause, after they saw the film." In view of this kind of statement taken from the reports, the final evaluation of the impact of the
film is that "it held a power within its grasp." If the film had been
promoted more extensively, there might have been "a more favourable public reaction to the introduction of meat rationing in Canada
at a time when it was imperative that Canada fulfil a moral obligation to her starving cousins in Europe." That "moral obligation"
became integrated in the postwar ethics of collective solidarity. If
Canada intended to play an international role, it could not remain
indifferent.

When specific relief campaigns were organized, film programming
was coordinated with them. *Friends in Need*[69] was produced during
the late summer of 1945 to launch an urgent appeal for clothing
relief during the National Clothing Collection Drive (1–20 October
1945), which had been organized by the Canadian United Allied
Relief Fund for UNRRA. The NFB ordered thirty-five French prints,
180 English prints, and one dozen to be charged to UNRRA.[70] The
film was shown in movie theatres (35mm) and on the nontheatrical
industrial and rural circuits of the NFB (16mm). Where the prints
charged to UNRRA were shown is not specified, but UNRRA needed
material on campaigns related to its relief action, just as it had used
newsreel material from different agencies – the NFB, the US Signal
Corps, the Soviet Film Committee – prior to the organization of its
own film service, for public information purposes in its formation
and relief centres.[71] The NFB was also involved in producing newsreel material depicting the clothing drive.[72] The audience was
reminded to be selective and that the clothes donated could not be
replaced immediately.

Another film coordinated with a large relief campaign was *Suffer Little Children*,[73] a short documentary film that depicted the story of children, alone, hungry, abandoned, or lost in Europe; it was scheduled with the national campaigns "Food Preservation" and "National Clothing Drive" of the fall of 1945.[74] Made at the request of the US Department of Agriculture for its UNRRA contribution and action, this short film was widely distributed in 1946; the department used 300 prints of *Suffer Little Children* in connection with the action of its Famine Emergency Committee[75] and 200 film libraries were cooperating with the department in motion picture distribution.[76] It was accompanied by a nine-minute discussion film in which a representative group of Canadian women consider how Europe's crisis affects them and what practical steps they can take to relieve the situation. *Suffer Little Children* and its discussion trailer "translate what to many is still only a vague and far-off story into a very urgent and immediate problem for Canadian women. The connection between food today and peace tomorrow is emphasized."[77]

This was an urgent issue since food supplies for that year were especially disastrous following periods of drought in the southern hemisphere that left very few agricultural producers capable of helping European populations. In early April 1946, UNRRA held an emergency conference in London to launch a desperate appeal to all countries, even those that were not members of UNRRA, to help alleviate the grave crisis in food supplies foreseen for the spring and summer of 1946.[78] Some countries, visited in May 1946 by Ira Hirschmann – passionate defender of UNRRA and envoy of its new director, Fiorello H. La Guardia – were not fulfilling their pledges or would not participate in the rescue effort even when they had large surpluses of cereals and other essential foods; Egypt and Turkey were among those.[79] Everyone feared that severe food shortages would occur in 1947 as well.

Some of the films made about and for UNRRA by the National Film Board of Canada were not only shown in the Americas and the British Empire or in countries that were suppliers of relief goods and services but also in countries that received help and their neighbouring territories. Such was the case in France, Belgium, Luxembourg, and Italy[80] with direct evidence concerning France. At least three titles from the NFB, which appear on the *Union List of U.N.R.R.A. Film* (March 1949), had also been distributed in France through the theatrical network. They were *Suffer Little Children* (*Les héritiers de*

la paix), *Food – Secret of the Peace* (*La faim, spectre de la paix*), and
Out of the Ruins (*À l'ombre de l'Acropole*). These films were viewed
by the French film control board, the *Commission de contrôle des
films cinématographiques*, and authorization was issued for their
release in France by *Les Artistes Associés*, the French branch of
United Artists. *Suffer Little Children* received its French release visa
on 26 August 1946; *Food – Secret of the Peace*, on 3 September 1946;
Out of the Ruins, on 22 June 1948,[81] one whole year after the end of
UNRRA operations in Europe. The *sortie de guerre*, it seems, was far
from over. United Artists distributed *Suffer Little Children* in England,
France, French North Africa, Belgium, and Switzerland.[82] Numerous
other films from the NFB had entered Europe before the end of military censorship, which occurred in France on 3 July 1945. Visual
material entering the country before that date had been chosen and
cleared by the Allies for immediate distribution and screening.

One of the last UNRRA productions, *Out of the Ruins* (1946),
made use of the visual material shot by Nicholas Read who had been
sent to Greece to document the plight of civilians in this region ravaged by the Second World War and by civil war. The film was made
under a special financial arrangement with UNRRA and intended for
UNRRA's use. This elaborate production started in December 1945
and was completed on 1 May 1946.[83] When screenings began during
the fall of 1946 and the following winter, the enthusiastic mood that
had prevailed in 1944 and 1945 had faded. The images were still
accurate because the Greeks were in dire need of relief, but the hopeful commentary was already outdated:

> [With] UNRRA at an end, civil war raging, and thousands of the
> ordinary folk exiled, imprisoned or seeking sanctuary in the
> mountains, one can only feel shaken and shamed by the frustra-
> tion of all the ideals and plans so enthusiastically portrayed in
> the film. The Canadian Film Board have turned out a good film,
> but they have done more than that. Perhaps inadvertently they
> have challenged the consciences of the freedom loving peoples
> of the world.[84]

On 7 May 1947 the film was shown to an audience of volunteers
and sympathisers of the International Voluntary Service for Peace in
London. UNRRA ceased operations in June 1947. Its end had been
foreseen from the start since its creation had served a temporary

purpose; yet it ended abruptly before the conclusion of some relief operations, especially in Austria and Italy, and there still remained a large number of displaced persons in Germany. The film continued to be shown in 1948, both in community screenings with discussion groups and in European theatres as mentioned above for the French market.

The international status of some of these films needs to be mentioned and carefully assessed, as it provides indirect evidence of distribution in Germany and Austria. One film examined above, *Suffer Little Children*, was made at the request of the United States Department of Agriculture. Produced by the NFB, it is listed in the pool of films of the American OWI. Similarly, the OWI collection includes the title UNRRA (1944),[85] which is the American version of the short documentary *In the Wake of the Armies: UNRRA*. The distribution of those titles was increased accordingly in all locations where Americans were present, and they were most likely offered in the territories of Germany and Austria where the Allies held absolute authority – a *de facto* monopoly – over all forms of public information that circulated in their zones of occupation. The OWI, along with the army and State Department, was involved in the motion picture segment of the American campaign. The feature films selection fell short of its objectives but, as reported by an experienced film journalist touring the American zones of occupation, "[t]he repertoire of documentaries has increased to fifty and has been well received and [...] the newsreels have improved."[86] In addition, the UNRRA Visual Media Branch reported that five film libraries had been opened in UNRRA Displaced Persons camps in the US Occupation Zone in Germany.[87] The circulation in Allied-occupied zones of Germany and Austria of other films that were not part of this American pool, despite having been produced at the request of the United Nations, was not so easily obtained. The first secretary general of the United Nations Organization, Trygve Lie, had to suggest that all films commissioned by the UN on its own work should circulate in the Allied zones of occupation as a contribution to the programs of reeducation and political reorientation promoted by the four occupying powers.[88] The unspoken objectives of Trygve Lie were to break the American monopoly, to encourage international cooperation by allowing diverse sources of information within the zones, and to counter ideological polarization at a time when Europeans were beginning reconstruction. Therefore, the occupied zones of Germany and Austria, the displaced persons camps, and the broad objectives of the UN in Europe provide additional information on the distribution of such film material. More research is needed to fully corroborate the information presented here, but indirect sources point to a significant broadening of the circulation of NFB material in postwar Europe.

The reception of films is the tricky part in such research: it is difficult to assess, especially outside Canada. In the case of the NFB films, some information is available, mostly for the nontheatrical showings that were usually followed by discussion and often accompanied by a questionnaire if the presentation was planned for a focus group: community leaders, teachers, union officials, civil servants, etc. The individuals in charge of a showing, for example at a local club or church, would also collect some verbal reactions from viewers and send a digest to the NFB. The reception of films that opened on theatrical circuits is even more difficult to document, however, since the general and specialized press rarely mention short documentary films, which were most often coupled with the newsreel and presented before the main feature film; only the latter gets the attention of other media. Nevertheless, scholars can rely on some indirect information. Press reaction abroad was collected by Canadian embassy personnel or NFB officers in Europe and forwarded to Ottawa. *Suffer Little Children* is one film in this series for which reception abroad was documented and it has been especially well received.[89]

3 CONTRIBUTION TO INITIAL POSTWAR RELIEF

The *carte blanche* attitude of the Canadian government towards its film board translated into the assertiveness of democratic ideals, the sense of purpose, and the direction taken by the NFB during the war. Towards the end of the conflict, however, this all appeared to go beyond what the government was willing to accept in the new world order that was taking shape.[90] Already the group of liberal propagandists who worked for the United States Office of War Information overseas program had met much greater political obstacles and resistance to their vision of the war from the American administration. The OWI propagandists saw "the struggle as a people's war, a necessary war that could reaffirm the values they held most dear."[91] On the other hand, this change of attitude did not mean the withdrawal of earlier productions nor did it forbid the internationalist point of view from being part of the 1945–46 productions. Ideas and objectives that do not prevail are nonetheless significant and contribute to a more complete understanding of the period for the reason that much of its complexity was lost in later accounts because of the bipolar opposition of the Cold War. Nevertheless, what struck immediate observers and somehow encouraged them in their hope that things could take a different turn was precisely that such films existed at all and that the power of the visual mass media could be put at the service of peaceful ambitions. The creation and purpose of UNRRA were great challenges, and the relief operation in war-torn areas amounted to the greatest relief operation in history:

> Upon its success depended not only countless human lives, but the future of international co-operation as an instrument of peace. Here was a beginning – a test of whether we could co-operate after the war in *saving* as well as we had during the war in *killing*. It was the first arm of the United Nations.[92]

This challenge was at the heart of the kind of film production discussed here, part of it made by the NFB and the rest produced by Allied agencies sharing the same objectives. This was new. After the First World War, the League of Nations had been looking into the use of mass media to further its work for world peace. It relied mostly on the written press and was not entirely ready for the extensive use of radio and film although it was very active in discussing their potential for peace education, literacy, and modernization at the international level.[93] The destructive experience of the Second World War, the uses of all media – old and new – for war propaganda purposes, and the magnitude of help needed afterwards transformed this hesitant attitude into a bold statement for change. Series of films such as *The World in Action* stimulated another kind of comprehension of world issues and understanding among the peoples of the world. The series "analysed post-war problems and dramatised the concept of the United Nations as a working partnership dedicated to the co-operative solution of such problems."[94] In early 1946, Grierson continued to believe that there was an enormous market for "Peace Films"[95] although he soon realised that he had been wrong: "[L]et me admit that for a short period I missed the point," he wrote in 1951, "[...] the war was on before the peace was started."[96]

The problems were obvious enough as stated by Richard Griffith about the film *Food – Secret of the Peace* (1945), which "predicted accurately the challenges to statesmanship which would occupy the stage within the next decade";[97] it was the solution of such problems through international cooperation that needed to be asserted. Some observers understood the novel contribution of films: "The use of the informational film by international organization deserves notice. The visual and film programme of the United Nations Relief and Rehabilitation Administration, for example, is one of the most significant of all present public international activities."[98]

The specific contribution of this series of films to postwar European relief and initial reconstruction can be summarized under three themes that together formulate a new experience to be shared. The first one was collective solidarity and mobilization for a renewed attempt at long-term international cooperation. The first director of UNRRA, Herbert Henry Lehman, the Democrat governor of the State of New York and friend of President Franklin D. Roosevelt, had declared at the founding meeting of November 1943, "We failed once. We dare not fail again," referring to the errors made after the First World War – errors that amounted to the humanitarian, economic, and political abandonment of war-wary Europeans. This solemn declaration is shown and heard in the film *In the Wake of the Armies: UNRRA*. Therefore, significant links had to be established among distant populations, otherwise living under very different conditions, but connected by their common experience of the war – an event of extraordinary magnitude. If there was a large collection of visual evidence about the military actions during the war, there was a discrepancy when the living conditions of civilians were concerned. Footage collected for UNRRA by various agencies or by its own cameramen was intended to remedy this difference in visual presence of all concerned by the effects of war.

Mass mobilization for international cooperation needed visual support, in film and still photographs, to expose viewers to the personal testimonies and war experiences of individual civilian victims. In addition, the international distribution of this series of films, including in Europe and in refugee camps, introduced the suppliers of relief to the victims, not anonymous governments and organizations only but also ordinary people, civilians like them, working to help them. The narration always stressed the viewers' relationship to "neighbours half the world away."[99] The careful editing also served to prevent negative reactions in Canada to the anticipated duration of rationing (food, textiles, etc.) and to the collective effort needed for long-term intervention abroad. Following the end of hostilities, a two-year effort would be needed to support European populations.

The cameraman Nicholas Read was sent overseas by *World in Action* to get on-the-spot coverage of "a battle still to be won." Staying away from victory parades, he traveled through Italy, France, Austria, and Yugoslavia, "assigned to go after the first film story for showing in Canada of the post-V-E fight of Europe's people for existence." The statement was clear: "Europe's people need food. Without it, millions will starve, and the rest will split into warring factions – each suspicious of the other and all hostile to their liberators."[100]

The second theme, particularly significant for foreign audiences, was greater exposure to western political values – democracy and humanism – presented as the best way to achieve freedom, strong democratic institutions, and an exceptional standard of living. It is here, in the film series examined in this chapter, that different political attitudes towards the Soviet Union came to light, although the Soviet Republics of Ukraine and Byelorussia received UNRRA supplies as late as the winter of 1947. Regarding the political changes in Europe at the time, it appears that multiple versions of some films were introducing different political overtones. *Food – Secret of the Peace* was one example of a film with an American version and a Canadian / *World in Action* version, both of which did not emphasize the same issues. The *World in Action* version, distributed worldwide, indicated the strain placed upon Soviet and Eastern European food resources that prevented any contribution from these areas to the relief of Western Europe. No such mention is found in the American version. Yet, there is no hiding the fact that there could be a political cost to Western allies if food supplies did not improve. The information sheet prepared by the NFB for the opening of *Food – Secret of the Peace* already explained this line of argument quite eloquently in the summer of 1945. Nicholas Read had accompanied the Italian police on a raid of black marketers in Rome, and then he went to Yugoslavia only a week after its liberation. Powerful images were shot for use in the film, which depicted food shortages in six European countries, underlining the political danger: "Black markets like this in Italy mean hungry people in Europe electing governments for peace may choose representatives hostile to the Western Allies if they are not fed quickly enough."[101] Food controls and rationing in

Canada were indispensable to alleviate food shortages in Europe because, "[o]nly by feeding the nations of Europe can the struggle for their liberation be completed and their friendship secured in the new world of peace and reconstruction."[102] The distribution described above suggests that this political message featured prominently not only in the training of UNRRA teams and to inform civil servants but access to theatrical and nontheatrical networks put national and foreign audiences within reach and in a timely manner.

The third theme was to open a space for future cooperation among different peoples, including even those from ex-enemy countries. Victors and vanquished could not avoid cooperation, despite the terrible loss of life, the widespread destruction, and the ultimate failure of civilization. The films used narrative and visual strategies that strove to counter the thesis of collective guilt of whole nations – the Italians and the Germans – for waging war and committing war crimes. In so doing, it followed in the steps of earlier productions referring to Italy. An effort was made to dissociate the army and the Fascist party from the Italian people. *The Gates of Italy* (1943), part of the series *The World in Action*, was preparing for the moment when the Allies would land. In a daring approach, it led public opinion to perceive Italians as future members of the United Nations community.[103] Similar strategies were used in subsequent films, including those made for UNRRA. In this case also, there was a need to prepare public opinion for the future integration of all nations into the postwar international community. Behind this attitude one could read a resolve not to repeat the errors of the aftermath of the First World War when Germany and Bolshevik Russia were treated as pariahs. Specific national groups were most often not identified in the series of films examined here, although the geographical environment, clothing, and physical outlook can provide clues. Of course, it was understood that UNRRA was intended to work in *liberated* areas only, helping the *victims* of a war inflicted upon them by Nazi Germany and Fascist Italy. The Italian population, however, was in a desperate situation and needed help[104] while millions of displaced persons were in Germany. Needs were also great in Austria. UNRRA sent its cameraman, Peter Hopkinson, to film the search for food by the hungry in Vienna.[105] Yet, the geography of UNRRA's Health Division interventions was directly connected to theaters of war and to the victim/enemy divide. Health assistance was provided for countries which had been liberated from the enemy and did not have enough foreign exchange to buy medical supplies; other countries, such as the ex-enemy countries (Italy, Austria, and Hungary) received help according to strict UNRRA's conditions; finally, in Germany, only displaced persons were to receive medical help.[106] If the four occupiers (Britain, the United States, the Soviet Union, and France) considered at first that German public health was a secondary matter, the immediate postwar situation soon revealed that it was rather an urgent priority.[107]

The solution to international problems called for international cooperation; therefore the films' objective was to focus on the common lot of *civilians* in distress, not to make distinctions between victims and perpetrators. This long-term perspective on the situation indicates some differences between the work of the National Film Board and the more restrictive policy of UNRRA, which was selective as to who should receive help; the overall relief operation, however, was entirely focused on civilian issues. The NFB also made use of visual strategies that underlined the extraordinary resilience of women and children who were shown prominently in many of its films. Most often, their nationality was not mentioned. Finally, the strong visual presence of children focuses the attention of viewers towards the future and contributes to dispelling the idea that a whole people could be collectively considered war criminals.

CONCLUSION

From its very beginning, UNRRA had decided to use to its fullest ability the mobilizing capacity of film as a mass medium. The administration had access to important visual collections (films and photographs), highly qualified technical personnel, reputable production units, and, finally, well organized international commercial and nontheatrical distribution networks. All this was put to the service of common objectives: to circulate vital information and educate the masses about the necessity of international cooperation, connect distant audiences and make them aware and involved with what was happening half the world away, and promote a system of values with the high hope of a lasting, peaceful, legacy.

These films were soon overlooked because of the onset of the Cold War that destroyed part of the idealism that was so present in the immediate postwar period. Nevertheless, they tried to create and sustain a collective sense of responsibility, a mass solidarity, and to connect North American audiences – soon to be participants in relief effort campaigns – with the civilians of war-ravaged areas. Images became an essential component of this major intervention and mobilization. The open reference to a system of moral and political values that could connect populations unknown to each other, the will to truly penetrate the social body, to initiate a process of active contribution and participation, were key elements of postwar idealism.

International cooperation was an important principle, but it needed to be built from the bottom up, it had to be created, it required massive involvement and commitment by responsible citizens. The coherent and concerted film production, as described above, worked towards this crucial transition from war to peace. It encouraged a public opinion that was favourable to the necessary task of rebuilding Europe, including its democratic culture, by stressing that peace, freedom, political rights, and security were immediately connected to the initial recovery of European civilians who would soon be called upon to reorganize their political institutions and overcome their divisions. These aspects were always strongly expressed in discussion trailers and focus groups, and the long-term issues were never separated from the depiction of daily life. The National Film Board of Canada created a visual education program that may not have been as demonstrative as Nazi power propaganda had been, according to Ben Shepard, but this series of films presented a discourse on international cooperation and the urgent action needed by ordinary citizens during a critical phase of transition. It was propaganda, not the highly emotional kind that audiences had been fed during the war years, but propaganda for peace and for peacetime.

APPENDIX

Select filmography

Descriptions are taken from the NFB Film Guide, *The productions of the National Film Board of Canada from 1939 to 1989*, The National Film Board of Canada, 1991. The dates indicated are the release dates. All films are in black and white, with sound (and voiceover narration).

In the Wake of the Armies: UNRRA, August 1944, 14 minutes, black and white, series *Canada Carries On*. Director/editor, Guy Glover; narrator, Lorne Greene.

A description of the aims and purposes of the United Nations Relief and Rehabilitation Administration. In the wake of World War II, Europe is in desperate need of food, clothing, medical supplies and, especially, agricultural supplies. As countries are liberated UNRRA is stepping in to help meet these enormous needs.

Archival film

(Note: contrary to the title appearing on film and paper archives concerning this film, it is listed in this NFB Guide under *UNRRA – In the Wake of the Armies*)

Getting the most out of a film: UNRRA – In the Wake of the Armies, 1944, 3 minutes, b&w, series *Getting the most out of a film*. Producer, Stanley Hawes.

Trade union representatives discuss the work of the United Nations Relief and Rehabilitation Administration as illustrated in the film *UNRRA – In the Wake of the Armies.*

Archival film

Now – the Peace, May 1945, 20 minutes, b&w, series *World in Action*. Producer/script/editor, Stuart Legg.

This film looks at the plans made at Dumbarton Oaks in 1945 for a renewed international organization devoted to world peace – the United Nations.

Archival film

Getting the most out of a film: Now – the Peace, 1945, 10 minutes, b&w, series *Getting the most out of a film*. Producer, Stanley Hawes.

Produced as an introduction to the NFB film *Now – the Peace*, this film features discussion among members of various unions in the Vancouver area. They express hope that the newly established United Nations, with its Economic Council, will be able to reduce the threat of war and increase the security and prosperity of workers everywhere.

Archival film

Food – Secret of the Peace, July 1945, 11 minutes, series *World in Action*. Director/producer/script/editor, Stuart Legg.

This film presents an analysis of the chief postwar problem in liberated Europe. Opening with scenes of food queues and hunger riots in famine areas, this film points out the political danger that lies in starvation conditions. Causes of food shortages and measures taken by the Allies to solve these problems are described.

Archival film

Food – Secret of the Peace [Discussion Trailer], 1946, 5 minutes. Producer, Stanley Hawes.

A group discussion of the issues raised in the film, which points out the social and political dangers of starvation conditions.

Archival film

Friends in Need, September 1945, 9 minutes, b&w. Producer, Alan Field.

A plea to Canadians to help provide textiles and much-needed clothing for those left destitute, homeless and hungry by World War II. Produced by the NFB in cooperation with the Canadian United Allied Relief Fund.

Archival film

Suffer Little Children, December 1945, 10 minutes, b&w, series *Canada Carries On*. Director/producer/editor, Sydney Newman; script, Len Peterson; photography, Nicholas Read; narrator, Lorne Greene.

At the end of World War II there were sixty million sick and starving children in Europe. Clothes and toys from every village and town in the United States and Canada helped to bring comfort and cheer, but this met only a small part of the demand. The United

Nations Relief and Rehabilitation Administration undertook to provide food, clothing, shelter, medical care, education and sympathetic attention to these terrorized victims of war.

Archival film

Out of the Ruins, August 1946, 32 minutes, b&w. Director, Nicholas Read; producer, Tom Daly; script, Rita Greer and Robert Greer. Produced by the NFB with the financial assistance of UNRRA.

Greece was ravaged first by World War II, and then by civil war. This film looks at the economic and social problems that resulted, and at the need for peace in this war-torn land. The efforts of the United Nations Relief and Rehabilitation Administration to provide effective aid are highlighted.

Archival film

Filmstrip

UNRRA goes into action, 48 frames filmstrip, July 1945, with 1 sound disc: analog, 33 1/3 rpm, mono.; 16 in.

NOTES

1 This research was supported by a grant from my home institution, Glendon College (York University, Toronto). I also wish to thank two archivists who generously helped me several years ago when I wanted to explore and bring together national and international archival material: Bernard Lutz (1944–2011) who was the archivist at the National Film Board of Canada in Montreal, and Angela Schiwy, the former chief archivist at the United Nations Organization – New York; without them, this research project could not have been carried out.
2 The titles of six films, one filmstrip, and three discussion trailers produced by the National Film Board of Canada for UNRRA-related contributions are listed in the appendix at the end of this chapter.
3 *Union List of U.N.R.R.A. Film. A Guide to Motion Picture Records Produced by Agencies throughout the World on the Activities of the United Nations Relief and Rehabilitation Administration 1943–1947,*

Lake Success, New York, Archives Section, Communication and Records
Division, United Nations, March 1949, 21.

4 United Nations Archives (hereafter UN Archives), PAG-4/1.5.0. United
Nations Relief and Rehabilitation Administration, Office of Public
Information (hereafter UNRRA, OPI), General Files, Box 2, Visual Media
Branch Report, September–October 1946, 1.

5 See in particular *The Grierson Effect: Tracing Documentary's
International Movement*, eds. Zoë Druick and Deane Williams (London:
British Film Institute/Palgrave Macmillan, 2014).

6 George Woodbridge, UNRRA: *The History of the United Nations Relief
and Rehabilitation Administration* (New York: Columbia University Press,
1950).

7 In numerous reviews and articles in the general and specialized press and
even in an early scholarly study: Patricia Joan Torson, "The Film Program
of U.N.R.R.A. A Study in International Cooperation for the Promotion of
International Understanding" (MA thesis, Dept. of International Relations
and Organization, American University, Washington DC, 1947).

8 Torson, *The Film Program of U.N.R.R.A.*, ii.

9 The Center for the Moving Image (Edinburgh): http://www.edfilmfest.org.uk/.

10 "Reconstruction in the Immediate Aftermath of War: A Comparative
Study of Europe, 1945–50" was historian Eric Hobsbawm's Balzan
research project established at Birkbeck College (University of London).
Four international workshops were held between 2005 and 2007, the final
conference took place in 2008. http://www.balzan.org/en/prizewinners/
eric-hobsbawm/research-project-hobsbawm.

11 See in particular the research of Jessica Reinisch who directed the special
issue of the *Journal of Contemporary History*, 43 (July 2008), in connection with the Balzan research project mentioned above; in that issue of the
JCH, her articles "Introduction: Relief in the Aftermath of War," 371–404,
and "'We Shall Rebuild Anew a Powerful Nation': UNRRA, Internationalism and National Reconstruction in Poland," 451–76, are important contributions in the history of UNRRA, a necessary reappraisal, and a more
nuanced understanding of what UNRRA was able to accomplish in
extremely difficult circumstances. See also the work of Sharif Gemie and
Louise Rees, "Representing and Reconstructing Identities in the Postwar
World. Refugees, UNRRA, and Fred Zinnemann's Film, *The Search*
(1948)," *International Review of Social History* 56, no. 3 (December 2011):
441–73. The authors consider this film as an exception because it did
explore the social and political issues of the massive presence of displaced
persons in postwar Europe, it was a commercial success, and is the only

feature-length film of the 1940s that puts the work of UNRRA at the center of its dramatic narrative (448). Like Reinisch, the authors stress that UNRRA deserves more study by historians. It must be mentioned that *The Search* is listed in the *Union List of U.N.R.R.A. Film*, 6; this 90-minute film was produced by Praesens Films AG, based in Zurich (Switzerland).

12 One such example is the action of UNESCO (founded in London in November 1945) in relation to reconstruction. See Chloé Maurel, "L'action de l'Unesco dans le domaine de la reconstruction," *Histoire@ Politique* 2013/1 (n19), 160–75. The Food and Agriculture Organization (FAO) was created in October 1945 in Quebec City; the World Health Organization (WHO) followed in April 1948. During the very first weeks of its existence, UNESCO was called to join UNRRA in providing aid to areas devastated by the war. At the time, however, UNESCO was unable to pinpoint the exact nature and scope of its responsibilities in that area. Nor could the organization, itself in a preparatory phase and without an established program, commit any resources (UNESCO archives, AG3 Preparatory Commission, London–Paris, 1945–46, vol. 6, Subcommittee on the needs of devastated areas, documents from January to June 1946) in S. Langlois, "And Action! UN and UNESCO Coordinating Information Films 1945–1951," in *A History of UNESCO: Global Actions and Impacts*, Poul Duedahl, ed. (Palgrave Macmillan, 2016), 73–94.

13 Ben Shepard, *The Long Road Home: The Aftermath of the Second World War* (New York: Alfred A. Knopf, 2011), 8. In an earlier article, Ben Shephard differentiated between the rhetorical, political, and military planning, the latter being the most important. During the winter of 1943–44, it became clear that the military was reluctant to "do welfare," thus UNRRA was created, but, for Shepard, it remained a weak organization. "'Becoming Planning Minded': The Theory and Practice of Relief 1940–1945," *Journal of Contemporary History* 43, no. 3 (July 2008): 405–19.

14 Mark D. Alleyne, *Global Lies, Propaganda, the UN and World Order* (Basingstoke, UK: Palgrave Macmillan, 2003).

15 See the recent biography of Grierson by Jack C. Ellis, *John Grierson: Life, Contributions, Influence* (Carbondale and Edwardsville: Southern Illinois University Press, 2000).

16 Jean-Pierre Jeancolas, "N.V.D. 28, appel à témoins," *100 Années Lumière* (Paris: AFAA Intermedia, 1989), 20.

17 John Grierson, "The Nature of Propaganda" (1942), Richard Meran Barsam, ed., *Nonfiction Film Theory and Criticism* (New York: E.P. Dutton & Co, 1976), 33–4.

18 Gary Evans, *John Grierson and the National Film Board: The Politics of Wartime Propaganda 1939–1945* (Toronto: University of Toronto Press, 1984), 4.

19 John Grierson, "Postwar Patterns," *Hollywood Quarterly* 2 (January 1946), 161–2.

20 Ibid., 162.

21 Ibid., 164.

22 Ibid., 163.

23 William Goetz, "The Canadian Wartime Documentary: 'Canada Carries On' and 'The World in Action,'" *Cinema Journal* 2 (Spring 1977): 59.

24 Quoted in Evans, *John Grierson*, 169.

25 Archives of the National Film Board of Canada (hereafter NFB Archives), *Memorandum to Mr. Salisbury on UNRRA's film activities following special work by representatives of the National Film Board of Canada, lent to UNRRA as advisers on a film program*, 15 July 1944. Morse Salisbury was the director of the Public Information Division of UNRRA from April 1944 until February 1946.

26 Woodbridge, *UNRRA: The History of the United Nations Relief and Rehabilitation Administration*, I, 284.

27 Such was the case in France where all professionals concerned, whether in the press, radio, cinema, information cooperatives, or war correspondents, were given specific orders by the government. *Textes essentiels concernant la presse, la radiodiffusion, le cinéma, les coopératives d'information, les correspondants de guerre*, Gouvernement provisoire de la République française, Secrétariat général, Commissariat à l'Information, n.d., "Instructions au cinéma," 43–52; also "Le cinéma allié," *Le film français* 8 (December 1944): 10.

28 UN Archives, PAG-4/1.5.0. UNRRA, OPI, General Files, Box 2, Visual Media Branch Report – October 1945, 1.

29 Gary Evans, *In the National Interest: A Chronicle of the National Film Board of Canada from 1949 to 1989* (Toronto: University of Toronto Press, 1991), 7.

30 Evans, *John Grierson*, 301.

31 UN Archives, UNRRA, S-0554-0002, "UNRRA Films," March 1946, 2 p. The NFB films were *In the Wake of the Armies: UNRRA* (1944); *Food – Secret of the Peace* (July 1945); *Suffer Little Children* (December 1945).

32 Bruno Cabanes, *The Great War and the Origins of Humanitarianism 1918–1924* (Cambridge University Press, 2014).

33 They are listed in the *Union List of U.N.R.R.A. Film*. March 1949.

34 United Nations Relief and Rehabilitation Administration, UNRRA:
   Organization, Aims, Progress (Washington, DC: 1944), 30.
35 UNRRA: Organization, Aims, Progress, 11.
36 Goetz, "The Canadian Wartime Documentary," 63.
37 UN Archives, PAG-4/1.5.0. UNRRA, OPI, General Files, Box 2, Visual
   Media Branch Report, December 1944. Overall, the recommended contribution of each member country for UNRRA's relief operations was 1 per
   cent of its national income for the year ending 30 June 1943; for Canada
   this amounted to an authorized contribution of $77,000,000 (Some Facts
   about UNRRA, Office of Public Information, Washington, 1 November
   1944, 6).
38 In the Wake of the Armies: UNRRA, NFB, 1944, 14 minutes, series
   Canada Carries On, Director/editor, Guy Glover; narrator, Lorne Greene.
39 NFB Archives, Memorandum..., 15 July 1944, 5–6. Also PF 1042 and a
   short 8-page guide, "In the Wake of the Armies. Raw material for screen
   writers, directors, producers, story editors," March 1946.
40 Torson, The Film Program of U.N.R.R.A., 105.
41 Ibid., 87.
42 NFB Archives, PF 1042, In the Wake of the Armies: UNRRA, press release
   by UNRRA, Washington, DC, 19 June 1944 for release to morning papers
   of Wednesday 21 June. Copy forwarded by the Canadian Embassy.
43 NFB Archives, PF 1042, In the Wake of the Armies: UNRRA, Information
   Sheet, August 1944.
44 UNRRA: Organization, Aims, Progress, 4, 11.
45 Some Facts about UNRRA, Washington, DC, Office of Public Information,
   1 November 1944, 6–7.
46 Ibid., 9.
47 Woodbridge, UNRRA, I–280.
48 Union List of U.N.R.R.A. Film, 14.
49 Goetz, "The Canadian Wartime Documentary," 73.
50 Evans, John Grierson, 224–5.
51 Torson, The Film Program of U.N.R.R.A., 124.
52 UN Archives, PAG-4/1.5.0. UNRRA, OPI, General Files, Box 2, Visual
   Media Branch Report – February 1945.
53 Cine-Citta Camp (NFB, Rome, 1945, camera: Read, 530 feet, unedited).
   Note: all the film material mentioned in the Union List of U.N.R.R.A.
   Film (negatives and positives) is of 35 mm film stock. In this case, 530 feet
   of 35 mm film lasts about 6 minutes. The NFB keeps the original negative;
   UNRRA gets a fine-grain master positive. The 35 mm films are intended

for commercial movie theaters; the 16 mm format is intended for nontheatrical showings.

54 NFB Archives, Information sheet, *Getting the most out of a film: UNRRA
– In the Wake of the Armies* (trailer).

55 NFB Archives PF 1042, *In the Wake of the Armies: UNRRA*. Booklet *Film
Programme B 3*[rd] *Series.*

56 90,000 feet of 16 mm film stock are the equivalent of 2,500 minutes
of film. The 150 copies of the 14-minute film would take up about
75,600 feet.

57 UN Archives, PAG-4/1.5.0. UNRRA, OPI, General Files, Box 2, Visual
Media Branch Report, March 1945, Summary.

58 NFB Archives, PF 1042, *In the Wake of the Armies: UNRRA*, NFB internal
memo from Dan Wallace to Kay Young (*Canada Carries On*), 21 May
1945.

59 NFB Archives, PF 1042, *In the Wake of the Armies: UNRRA*, letter from
William H. Wells (UNRRA) to Ross McLean (NFB), 29 January 1946.

60 *UNRRA goes into action*, filmstrip, NFB production, April–May 1945.
Filmstrips are sometimes referred to as "slide films"; they were an inex-
pensive, light, and versatile technology making use of photographs, draw-
ings, or charts mounted on a continuous strip of film. They should be
considered among the major media of the twentieth century. In May 1945,
an initial twenty-five prints with a sound recording were made for UNRRA
(UNRRA, OPI, Visual Media Branch Report, Maurice Liu to Morse
Salisbury, 4 June 1945). *The Monthly UNRRA Review*, no. 10, June 1945,
18, indicated that the filmstrip was accompanied by a mimeographed
commentary and that a disc recorded commentary was in preparation.
Maurice Liu was the narrator and he describes the role of UNRRA in helping to provide food, clothing, medical supplies, blankets, and tools to liberated people who suffered during the Second World War. The sound
material includes music by the Yugoslav Chorus of the UNRRA Refugee
Camp in El Shatt, Egypt, as originally recorded by the British Broadcasting
Corp. I have found the filmstrip (images only) at the NFB archives and the
sound commentary on disc at the Library of Congress in Washington, DC.
This is but one example of the challenges and requirements of doing
research in international organizations' material which was routinely
commissioned to production units located in different countries.

61 Goetz, "The Canadian Wartime Documentary," 72, 76.

62 NFB Archives, PF 01-010 *Now – the Peace*, leaflet from Brandon Films,
Inc.

63 NFB Archives, PF 01-010 *Now – the Peace*, Educational Film Library Association evaluation, February 1946.

64 See in particular the work of Mark Mazower, *No Enchanted Palace: The End of Empire and the Ideological Origins of the United Nations* (Princeton: Princeton University Press, 2009).

65 Torson, *The Film Program of U.N.R.R.A.*, 125.

66 NFB Archives, PF 01-011 *Food – Secret of the Peace*, text for *The World in Action* series, 1.

67 NFB Archives, PF 01-011 text for the American version.

68 NFB Archives, PF 01-011 *Food – Secret of the Peace*, Report on promotional aids sent out and results received on "Food – Secret of the Peace," 2, Reports from field representatives.

69 *Friends in Need* (NFB, September 1945, 9 minutes).

70 NFB Archives, PF 04-904, *Friends in Need*, memo from M. Ross to Alan Field, n.d.

71 NFB Archives, *Memorandum…*, 3.

72 The *Union List of U.N.R.R.A. Film* (7) includes newsreel and cuts under the title *Canada Donates 12 Million Pounds of Used Clothing to UNRRA* (NFB, December 1945, 565 feet). The mention "Newsreel" indicates an edited, released newsreel.

73 *Suffer Little Children*, by Sydney Newman (NFB, December 1945, 10 minutes).

74 NFB Archives, PF 01-533 *Suffer Little Children, Utilization Analysis of National Film Board Production*, "Suffer Little Children," report sent to Sydney Newman, 16 August 1946.

75 NFB Archives, PF 01-533 *Suffer Little Children*, memo from the liaison officer of the Canadian embassy in Washington (L. Savage) to Sydney Newman, 16 April 1946.

76 NFB Archives, PF 01-533 *Suffer Little Children*, Release information, USDA, 25 April 1946.

77 NFB Archives, PF 01-533 *Suffer Little Children*, Press story. Film showing for housewives on Europe's food situation.

78 *Emergency Conference on European Cereals Supplies Held in London from 3rd to 6th April 1946* (London: 1946), 77–9.

79 Ira A. Hirschmann, *The Embers Still Burn* (New York: Simon and Schuster, 1949), 25–7.

80 Arch A. Mercey, "Social Uses of the Motion Picture," *Annals of the American Academy of Political and Social Science*, 250; Communication and Social Action (March 1947), 102; Evans, *John Grierson*, 301.

81 Centre national de la cinématographie (Paris), Archives de la Commission
    de contrôle des films cinématographiques, files of *Suffer Little Children,
    Food – Secret of the Peace* and *Out of the Ruins.*
82 UN Archives, PAG-4/1.5.0. UNRRA, OPI, General Files, Box 2, Visual
    Media Branch Report, April 1946, 2.
83 NFB Archives, PF 01-002, *Out of the Ruins.* Four reels of 35mm film, an
    elaborate musical score, and recording session with an orchestra, for a
    total cost of 26,000 dollars.
84 *Documentary News Letter,* June–July 1947.
85 United States National Archives & Records Administration, RG 208,
    Office of War Information, Series Propaganda, Information, and
    Documentary Motion Pictures, 1941–45.
86 Gladwin Hill, "Our Film Program in Germany: 11. How Far Was It a
    Failure?," *Hollywood Quarterly* 2 (January 1947), 135.
87 UN Archives, PAG-4/1.5.0. UNRRA, OPI, General Files, Box 2, Visual
    Media Branch Report, April 1946, 2.
88 UN Archives, Central Registry, RAG-1, files 1001-9-1/2/3/4, letter from
    Trygve Lie to Georges Bidault (France), Ernest Bevin (UK), George C.
    Marshall (USA), Andrej Gromyko (USSR), 21 February 1947.
89 NFB Archives, PF 01-533, *Suffer Little Children,* excerpt from the *London
    News Chronicle,* 2 March 1946; memo from Janet Scellen (NFB Ottawa)
    to Ross McLean, 21 March 1946.
90 Evans, *John Grierson,* 224–5.
91 Allan M. Winkler, *The Politics of Propaganda: The Office of War
    Information 1942–1945* (New Haven: Yale University Press, 1978), 73–4.
92 Hirschmann, *The Embers Still Burn,* 6.
93 See Zoë Druick, "'Reaching the Multimillions': Liberal Internationalism
    and the Establishment of Documentary Film," Lee Grieveson and Haidee
    Wasson, eds., *Inventing Film Studies* (Durham: Duke University Press,
    2008), 66–92.
94 Richard Griffith, in *Documentary Film,* Paul Rotha, ed. (London: Faber
    and Faber, 1952), 333.
95 UN Archives, DAG – 12/1.0 Box 2, Office of Public Information, Sub-
    Committee of technical advisory Committee on Information, "Information
    policy – London," Points raised by J. Grierson, 4 January 1946, 2.
96 Preface by John Grierson for the third edition of Paul Rotha, Sinclair
    Road, and Richard Griffith, *Documentary Film: The Use of the Film
    Medium to Interpret Creatively and in Social Terms the Life of the People
    as It Exists in Reality* (London: Faber and Faber Ltd., 1951, 1st ed. 1935),
    21.

97 Griffith, *Documentary Film*, 333.

98 Mercey, "Social Uses of the Motion Picture", 102.

99 *Out of the Ruins* (NFB, 1946, 32 minutes).

100 NFB Archives, PF 01-011, *Food – Secret of the Peace*, NFB news briefs, 1.

101 NFB Archives, PF 01-011, promotion leaflet for the film *Food – Secret of the Peace*, NFB, Stuart Legg, July 1945, 11 minutes, *World in Action* series.

102 Ibid.

103 Goetz, "The Canadian Wartime Documentary," 67.

104 *UNRRA. Organization. Aims. Progress*, 23.

105 UN Archives, PAG-4/1.5.0. UNRRA, OPI, General Files, Box 2, Visual Media Branch Report, June 1946, 2. It was the same British cameraman, Peter Hopkinson, who was later sent by UNRRA to Ukraine and Byelorussia in the fall and winter 1946–47.

106 Wilbur A. Sawyer, "Achievements of UNRRA as an International Health Organization," *American Journal of Public Health*, no. 37, January 1947, 44.

107 For more on this topic, see the excellent monograph by Jessica Reinisch, *The Perils of Peace: The Public Health Crisis in Occupied Germany* (Oxford University Press, 2013).

3

Canadians and the "First Wave" of United Nations Technical Assistance

David Webster[1]

The United Nations was born with great hopes that it would play a central role in maintaining global peace and security. But as the ambiguous cooperation of the Second World War chilled and then froze into full-scale Cold War, the UN was unable to carry out this task. The two greatest powers, the United States and the Soviet Union, were at odds with each other around the globe. To be effective as a guarantor of peace and security, the UN needed the permanent members of the Security Council, and especially the two superpowers, to work in harmony even if not full friendship. The Cold War made this impossible.

So was the UN as doomed as the League of Nations that had come before, ineffective in the security realm and thus irrelevant in the great affairs of the globe? It was not. In the realms of economic and social affairs, in fact, it proved to be vital. In this, it echoed the league that had come before. Several recent historical studies reveal the league not as a colossal failure but as a world organization that was influential and vital in economic and social issues, even while it failed in the end to ensure global peace.[2] The same case can be made for the UN, and there is a growing literature that makes precisely that case.[3] The most careful study of Canada's role in the formation of the UN, too, concludes that Canada and Canadians were influential in the UN in economic affairs and helped make it a vital organization more through the Economic and Social Council (ECOSOC) than the higher profile Security Council.[4]

While the Cold War split the world on an East–West line of tension, the UN was a major arena allowing the world to be seen more in North–South terms, with the majority world rendered visible and given agency. Through Cold War lenses, the global South was a battleground. Even as many of its governments sought a path of nonalignment, the very concept of nonalignment implied a Cold War world. In the UN – especially the General Assembly and also in ECOSOC – the countries of the global South could speak and at times be heard more clearly in global politics.[5] This helped the world body, too. As the UN struggled to be relevant in global politics during the early Cold War, it found a new global mission in pushing for the decolonization of less developed countries and then promoting their economic development after independence. The chosen tool in the early years was technical assistance – the attempt to transfer expertise and models from wealthy countries to less developed countries and thus advance a mission of worldwide economic development. In this great mission, Canadians were prominent. Technical assistance, especially in the first wave before the formation of the UN Development Programme in 1965, shows Canada and Canadians playing a substantial role in one of the major tasks of the United Nations in its early years. This chapter illustrates this through four Canadian exemplars: UN Technical Assistance Administration chief Hugh Keenleyside; industries and planning advisor George Cadbury; poet, professor, and planning advocate F.R. Scott; and mining engineer Gilbert Monture. Their technical assistance journeys are not a full story, but they sketch a picture of Canadian involvement in what was perhaps the most important venture of the UN's first decade: technical assistance for economic development in the global South.

Studies of the history of development have tended to centre on individual donors, especially the United States, and to stress the foundational role of US President Harry Truman's "Point Four" in the creation of technical assistance.[6] This is not wrong, but the UN must be read back into the story as a central actor and nexus. Technical assistance was not only Truman's Point Four but also Point Six of Trygve Lie's program for achieving peace through the UN.[7] Lie, a Norwegian Labour Party politician, was one of those who promoted a technical assistance model inspired less by American New Deal liberalism than by European and Commonwealth social democratic thinking.

Trygve Lie's account of the origins of UN technical assistance traces its origins to his first trip to Latin America in 1947. On returning to

New York, he wrote, he had been overcome by the message delivered "not by statesmen or other leaders, but by the thousands of dirty, ragged figures that never attended a reception or raised their voices in any fine declaration of faith. I was distressed by the sight of poverty and ignorance on such an unexpected scale – and on the very doorstep of the richest nation on earth. The contrasts to be seen in a single city, or in a single city block, were hardly to be believed." There was urgency in this poverty, he recalled. "The creation of a firm and lasting structure that would help preserve world peace implied all possible help to nations grappling with problems like those we had just witnessed. Here was a field where we would have to take the initiative; and we could not afford to wait."[8] Lie summed up the sense of mission in his memoirs:

> My 1947 visits to Latin America had left me with a sense of impotence, distressed by what I had seen, but even more so by the necessity of forever being forced to deal in terms of assurance and promises. Here were millions of people whose support we needed, and whose confidence in the United Nations could be strengthened, if only we were in a position to act. Their needs were not reflected in the vocabulary of military security that so fully occupied the world's statesmen. Their needs were for economic and social assistance in the countless areas where they themselves could not hope to make a start without outside help. Now, we had at least begun.[9]

The result was a small technical assistance program administered through the UN, which broadly continued earlier League of Nations technical assistance to such countries as China.[10] This scheme suffered from low profile and meagre funds. Both these troubles vanished when Harry Truman declared American government support for a big global technical assistance push, in which he envisioned the UN as a major actor. The result was an Expanded Programme of Technical Assistance (EPTA) accountable to the UN Economic and Social Council, delivered through the UN itself and such specialized agencies as the World Health Organization and the Food and Agriculture Organization.

The channel for UN "Point Six" aid was the UN Technical Assistance Administration (TAA), which operated from 1950–59 under the leadership of Hugh Keenleyside, a Canadian civil servant. Keenleyside had been an important Canadian diplomat before the Second World War, influencing Canada–Asia relations in particular. In 1947, he was recalled from his perch as ambassador to Mexico to become deputy minister of Mines and Resources in Ottawa, a job that also made him commissioner of the Northwest Territories. In effect, he ruled the territories from his Ottawa office. In a three-year tenure, he "transformed the somewhat laissez-faire style of northern government into one of active intervention supported by major financial investment."[11] From ambassador to a less developed country, he became the chief official mapping out an activist economic development strategy in a northern, semicolonial periphery of his home country. Keenleyside went on from his northern tenure to lead one of the first UN technical assistance missions, in Bolivia in 1950. He parlayed that into a job as director-general of the UN Technical Assistance Administration. The Canadian colonial North, for him, became a laboratory for policies to be applied to the decolonizing global South.

Under Keenleyside's leadership, the UN technical assistance mission to Bolivia set the pattern for UN technical assistance as a whole. It was not the first such mission, but its influence went far beyond the country it addressed directly. The UN dispatched a presurvey team to Bolivia in 1949. While it was there, a revolution broke out. Though that uprising was put down, the mission noted mildly, "the conditions for rendering technical assistance did not seem very propitious."[12] Bolivia asked for experts in mining and taxation policy, but the UN insisted on a full, twenty-two-man survey of the national economy by foreign experts and chose Keenleyside to head it.

Why, the mission's final report asked, was Bolivia underdeveloped in spite of its abundant mineral resources? "It was the first duty of the United Nations Mission to find a satisfactory explanation of this paradoxical contrast between the potential wealth of Bolivia and the failure of its people to translate that wealth into the concrete evidences of a prosperous national economy. *It is now the belief of Members of the Mission—and in this belief they are supported by the opinion of every Bolivian with whom the matter was discussed—that the explanation of the paradox is to be found in the governmental and administrative instability that has consistently marked the history of the nation.*" The obstacles lay in poor governance, in other words, *not* in international systemic factors or domestic political developments. With the injection of expertise, the team argued, it would be "possible to telescope into a single generation or less the

economic and social advance that will otherwise involve a slow pro-
gression over many decades." That expertise could only come from
abroad. Therefore, the key recommendation was that the United
Nations provide "a number of experienced and competent administrative officials of unquestioned integrity drawn from a variety of
countries, and that the Bolivian Government appoint these officials
on a temporary basis to positions of influence and authority as integral members of the Bolivian civil service." Without such a "bold and
dramatic step," Bolivia would face centuries more underdevelopment; *with* the experiment for international civil servants in place,
Bolivia could advance rapidly. Granted, this was a risk and a new
type of UN assistance. Yet, in the mission's view, it offered "the only
real hope of success."[13] The report stressed apolitical themes of economic development, paying no attention to the fact that Bolivia's
government was clinging to power by a thread against a strong opposition party, the National Revolutionary Movement (MNR), backed
by the mining unions vital to Bolivia's main export industry.[14]

Obviously, there would be fears of foreign control if foreign advisors were to staff Bolivian government offices. To defuse that,
Keenleyside pointed to the multilateral aspects of the advisors: "The
fact that they would come from a number of countries and would
serve in a sense under U.N. auspices would, we believed, counteract
charges that the programme was just a continuance of the old colonial
system."[15] One newspaper, on the other hand, called this program a
"test-run for the whole world-wide program of technical assistance."[16]
In other words, multilateralism – the fact that the UN would recruit
and pay advisors – meant that the oversight by definition could not be
colonial. Some disagreed, with UN social affairs chief Henri Laugier
saying the program would be a disaster drawing hostility from all
recipient governments. But Keenleyside's proposal was backed by
David Owen's economic affairs division and, after Keenleyside became
director of the Technical Assistance Administration, by the TAA itself.
Bolivia became a top UN field: in its first five years, third in the world
among TAA projects after Yugoslavia and Iran. In the late 1950s, it
was still the largest TAA project in Latin America, getting more than
double the funds going to second-place Colombia.[17]

The project raised issues of control and tutelage by the UN over an
independent country. Thus the opposition MNR opposed it. Yet when
the MNR managed to take power in 1952, the UN was able to negotiate an agreement for "technical consultants" after all. By 1956, MNR

president Victor Paz Estenssoro was praising the UN mission for its assistance to his government in terms as strong as any ever used by his predecessor. The change of government did not ruffle UN planning and publicity, which reported as if there had been no transfer of power, in keeping with UN claims that its technical assistance was apolitical. UN advice aided the tendency of the revolutionary government to become a modernizing technocratic administration.

This was true not only in Bolivia but also globally. Development was foundational to the UN, providing a mission for the world body that promised more success than its faltering security function as the Cold War set in. Yes, the United States sponsored the resolution creating a UN technical assistance program, and paid 40 to 60 per cent of the bill in the early years, but more than half the experts came from Western Europe with the US share falling from 17 per cent to less than 10 per cent.[18]

Canadians, on the other hand, were prominent, part of a Canadian embrace of the UN as a whole. When the Commonwealth established its "Colombo Plan for Cooperative Economic Development in South and South-East Asia," the Liberal government headed by Prime Minister Louis St Laurent was highly sceptical, wondering why aid should be dissipated through Commonwealth channels rather than focused through the UN's new technical assistance machinery. Ottawa was careful to give more to UN technical assistance than its Commonwealth counterpart, and St Laurent urged that the Commonwealth scheme be folded into UN-run technical assistance.[19] Technical assistance, like support for the UN as a whole, was seen as being in the Canadian interest. A cabinet memorandum summed it up:

The Expanded Programme [EPTA] is a constructive United Nations plan to confer on the more backward peoples of the world some of the technical advantages of Western production and organization, and thereby enable them to develop self-reliance and to learn how to improve their standard of living by their own efforts. This will, at one and the same time, meet the widespread demand amongst under-developed peoples for a share in the benefits of western progress and offer a concrete retort to the promises and allure of Russian Communism.

Participation in the Programme will also extend the knowledge of Canadian technical achievement and assist in developing markets for Canadian exports. It will give an opportunity for

Canadian experts to be employed in various fields abroad; and
students coming to Canada for training under the Programme
will take back with them firsthand knowledge of Canadian
industry and production.[20]

At the same time, the UN wanted Canadian involvement badly: no
country would object to Canadian experts, the TAA argued, particularly since they could advise in English and French, the two languages
most in demand.[21]

Technical assistance offered the world body a grand new mission:
in Trygve Lie's words, "a worldwide crusade against poverty." Here
the UN had a unique role that no one government or group of states
could play. Lie declared, "Under the United Nations programme,
technical assistance for economic development cannot be used for
purposes of domination or imperialism." Keenleyside called technical
assistance "the most important job the UN could do."[22]

The UN was one element in a multilateral aid universe alongside
the United States, the Colombo Plan for cooperative economic development in South and Southeast Asia, Japanese, and European aid
schemes. It had its own unique flavour, one that was above all social-
democratic. This meant members of the Co-operative Commonwealth
Federation, forerunner to today's NDP, and other moderate leftists in
Canada were especially prominent in the TAA. There they were part of
an alternative transmission belt for development thinking, independent of any government. Although it did not displace neoclassical economics, a new field of development economics, with a central role for
the UN as transmission belt, was emerging in this period. Positivist
ideas going back to the elite-driven socialism of Henri Saint-Simon
and Robert Owen were transmitted through British Fabians and
through other European and Commonwealth social-democratic networks. Arthur Lewis, from the Caribbean island of St Lucia, could use
UN channels to move from his role as a social-democratic economist
in Britain, where he was influential in Labour party circles, to key
positions advising on development planning in Ghana and other
countries. He would later head the Caribbean Development Bank and
win a Nobel Prize in economics. Another Nobel economics laureate,
Gunnar Myrdal, moved between academic jobs, UN-linked positions,
and Sweden's Social Democratic Party. German-American scholar
Albert Hirschmann was a prolific author on development economics
partly on the strength of his job as advisor on economic planning to

the government of Colombia, a job that would have been arranged through the UN. German-British thinker E.F. Schumacher developed his ideas on "Buddhist economics" while advising on the UN's behalf in Burma. Argentine economist Raul Prebisch made his name at the UN-linked Economic Commission on Latin America, where leftist alternatives to neoclassical economics were allowed to flourish under his leadership. He would later head the UN Conference on Trade and Development (UNCTAD). Hans Singer's influential work in economics benefitted from the space provided by a succession of posts in the UN secretariat and elsewhere in the UN system. In short, few development economists did their work without some sort of UN link. The UN provided space for their thoughts to develop and for a social-democratic perspective on development economics to emerge outside a field that might otherwise have been dominated by the United States academy, government, and foundations.[23]

The TAA's operations director George Cadbury furnishes a Canadian example of this process. Cadbury's is one of the "life stories" of CCF members and other Canadian social democrats who worked as technical advisors through the UN TAA.[24] A British Fabian industrialist, Cadbury moved to head the Economic Planning Board of the government of Saskatchewan, formed by Tommy Douglas's CCF government in 1945, the year after it came to power. The Saskatchewan board was, in his words, "the marriage of the politician and the technician" and "the first comprehensive economic and social planning mechanism in a democratic country." (It did in fact form before similar national planning agencies in Western Europe, though Puerto Rico can claim pride of place in having a planning board slightly earlier.)[25] The Saskatchewan CCF relied heavily on a doctrine of social-democratic planning, with the planning board as the early nerve centre. But it also had to face the reality of having to function within a capitalist economy. It therefore abandoned calls for nationalization and sought private capital investment in order to deliver employment and develop natural resources. Frank Scott, at the time president of the national CCF, was involved in this shift, recommending the use of private investors to develop Saskatchewan's oil reserves. So the government in 1947 embraced a "four-year plan" to develop resources using outside investment.[26] This was a pragmatic decision based on perceived needs and the context of North America, rather than an ideological softening. The stated commitment to socialist planning remained. When Cadbury moved from

Saskatchewan's planning board to the UN Technical Assistance Administration, he wrote that there were "shades of Saskatchewan" in his new task.[27]

The TAA found itself top-heavy by the mid-1950s. Thus operations director Cadbury went into the field in 1954, with long-term field trips in Asia. The TAA tried to place him as head of the State Planning Bureau of Indonesia, but the Indonesian government chose not to accept a "chief planner" for fear of losing control of its own development planning. Instead Cadbury became advisor in Sri Lanka, then known as Ceylon. Ceylon was perhaps the keenest country in Asia to hear "the gospel of technical assistance," in the words of Beatrice Keyfitz, the Canadian wife of another technical advisor. It took this help "very seriously; the number of foreign experts per head of local population must set a world record."[28] Ceylon raised, in Keenleyside's words, "one original problem with which we are faced, namely how far we can go in urging policies upon governments."[29]

Cadbury felt that Ceylon's government lacked a clear idea of its own needs and thus laid them out in an early memorandum for the minister of industries: privatize government enterprises in order to generate capital for development, remove the need for annual budget appropriations for industry in favour of self-supporting industrialization, and increase the efficiency of those enterprises remaining under government control and encourage their transformation into cooperatives. Given that few industries would sell for much money, his stress was to find efficiencies.[30] He pressed for a development plan and offered detailed recommendations on specific industries. His reports on leather and ceramics industries provide an illustration of the overall view he was pushing on Colombo. It opened with an overview of the problem of development:

> The problems confronting any agricultural community which desires to increase the industrial activities in its area are very much the same all over the world. There is the same desire to emulate the great industrial countries like the United States of America, Great Britain and Japan and to achieve a resulting increase in the standard of living. To get results however one must not ignore economic or historical facts and must be careful to separate them from the product of wishful thinking.[31]

But much more than skills and capital were needed before Colombo could "become another Chicago." These included above all "the creation of a new attitude to industry in Ceylon itself."[32] Cadbury ended his Ceylon time in frustration – the industry department "just don't know what they are doing" and thus advice was close to pointless, he reported to New York.[33] "Ceylon is a discouraging place and as events go now there would be absolutely no point in continuing here."[34]

The following year, Cadbury left for a more rewarding contract in Jamaica, where he was seconded from the TAA as "Consultant and Adviser on Economic and Social Development" to Norman Manley, chief minister of the British colonial territory. In Kingston, he would have powers echoing those he had wielded at Saskatchewan's Economic Advisory and Planning Board but been denied on his TAA field assignments: access to all government documents and information backed by the right to prepare advice on request or on his own initiative.[35] Yet he found his efforts continually stymied by interference from the British colonial authorities. The constraints of a colonial territory echoed in some ways the constraints Cadbury had suffered in a Canadian province: the ultimate authority lay elsewhere, limiting local ability to plan.

Cadbury's letters to former colleagues in Regina show him trying to make links between the socialist-governed British colony and the lone socialist province in Canada. In one letter to Premier Tommy Douglas, with whom he maintained an active correspondence, Cadbury argued, "it makes a lot of sense for two Governments like Saskatchewan and Jamaica to help one another. How about your grapefruit problems!"[36] Joking aside, Cadbury wanted to bring in experts and examples from Saskatchewan to bolster his efforts in Jamaica, seeing parallels in the two units developing status and their political status. He was trying to position Saskatchewan as a source of advisors and a model. Social-democratic Saskatchewan, he believed, offered lessons from a provincial resource economy to the global South, which was home to quite a few similar resource-producing, dependent economies.

What the Saskatchewan CCF did provincially, the federal CCF tried to do nationally under the leadership of party president Frank Scott, the McGill University law professor and poet. Scott in 1952 became one of the UN's first Technical Assistant Resident Representatives. He was sent to Burma, one of the largest TAA programs in Asia.[37] Burma was a major consumer of UN technical assistance after its independence from Britain in 1948, coming to rank third among UN programs. Like Cadbury, Scott preached democratic planning on socialist lines. In 1944, amidst national mobilization to fight the Second World War, he had argued that "free enterprise" failures showed the need for a new system that continued wartime planning into peacetime. Thus he called for a National Planning Commission, "a small body of experts who will co-ordinate the plans coming from communities and industries, and who will propose developments of national importance." This would be "democratic planning" since the "people's representatives" in parliament would make the ultimate decisions.[38]

In both Canada and Burma socialism in this period meant internationalism, including freer global trade. Burma's Socialist Party, dominant in the national government, shared CCF faith in planning and expertise that located Burma very much in the global context and opted for internationalist rather than nationalist methods, exemplified through the close link with UN technical assistance machinery. Talk of development and social justice helped Burma's government, dominated by the Socialist Party, beat back challenges from communists and other rebels.

Prime minister U Nu was willing to welcome foreign investment in order to boost production. "Nationalization is not an end but only a means in the socialist scheme of things," he told critics that accused him of backsliding away from socialism.[39] Burma welcomed UN aid because it was seen as social-democratic in nature and independent of the former colonial power and the world's dominant power. A bad taste often clung to US aid, as Scott noted soon after his arrival in Rangoon in 1952. This was a problem because it increased suspicion of all Western aid – a category in which he placed the UN's own programs.[40] Burma, meanwhile, sought aid that was neither too communist nor too capitalist in nature. One top Burmese Socialist leader expressed a desire "to transform Burma into the Yugoslavia [of] Asia." (Yugoslavia meanwhile treated Burma as its window on Asia and provided substantial military equipment in exchange for Burmese rice.)[41] Israel also maintained its "most active Asian post" in Rangoon where relations were especially cordial with the Burmese Socialist party and army. Thus Israel was one of the major technical assistance providers to Burma. Army chief Ne Win and Israel's president exchanged visits as late as 1959, pointing to a relationship important to both governments.[42] Despite the significant and overlooked role of these two smaller states, Burma's major advice in the early years came, inevitably given availability of funds, from the West. With

American aid suspect – in fact Burma refused to accept any US money for much of the 1950s – this meant the United Nations and the Colombo Plan. Canada was important in both of these. Scott saw Canada, "a country which has not yet fully awakened from the sleep of colonialism," as offering possible lessons for Burma.[43]

Technical assistance, for all the UN's protestations, was not neutral or apolitical. Instead, it was implicated in the Cold War. For Scott, as for most UN resident representatives, it was important to defeat communism. As he wrote in one letter home, "What makes technical assistance in Burma so important is that it makes the success of [Burma's] democratic experiment more likely."[44] After all, "the way of life Burma is trying to establish – tolerant, religious, democratic and socialist – is conceivable only if communism is contained."[45] UN advice was central to the 1952 "Pyidawtha" development plan. One Burmese writer translates Pyidawtha as the Pleasant Land – pleasant in the sense of "a pleasing view or an agreeably furnished home. It was a social democratic vision of the future, of a welfare state and government-managed development within the framework of a parliamentary democracy."[46] It would require "a high level of international trade," the government conceded, adding, "Burma can remain economically *independent and self-supporting*, but can never become *economically self-sufficient.*"[47]

Scott finished his term as TAA resident representative early, suffering from dysentery and overwhelmed by the enormity of Burma's challenges. His faith in technical assistance was undimmed by his term in Burma, but he felt "the foreigners are like foam on the surface of a stream" even in Rangoon.[48] Attention turned to a small industries program headed by Chinese-Canadian York Wong, in which UN headquarters placed great hopes. The small industries program, however, tended to become larger and larger, despite the efforts to keep it small by such UN advisors as E.F. Schumacher, who would later author the book *Small Is Beautiful*.[49] The international way to socialism in Burma did not bear fruit. As the 1950s wore on, the high hopes vested in foreign experts seemed to be dashed at every turn. In Rangoon, U Nu's government wavered on many things but never on the instance that a socialist economy in Burma had to act pragmatically in the international context and draw heavily on foreign technical experts. The UN was the most acceptable channel, and UN and Burmese government visions meshed well. That changed when the

Burmese military, frustrated at the apparent failure of the government's plans and especially at its alleged openness to the claims of ethnic minorities, seized power in 1962. The bright hopes of 1952, a decade later, were a foil that the new military regime reacted against. The regime's claimed basis of legitimacy rested in a straightforward rejection of the "internationalist way to socialism" pursued under civilian governments. Instead, they substituted "the Burmese way to socialism," grounded in autarky and strict military dictatorship.

Development abroad, again and again, linked to development at home. From Keenleyside's work in the Northwest Territories to Cadbury's in Saskatchewan, Canadian peripheries provided models for Canadians embarking for global peripheries. Another example comes in the form of the second Canadian on the Keenleyside mission to Bolivia, mining engineer Gilbert Monture. "This descendant of countless generations of savages is going off to give technical assistance to one of the oldest civilizations in the world," recalled Jack Pickersgill, a minister in the St Laurent government, as Monture headed to Indonesia in the mid-1950s.[50] Alone among the first generation of technical assistance advisors from Canada, Monture was a Mohawk from the Six Nations territory near Brantford, Ontario. His origin seldom escaped the notice of his Ottawa colleagues. For several of them, as Pickersgill's recollection indicates, he embodied in his own life's progress the civilizing arc of economic development. Monture was, in his own words, "one of the Indians who have broken away from the old mode of life but are still proud of their racial ancestry."[51] That was a pattern he saw as entirely appropriate for the global South: cultures should be preserved, but economics shifted radically.

As deputy minister of mines and resources from 1947 to 1950, Keenleyside was Monture's boss. Offered the job of running the UN's technical assistance mission to Bolivia in 1950, Keenleyside picked Monture as one of the team members, the only other resident of Canada to be chosen. Subsequent missions sent Monture to Afghanistan for the UN, Indonesia for the Colombo Plan, and finally to Jamaica on Cadbury's invitation. "The Third World was calling him," his cousin Enos Montour wrote. He saw the underdeveloped world as needing to pull itself up by its bootstraps, as he had done. Like Third World farmers, he had walked behind a plough. "Surely he could raise their way of life, at least to the average of the Canadian Indian farmer," his cousin summarized his thinking.[52]

In common with many writers of the day, Monture saw the Commonwealth as an especially useful North–South bridge and technical assistance as one way to strengthen that bridge. This meant sending expert advisors from North to South. These experts, he said, had to be "sincere, sympathetic, and understanding of heart, with almost missionary zeal who assist in any part of the Commonwealth. They would be of great assistance on their return, between assignments[,] in providing to the Government first hand coun[sel] and advice." In other words, what was needed was an international civil service of flying experts.[53] The proposal drew on Monture's experience on the 1950 Bolivia mission, which had recommended international "administrative assistants" to staff Bolivia's governmental ranks, and transposed it onto the frame of the whole global Commonwealth.

Monture's role in Indonesia, where he was bound when Pickersgill encountered him and thought of the descendant of "savages" advising an ancient civilization, illustrates his place in the technical assistance universe. As in so many countries, the issue was how much control the local government would have over technical assistance plans and how much would belong to the UN itself. It came together in a single family at times: when Hugh Keenleyside visited Indonesia as part of his round-the-world technical assistance diplomacy, he stopped in to visit his brother Miles who was there trying to sell the Indonesians aerial surveys that might find future resources – the same aerial surveys that were a top item of Canadian government technical assistance to Asia. Canada's Colombo Plan assistance grappled with issues of local or international control and was entangled in trade hopes, even as Canadians pointed to the plan as driven by recipient needs above all.

Canada's capital aid in the early years concentrated on areas of perceived Canadian expertise, which not coincidentally might open the doors to subsequent Canadian trade. Thus early Canadian aid featured hydroelectric projects, in which Canada helped fund and build dams that would generate power and allow improved irrigation. As aid official R.G. Nik Cavell said, "we are probably the world's most experienced people in hydro electric generation." So Canada supported several hydro projects in India and Pakistan, which by the end of the 1950s accounted for more than 40 per cent of total Canadian Colombo Plan spending.[54] Transportation and telecommunications equipment and technical training also loomed large. Indonesia had some hopes of this sort of aid from Canada, but

Ottawa did not rush to meet those hopes. "The greatest need in Indonesia at the present time is for technical assistance rather than capital aid," one Canadian aid official concluded after visiting the country, because people trained for large capital projects were not yet in place.[55] Canadian expertise was already flowing at this time: The TAA had sent nine experts to staff the Indonesian State Planning Bureau, tasked with developing the broad outlines of an economic development program. Heading them in the early years was McGill University economist Benjamin Higgins. He was backed by Nathan Keyfitz, seconded from the Dominion Bureau of Statistics, and others. Though it never showed up in the early figures, since funds and experts went via Keenleyside's TAA, the State Planning Bureau represented the major Canadian contribution to technical assistance in Indonesia.

In 1954, inspired in part by his Canadian advisors, Planning Bureau chief Djuanda Kartawidjaja made a targeted request designed to appeal to Canadian interests: college level vocational training for Indonesian students in such areas as electricity, mechanics, mining, paper manufacture, aluminum production, and timber.[56] This quickly came together with a suggestion that Canada assist in helping Indonesia improve its engineering schools, which would build on the work of J.F. McDivitt, a Canadian teaching engineer at President Sukarno's alma mater (now called the Bandung Institute of Technology).[57] Djuanda wanted more Indonesian engineers, opting to send them overseas as hopes faded for foreign funding to a new engineering faculty in Indonesia.[58] After Australia announced 200 spots for science undergraduates (a number reduced later to 110), Ottawa offered ten spots in Canada on a trial basis.[59]

In the long run, there would be more bang for the Canadian buck through increased engineering training in Indonesia: an Indonesian coming to Canada learned the skills for himself, but a Canadian expert or an Indonesian trained at the postgraduate level could train many more people in Indonesia. So the idea of Canada aiding an engineering faculty in Java remained a live one. Thus Colombo Plan officials in Ottawa sent Monture, along with the president of the Nova Scotia Technical College (now part of Dalhousie University), to pass judgment on the Indonesian request.[60] The duo carried a wider brief to advise on Canadian technical assistance in general and recommended support for aerial surveys and other local needs such as paper for printing books and gypsum for a cement plant. But they

judged Canadian involvement in technical education, including engineering, to be premature given low levels of development on the
ground and shortages of educated people.[61]

Nevertheless, Monture felt that his recommendations would help
Indonesia and that Canada had a role to play in preventing Indonesia
from tipping into the communist camp. "Canada has great potential
in holding Indonesia against communism in the Far East," he told the
Carleton University Optimist Club after his return. "Canadians are
accepted whole-heartedly and with trust by the Indonesians. They
know we are not Americans and believe we are not commercial
exploiters." And Indonesia mattered: it was "the gap holding the red
invasion out of China, away from Australia and New Zealand."[62]
Technical assistance, in other words, was useful not only for its own
sake but also as a cold war weapon.

After his retirement, Monture turned his attention to indigenous
issues at home, becoming involved in the Indian-Eskimo Association
of Canada. He wrote that there was "no reason why Indian communities proud of their past traditions and culture cannot exist and play
their part as responsible citizens of Canada without forever depending
on handouts from Government or the contemptuous charity of white
do gooders." Where his own background had informed his technical assistance work overseas, Monture now saw his overseas work as
useful to his postretirement mission of helping aboriginal people in
Canada.[63] The development mission had come full circle. Where
Hugh Keenleyside and George Cadbury spoke and wrote of lessons
from the Northwest Territories and Saskatchewan to the "less developed countries," Monture saw his work in those countries offering
lessons for the poverty-stricken territories of Canada's first peoples.
Development at home and abroad were two sides of the same coin.

Other "life stories" of Canadian technical advisors would describe a
complex web of advisors to a multitude of governments in the global
South that shaped those countries' destinies well before American
modernization theory became the dominant development ideology
in the 1960s. These advisors spanned the spectrum from Jesuit educators in Ethiopia to agricultural modernizers in Thailand. The
agencies sending them included the Canadian government's own
bilateral aid programs, the Commonwealth's Colombo Plan, the
United Nations through its technical assistance machinery, and UN
specialized agencies such as the World Health Organization and the

Food and Agriculture Organization. They shared much in common. Reading their technical assistance stories together reveals a group with striking similarities. It helps to make visible the broad outlines of technical assistance as a postcolonial project that operated on North–South lines, attempting to "modernize" and transform "less developed" countries, and also on East–West lines, attempting to hold these countries to the Western side in the global Cold War.

Canadians who went overseas under UN auspices in particular were not mere technicians providing impartial and apolitical advice. Technical assistance repeatedly raised questions of how much control would go to UN-appointed advisors and how much to their host governments. Billed as apolitical and as a new UN mission to the global South, technical assistance also proved to be entangled in the Cold War. Canadian advisors tended to be well aware of this. At the same time, they were peddling Western and especially Canadian models of economic development, doing so in ways that heavily influenced much of what was coming in the 1950s to be called "the Third World." For good or for ill, Canadians mattered in these countries' histories, and the UN is the channel that, more than any other, got them there.

NOTES

1 Some material in this chapter was previously published in David Webster, "Development Advisors in a Time of Cold War and Decolonization: The UN Technical Assistance Administration, 1950–1959," *Journal of Global History* 6, no. 2 (2011): 249–72, and David Webster, "Modern Missionaries: Canadian Postwar Technical Assistance Advisors in Southeast Asia," *Journal of the Canadian Historical Association* 20, no. 2 (2009): 86–111. This research was supported by the Social Science and Humanities Research Council.

2 Patricia Clavin, *Securing the World Economy: The Reinvention of the League of Nations, 1920–1946* (Oxford: Oxford University Press, 2013); Akira Iriye, *Global Community: The Role of International Organizations in the Making of the Contemporary World* (Berkeley: University of California Press, 2002); Susan Pedersen, "Back to the League of Nations," *American Historical Review* 112, no. 4 (October 2007): 1091–1117; Daniel Laqua, "Transnational Intellectual Cooperation, the League of Nations, and the Problem of Order," *Journal of Global History* 6, no. 2

(2011): 223–47; Glenda Sluga, "The Transnational History of International Institutions," *Journal of Global History* 6, no. 2 (July 2011): 219–22; Daniel Gorman, "Liberal Internationalism, the League of Nations Union, and the Mandates System," *Canadian Journal of History* 40 (Dec. 2005): 449–77; Sunil Amrith and Patricia Clavin, "Feeding the World: Connecting Europe and Asia, 1930–1945," *Past and Present* 218 (2013) suppl. 8: 29–50.

3 Many of these are published under the auspices of the United Nations Intellectual History Project, http://unhistory.org/. They include Richard Jolly, Louis Emmerij, Dharam Ghai, and Frédéric Lapeyre, UN *Contributions to Development Thinking and Practice* (Indianapolis: University of Indiana Press, 2004); John Toye and Richard Toye, *The UN and Global Political Economy: Trade, Finance, and Development* (Indianapolis: University of Indiana Press, 2004); Richard Jolly, Louis Emmerij, and Thomas Weiss, *The Power of UN Ideas: Lessons from the First 60 Years* (Indianapolis: University of Indiana Press, 2005); Olav Stokke, *The UN and Development: From Aid to Cooperation* (Indianapolis: University of Indiana Press, 2009); Richard Jolly, Louis Emmerij, and Thomas G. Weiss, UN *Ideas That Changed the World* (Indianapolis: University of Indiana Press, 2009). Other examples include Sunil Amrith, *Decolonizing International Health: India and Southeast Asia, 1930–1965* (London: PalgraveMacmillan, 2006); Glenda Sluga and Sunil Amrith, "New Histories of the U.N.," *Journal of World History* 19, no. 3 (September 2008): 251–74; Poul Duedahl, "Selling Mankind: UNESCO and the Invention of Global History, 1945–1976," *Journal of World History* 22, no. 1 (March 2011): 101–33; Todd Shepard, "Algeria, France, Mexico, UNESCO: A Transnational History of Anti-Racism and Decolonization, 1932–1962," *Journal of Global History* 6, no. 2 (July 2011): 273–97.

4 Adam Chapnick, *The Middle Power Project: Canada and the Founding of the United Nations* (Vancouver: University of British Columbia Press, 2005).

5 Mark Mazower, *Governing the World: The History of an Idea* (London: Penguin, 2012).

6 Nick Cullather, "Modernization Theory," in Michael J. Hogan & Thomas G. Paterson, eds., *Explaining the History of American Foreign Relations*, second edition (Cambridge: Cambridge University Press, 2004); Gilbert Rist, *The History of Development: From Western Origins to Global Faith*, second edition (London: Zed Books, 2002); H.W. Arndt, *Economic Development: The History of an Idea* (Chicago: University of Chicago Press, 1987); M.P. Cowen and R.W. Shenton, *Doctrines of Development*

(London: Routledge, 1996); Michael E. Latham, *Modernization as Ideology: American Social Science and "Nation-Building" in the Kennedy Era* (Chapel Hill: University of North Carolina Press, 2000); Ruth Compton Brouwer, *Modern Women Modernizing Men* (Vancouver: University of British Columbia Press, 2002).

7 "Memorandum of points for consideration in the development of a twenty-year program for achieving peace through the United Nations," 6 June 1950, *Public Papers of the Secretaries-General of the United Nations, vol. I: Trygve Lie, 1946–1953* (New York: Columbia University Press, 1969), 301. On the centrality of Point Four in development, see for instance Gilbert Rist, *The History of Development: From Western Origins to Global Faith* (London: Zed Books, 2014).

8 Trygve Lie, *In the Cause of Peace: Seven Years with the United Nations* (New York: Macmillan, 1954), 132–3.

9 Lie, *In the Cause of Peace*.

10 Margherita Zanasi, "Exporting Development: The League of Nations and Republican China," *Comparative Studies in Society and History* 49, no. 1 (2007): 143–69; Jürgen Osterhammel, "'Technical Cooperation' Between the League of Nations and China," *Modern Asian Studies* 13, no. 4 (1979): 661–80.

11 Shelagh Grant, "Hugh Llewellyn Keenleyside: Commissioner of the Northwest Territories, 1947–1950," *Arctic Profile* 43, no. 1 (1990): 80–2, DOI: http://dx.doi.org/10.14430/arctic1594.

12 Note on UN Secretariat interdepartmental meeting, 30 August 1949, United Nations Archives (UNA) S-0441-1417-04; Memorandum on history of Bolivia requests, 1 October 1949, UNA S-039-0022-09.

13 Report of the UN mission of technical assistance to Bolivia, 1951, Library and Archives Canada (LAC), Hugh Keenleyside papers, 8/Bolivia [1].

14 James M. Malloy, *Bolivia: The Uncompleted Revolution* (Pittsburgh: University of Pittsburgh Press, 1970); Herbert S. Klein, *A Concise History of Bolivia*, 2d edition (Cambridge: Cambridge University Press, 2011); Glenn J. Dorn, "Pushing Tin: U.S.-Bolivian Relations and the Coming of the National Revolution," *Diplomatic History* 35, no. 2 (April 2011); Robert J. Alexander, *The Bolivian National Revolution* (Westport, CT: Greenwood Press, 1958).

15 Hugh Keenleyside, *Memoirs* (Toronto: McClelland and Stewart, 1981–82), 2: 336.

16 Walter O'Hearn, "Keenleyside Report on Bolivia Likely to Be Amazingly Frank," *Montreal Daily Star*, 17 August 1950.

17 List of experts appointed under Expanded Programme of Technical Assistance 1950–55, UNA S-0441-1423-04; TAA 1956 country targets, S-0441-1438-01; *Yearbook of the United Nations* 1951: 403.
18 Stokke, *UN and Development*, 74.
19 Extract from cabinet conclusions, 12 June, *Documents on Canadian External Relations (DCER)* 1950: 1226–7.
20 Memorandum from secretary to cabinet, cabinet document 158–60, n.d. *DCER* 1950: 621–2.
21 Canadian delegation to UN dispatch to Department of External Affairs, 15 July 1950, *DCER* 1950: 626–8.
22 Trygve Lie, address at University of Quito, Ecuador, 28 February 1951, in *Public Papers of the Secretaries-General* vol. 1, 383–4; Peter Stursberg broadcast for CBC News, 9 September 1950; LAC, Peter Stursberg papers, MG 31 D78/35, Keenleyside interview, 28 August 1980.
23 Michael Cowen and Robert W. Shenton, *Doctrines of Development* (New York: Routledge, 1996); Jolly et al., *UN Contributions to Development Thinking and Practice*; Robert L. Tignor, *W. Arthur Lewis and the Birth of Development Economics* (Princeton: Princeton University Press, 2006); Barbara Wood, *E.F. Schumacher: His Life and Thought* (New York: Harper & Row, 1984).
24 Amrith and Sluga, "New Histories of the United Nations," 271.
25 George Cadbury, "Planning in Saskatchewan," in Laurier LaPierre et al., eds., *Essays on the Left* (Toronto: McClelland and Stewart, 1971), 51–2.
26 Jean Larmour, "The Douglas Government's Changing Emphasis on Public, Private and Co-operative Development in Saskatchewan, 1955–1961," in J. William Brennan, ed., *Building the Co-operative Commonwealth: Essays on the Democratic Socialist Tradition in Canada* (Regina: Canadian Plains Research Center, 1984), 161–80.
27 Cadbury to Premier T.C. Douglas, 18 February 1951, Saskatchewan Archives Board (SAB), R-33.1 CXX-949.
28 Keyfitz family Christmas letter from Colombo, 1 November 1956, LAC, RG74, vol. 266, file 36-8C-K1[1].
29 H.L. Keenleyside to G.W. Cadbury, 21 September 1954, UNA, S-0441-1431-04.
30 Notes for discussion with the minister of industries, n.d., UNA, S-0441-1431-04.
31 Review of the Problems of the Government Tannery and Leather Factory July 1954, UNA, S-0441-1431-04.
32 Ibid.

33 Cadbury to Keenleyside, 26 August 1954, UNA, S-0441-1431-04.

34 Cadbury to Arthur Goldschmidt, 11 August 1954, UNA, S-0441-1431-04.

35 UN interoffice memorandum, 24 February 1955; Jamaican government request for technical assistance, 14 Feb 1955, UNA, S-0441-1416-06.

36 Cadbury to Douglas, 21 March 1955, SAB, R-33.1 CXX-949.

37 Sandra Djwa, *The Politics of the Imagination: A life of F.R. Scott* (Toronto: McClelland & Stewart, 1987); Burma contract, LAC, F.R. Scott papers, MG 30 D11, vol. 5, file 8; Scott, "The United Nations Programme of Technical Assistance," undated typescript, Scott papers, vol. 5, file 9.

38 F.R. Scott, "The Nature of Economic Planning," in *Planning for Freedom: 16 Lectures on the CCF, Its Policies and Program* (Toronto: Ontario CCF, 1944), 6, 10.

39 Louis J. Walinsky, *Economic Development in Burma 1951–1960* (New York: Twentieth Century Fund, 1962), 73.

40 Scott, "ECA does *this* damage," handwritten note in Scott papers, vol. 5, file 9.

41 Jovan Čavoški, Arming Nonalignment: Yugoslavia's Relations with Burma and the Cold War in Asia (1950–1955) (New Evidence from Yugoslav, Chinese, Indian, and US Archives) (Washington: Cold War International History Project) 4, 9.

42 Canadian embassy in Rangoon letter to DEA, 16 July 1960; Canadian embassy in Tel Aviv letter to DEA, 19 June 1959, both at LAC 5567-A-40.

43 F.R. Scott, "A Decade of the LSR [League for Social Reconstruction]," LAC, F.R. Scott papers, MG30 D211, vol. 5 file 9.

44 Scott's May Day report 1952, 1 May 1952; Scott's report to TAA for 1 May to 30 June, Scott papers, vol. 5, file 9.

45 Travel diary entry for 12 May 1952, Scott papers.

46 Thant Myint-U, *The River of Lost Footsteps: Histories of Burma* (New York: Farrar, Strauss and Giroux, 2006), 273.

47 *Pyidawtha: The New Burma* (Rangoon: Economic and Social Board, 1954), italics in original; Louis J. Walinsky, *Economic Development in Burma 1951–1960* (New York: Twentieth Century Fund, 1962).

48 Scott travel diary, 7 May 1952, Lashio, Scott papers, vol. 92; Scott to Terence Sheard, Toronto, 8 July 1952, Scott papers, vol. 5, file 9.

49 E.F. Schumacher, *Small Is Beautiful: A Study of Economics as If People Mattered* (Blond and Briggs, 1973), full text available at http://www.ditext.com/schumacher/small/small.html.

50 J.W. Pickersgill, foreword to Enos T. Montour, *The Rockhound of Jerusalem, Being the Saga of Dr. Gilbert Clarence Monture* (self-published

booklet, 1981), ii. Trent University Archives, E.E.M. Jobin fonds, 95-019/1/4.

51 G.C. Monture to Vivian Williams, executive secretary of National Commission on the Indian Canadian, Toronto, 23 July 1957, Trent University Archives, Gilbert Monture papers, 97-017-1-4.

52 Montour, *Rockhound*, 18–19.

53 Ibid.

54 "The Colombo Plan: A Progress Report, Cavell to House Standing Committee on External Affairs," 3 May 1956, *External Affairs* 8, no. 6 (June 1956), 165; "Canada and the Colombo Plan: The Warsak Project," *External Affairs* 11, no. 6 (June 1959), 125–7.

55 "Technical Assistance to Indonesia," report by D.W. Bartlett, Singapore, 17 April 1955, LAC, RG25, vol. 6604, file 11038-AB-2-40 [3.2].

56 Letter from Djuanda at Indonesian Embassy in Ottawa to Nik Cavell, 18 October 1954, LAC, RG25, vol. 6590, file 11038-4-40[1].

57 Secretary of state for external affairs (SSEA) telegram to Canadian embassy in Jakarta, 8 November 1955; Jakarta telegram to SSEA, 7 December 1955, LAC, RG 25, vol. 4299, file 11038-AB-2-B-40 [1]; Canadian embassy in Jakarta letter to SSEA, 8 December 1955, LAC, RG 25, vol. 4299, file 11038-AB-2-B-40 [1].

58 Canadian embassy in Jakarta letter to SSEA, 24 January 1955, LAC, RG25, vol. 7564, file 11038-AB-2-B-40 [4.1].

59 Under-SSEA letter to Canadian embassy in Jakarta, 7 Feb. 1955; Canadian embassy in Jakarta letter to SSEA, 15 Feb. 1955; USSEA letter to Canadian embassy in Jakarta, 16 June 1955, LAC, RG25, vol. 7564, file 11038-AB-2-B-40 [4.1].

60 George Heasman, Canadian ambassador to Indonesia, letter to Penelope Monture, 24 July 1945, Monture papers, 97-017-1-3.

61 Report of Technical Education team to Indonesia by G.C. Monture and A.E. Cameron, February and March 1956, transmitted to Cavell 24 April 1956, LAC, RG74, vol. 277, file 36-8GH-HI.

62 "Canada has vital role in helping Indonesia," 15 January 1957, Monture papers, 97-017-1-11.

63 Undated letter to Mr Albert Chatsis (?), Monture papers 97-017-1-1.

4

Save the Children/Save the World

Canadian Women Embrace the United Nations, 1940s–1970s

Tarah Brookfield[1]

In November 1961 Mrs Wayne Elwood, a California housewife, mailed a cheque for $1,000 to the UN, explaining in her letter to Secretary-General U Thant that this was the advertised cost to build a fallout shelter, but she preferred to invest her family's safety in the hands of the world organization. She specified that her donation be put toward the UN's nonmilitary operations, such as the Food and Agriculture Organization, the World Health Organization, or UNICEF. Inspired by Elwood's action, several of her friends and neighbours, along with twenty-eight families in North Carolina, agreed to pledge similar quantities because they believed the "United Nations was the only real shelter in a nuclear world."[2] This gesture made headlines across Canada, prompting Canadians to make similar promises. *Chatelaine* editor Doris Anderson applauded Elwood's "simple act" and was inspired by the initiative of an "ordinary citizen."[3] She called it a "positive gesture of faith that mankind will not embrace this final piece of madness" but will find a "sane just way to settle the world's tangled problems" in "these anxious times."[4] Not only was 1961 a time of heightened Cold War anxiety, having witnessed the Bay of Pigs invasion, the erection of the Berlin Wall, and the Soviet detonation of the most powerful thermonuclear weapon to date, it also saw the UN overwhelmed by a debt that put the future of its new peacekeeping responsibilities in question.[5] The fear of a crumbling UN prompted one Toronto woman, Brenda Smith, to follow Elwood's philanthropy with her own donation. She felt it was the obligation of "everyone who believes in the United Nations ... [to] send in as much money as they could afford."[6]

It is unknown how many other women followed Smith's appeal, but between 1945 and 1975 hundreds of thousands of Canadians raised millions of dollars for UN programs, including more than $21 million in private donations for UNICEF alone.[7] Although both men and women were drawn to ideologically and financially supporting the UN, the new world organization was characterized in one public relations study as appealing most strongly to women.[8] Using explicitly gendered language, Kay Livingstone, UN advocate and prominent member of many Toronto women's clubs elaborated on why Canadian women were so drawn to the UN: "No longer can women afford to let someone else look after the world while they look after their homes. To protect our homes we must look after the world. The UN is the only organization today which attempts to speak for mankind. The UNA [United Nations Association in Canada] is the only association in Canada designed to link the citizen with that organization."[9] Livingstone saw women, referenced in her quote above as both homemakers and citizens, as committed to internationalism, the belief that nations should cooperate politically and economically. She also saw women as critical players in Canada's foreign affairs. This spirit of internationalism was often punctuated with doses of maternalism, emphasizing women's expertise as nurturers and caregivers, and their global interest in children's health and safety. Given that international relations had long been perceived as a masculine domain, it is likely the activists' embracement of maternalism represented a genuine interest in saving children, as well as its uses as a pervasive "political strategy for women to claim a space and have their voices heard."[10]

In the aftermath of the Second World War and throughout the 1950s and 1960s, the UN prioritized improving the lives of children. Not only were children deemed more vulnerable than adults in time of war, poverty, and natural disaster, but, as Dominique Marshall explored in her analysis of the UN's postwar support for child rights, children's innocence generated the biggest sympathy from donor nations and was one of few issues that could neutralize Cold War tensions.[11] Widespread concern for child welfare was also an important part of Canada's new postwar welfare system and baby-boom culture. While orphaned, neglected, and sick children had always been the recipients of charity in Canada, programs such as the new

Family Allowance program addressed the universal ideology of the nation's postwar welfare state, funding the development of "normal" children as a preemptive measure to avoid developmental, health, or economic problems.[12] In the case of foreign aid, this attitude was expanded on, whereby it was hoped that if all children's basic needs were met, then Canada and by proxy the UN could influence the development of future generations, thus neutralizing threats, making peace, and winning allies. This attitude was emphasized in the 1946 UN film *Seeds of Destiny* in which the narrator proclaimed, it was critical that postwar children avoid the "ruin, doubt, defeatism and despair [that] will breed Fascism, more Hitlers, more Tojos"; instead, we must encourage the development of "Einsteins, Toscaninis, Manuel Quezons, Madame Curies, and Sun Yet Sens."[13]

Although most of the UN's child-focused campaigns served children in war zones and developing nations, they also involved children living in more prosperous and peaceful nations, such as Canada. The Trick-or-Treat for UNICEF campaign and Model UN clubs were considered to be a form of citizenship "training" for young Canadians, inaugurating them into Canada's new postwar commitment to internationalism by teaching them to be generous, cooperative, responsible, and globally aware citizens. In a sense, these programs were promoted as being just as much about shaping the character of Canadians as they were about building healthy bodies and minds in their overseas counterparts. Therefore children on both sides of the foreign relief equation, the young donors and the young recipients, were considered by the UN to be "seeds of destiny," future leaders who, if nurtured properly in terms of nutrition, health, education, and democracy, would grow up to be peaceful and productive citizens.[14]

While Canadian and non-Canadian children may have been seen as sharing an intertwined destiny, UN campaigns did not portray them as equal or alike but rather two sides of a problem/solution binary. Laura Briggs has demonstrated how the image of the "rail-thin waif, maybe with an empty rice bowl" became the standard representation of Third World need since the postwar period.[15] The salvation of these children was positioned as in the hands of the white, heterosexual, middle-class Western family, which was seen as "fundamentally caring and committed to the well-being of local non-white and working class children, as well as infants, youth and families around the globe."[16] In general, the young recipients of UN foreign relief, as well as those sponsored by other agencies' international foster parent plans, were conceived as weak, vulnerable, and in desperate need of Canadian attention, love, and financial contributions. Additionally, it was implied that any foreign child not helped by Canada could grow up to be a dangerous and destructive force. Meanwhile Canadian children participating in UN foreign relief projects as volunteers and donors were presented rather homogenously, as universally blessed with health and wealth, and enthusiastic in their quest to assist their underprivileged counterparts.

From UNRRA to UNICEF, this chapter will explore the different ways Canadian women engaged with the UN in Canada and overseas between 1945 and 1975, particularly through promotion and sponsorship of the organization's global child welfare efforts and UNA clubs. It will also consider the impact women's paid and unpaid labour, boosterism, and fundraising had in shaping the UN's mission in Canada and how these efforts represented one cohort of activist women's dual expressions of maternalism and internationalism in the postwar and early Cold War years.

UNRRA: PLANTING THE SEEDS OF DESTINY

As Allied armies liberated countries in Europe during the Second World War, they were followed by an international delegation of relief workers organized by the newly formed UN who were assigned to offer care and coordinate the dispersal of supplies to refugees. The high casualty rates and displacement of civilians became a rallying point in mobilizing support during the last year of the war; at the same time it demonstrated the new costs of modern warfare. Political ideologies and military strategies that deliberately targeted noncombatants, combined with the collapse of agricultural production and breakdowns in sanitation and housing, caused unseen levels of death, devastation, and disease. It has been estimated that the death toll in World War II was approximately sixty million people, with the majority of deaths attributed to civilians.[17] Even before the war was over, Allied governments collaborated to raise the necessary resources needed to repair the damage in Europe and Asia. Food, wheat, milk, cattle, poultry, seeds, machinery, medicine, blankets, clothes, and shoes were in high demand, as was construction material for the reconstruction of roads, bridges, and buildings. Operating between 1943 and 1947, the United Nations Relief and Rehabilitation

Administration (UNRRA) was the first of many UN agencies assigned to cater to the human side of reconstruction. It was hoped that, if successful, UNRRA would be able to "pump into the veins and arteries of stricken peoples around the earth the emergency items of relief and rehabilitation that serve as the plasma of peace."[18]

UNRRA was Canada's first involvement in what historian Adam Chapnick called "shaping the post-war world," a demonstration of the government's and the people's commitment to long-term internationalism.[19] After the Second World War, Canadians liked to emphasize their nation's special destiny in helping other people, significant as Canada spread its wings globally as a respected middle power. The nation's military and financial contributions during the war gave the government a legitimacy to continue acting upon its international interests and prompted a sense of responsibility to preserve what had been fought for. Unlike its allies, Canada was not faced with extensive postwar reconstruction, so it contributed to large-scale rehabilitation projects in war-torn Europe. The federal government donated more than $2 billion to European reconstruction, $90 million of which was channelled through UNRRA in the form of wheat, textiles, and farm implements.[20] The UN elected Canada to chair UNRRA's Suppliers Committee, which was responsible for coordinating countries assigned to pay for the relief and study the needs of receiver nations. Some UNRRA resources were also collected through private donations, such as the campaign led by Canadian actress Mary Pickford. Pickford advised housewives to purchase an extra canned good or package of food every time they went shopping and place it in a specially marked UN bin found in stores of major grocery chains. At the end of the day, the grocery stores would calculate the value of the donations, return the items to the store shelves, and use the equivalent value to purchase food in bulk quantities for UN relief.[21] Polls taken during and after the war suggest that the Canadian public supported UNRRA and their nation's continuing internationalist efforts, even if it meant the continuation of food rationing and conserving in the postwar years.[22]

In addition to sending agricultural resources, Canadians with experience in welfare service, administration, and health care, especially those with foreign language skills, were recruited to work for UNRRA. Hundreds of Canadian nurses joined UNRRA's nursing divisions, and several Canadian women rose high in the organization's administration, which proclaimed itself an equal opportunity employer.[23] The mobilization of women working overseas is reminiscent of an earlier form of women's international work, the missionary movement. In the late nineteenth and early twentieth century, women could be found at the heart of Canada's overseas missions in India and China. Overseas charity work was considered a respectable occupation for pious (and adventurous) women looking for a vocation or leadership opportunities they could not find at home. According to Ruth Compton Brouwer, the women who joined foreign missions had a "uniquely authoritative source of information and opinion about life in non-Christian lands and a congenial object for philanthropic zeal" as well as "a siren call to a vocation and to a larger life than any could contemplate in Canada."[24] As seen in the UNRRA careers of two Canadian women – Mary McGeachy, UNRRA's director of welfare, and Elizabeth Brown, UNRRA's chief of mission for the Middle East – this earlier missionary spirit was paired with the secularized form of internationalism.

McGeachy had been a long-time advocate of Canada's internationalism, a belief she cultivated as a member of the Student Christian Movement and Young Women's Christian Association (YWCA) in Toronto. She wove this interest into a career with the League of Nations (LON), where she was employed as an information section officer in Geneva between 1928 and 1940. After the dissolution of the LON, McGeachy found new work with the UN, where she became the most senior Canadian and the only woman to hold a high-level executive position. In her biography of McGeachy, Mary Kinnear recounts the challenges involved in managing UNRRA's welfare division, whose role was to administer care to the 150 to 160 million refugees living in displaced persons' camps across Europe. This work won the unmarried and childless McGeachy the title "Europe's no. 1 Foster Mother."[25] Kinnear notes that, throughout McGeachy's time with UNRRA, her authority was questioned by other UN officials who were uncomfortable with a woman holding such a senior position; however, she felt the bigger frustration lay in the fact that her "vision of relief could not be adequately measured in the terms of the budgets and personnel."[26] Whatever UNRRA's successes and failures, McGeachy believed it represented the greatest undertaking in international cooperation to date. After the agency folded, she left the UN to get married but remained involved in international work through her membership in and later presidency of the International Council of Women. Kinnear concluded that "McGeachy's accomplishments were unusual because she was Canadian, not rich or well connected, and female" and that her life showed the "opportunities, and the limitations, that the idea of international cooperation could offer to a woman."[27]

Brown's reflections on this period support Kinnear's contention that international cooperation projects offered a woman-friendly working environment. In 1943 Brown left her position as an employment advisor with the Department of Labour, citing disappointment in the lack of respect shown to federal women employees in Canada. She applied to UNRRA because she yearned to "do something in the present world situation" and had an "itchy foot" and the "wanderlust bug."[28] At age forty-two Brown thought there was little chance she would be accepted, yet she passed the medical screening and four weeks of training at the University of Maryland. Just as McGeachy experienced some gender prejudice, so did Brown. Her original UNRRA posting was changed from Yugoslavia to Jerusalem when it was made known that President Tito preferred male UNRRA workers in his country.[29] Between 1944 and 1947 Brown supervised the administration of food supplies, education, medical services, housing, and repatriation programs in refugee camps in Egypt, Palestine, Lebanon, and Syria and opened UNRRA's first Jerusalem office. Brown felt the Middle East was one of the most challenging UNRRA regions due to the high number of legal and illegal entries to the region and the considerable tensions connected to partition. Despite this, "Miss UNRRA Brown" as the locals called her, found great satisfaction in her work and accomplishments, something she found lacking in her work in Canada. She referred to her time with UNRRA as "a miracle," explaining that "this type of assignment, to organize and administer a program to help people, to carry the responsibility for relationships in the community, with the government, the military and any private groups touching on our work, to have the freedom of planning and carrying UNRRA's chart ... was a tremendous challenge, yet one I knew I could handle."[30]

Brown was forced to leave UNRRA in 1947 when the British pulled out of their commitments in Palestine, and she continued her relief work for the UN's International Refugee Organization in Turkey and Germany. In 1954 she was offered a position with the UN relief administration in postwar Korea, but she turned it down, acknowledging the agency's temporary nature and fearing as a single woman in her fifties, responsible for her own support, she needed more secure employment.[31] Instead Brown spent eight years working for an American nursing association before returning to work abroad in 1963 as director of the Saigon Foster Parents Plan International (FPPI) office during the height of the Vietnam War.

Interestingly, experience with UNRRA was viewed by other women as a stepping stone not only to additional international work but also to leadership opportunities in parallel Cold War movements seeking peace or security. In 1956 the Canadian Welfare Council recruited Molly E. Christie, a social worker with UNRRA's European program, for a position with the Emergency Measures Organization. The committee had put a specific call out to former UNRRA employees, explaining to recruiters that these skilled workers might not be aware of how much their experience in disaster management was needed to manage emergency preparedness in a nuclear war scenario.[32] UNRRA workers were also sought by the peace movement for their international experience and commitment to the UN. Ethel Ostry, a Jewish social worker and teacher, was a founding member of the Canadian women's peace organization, Voice of Women (VOW). One of the reasons she was selected to participate in VOW's 1963 peace mission to ten European countries in honour of International Co-operation Year was her postwar experience working for UNRRA in Germany, Austria, and Italy. Living abroad, being a witness to the consequences of war, and having experience in a workplace dedicated to cross-cultural understanding made Ostry a strong representative for Canada.[33] Although UN service work, peace activism, and civil defence shared different politics, each were contextualized as organizational leadership and professional opportunities for women in fields related to caregiving.

One of the significant tasks facing Brown and other UNRRA workers on the ground was the overwhelming responsibility of caring for the millions of children suffering from malnutrition and disease, those who had been crippled and blinded by shrapnel and other weaponry, and those traumatized by living through invasions, bombings, and the Holocaust. Amid the casualties were an estimated thirteen million unaccompanied children who had been orphaned, abandoned, or accidently separated from their parents.[34] UNRRA had a special division dedicated to child welfare, which provided care to mothers and their children, devoted resources to improving national child and maternal services, and attempted to reunite displaced children with relatives.[35] Generally there was great sympathy for all children affected by war, although Canadian UNRRA worker Marjorie Bradford recalls how in France she confronted social prejudice towards and the denial of citizenship rights of illegitimate children who had been fathered by Germans and children whose parents were accused of being French collaborators. Furthermore UNRRA workers felt the pressures of Zionism and strict Soviet repatriation policies when determining where to resettle displaced children. Whenever possible, Bradford tried to ensure the children's interests were placed first, above political or legal considerations.[36]

A handful of displaced children had been cared for during the Second World War in special nurseries in England financed by FPPI and supervised by psychologists Dr Anna Freud, daughter of Sigmund, and Dr Dorothy Tiffany Burlingham. These war nurseries offered residential childcare for European refugee children who had been evacuated to England without their parents and British children whose parents were engaged in war work or whose homes had been destroyed in the blitz. The nurseries were staffed by refugees trained in social work, health care, or education, and who, under Freud's and Burlingham's supervision, strove to ease the children's separation anxiety and minimize the impact of stress on their social development.[37] Research performed in the war nurseries provided analytical tools and guidelines for social workers and administrators working with young refugees. In 1943 Freud and Burlingham published *War and Children*, the first academic study about the effects of war on children. Their work represented the growing importance of child psychology, which recognized childhood as being a unique and fragile time in a person's life, a time when one needed to be nurtured and protected by parents. They concluded that "the care and education of young children should not take second place in wartime," arguing that "adults can live under emergency conditions and, if necessary, on emergency rations. But the situation in the decisive years of bodily and mental development is entirely different."[38] Freud's and Burlingham's research demonstrated the physical and psychological malformations found in children under severe stress from air raids, evacuations, and the shock of separation from their parents, especially their mothers. To minimize the impact of war on children, they believed there should be a concentrated effort to ensure that normal routines were not broken and that there were replacement forms of security (family, home, and school) available if the original ones vanished. The theories in *War and Children* would become a guide for

UNICEF, whose programs promised to intervene when parents and communities were unable to offer these elements alone, buffering the care with items of relief and the provision of schools, hospitals, and orphanages. UNICEF agreed with Freud and Burlingham that the "wartime care of children has to be more elaborate and more carefully thought out than in ordinary times of peace."[39]

War and Children was considered a landmark achievement among professional child welfare workers working with war-affected youth, but it was the documentary *Seeds of Destiny* that generated a tidal wave of response from the general public. In 1945, eight cameramen from the United States Army Signal Corps were assigned to film daily life in cities and refugee camps in fourteen European countries. (Although Asia is mentioned in the film, it is not visually represented because filming started before the war in the Pacific was over.) What struck the filmmakers was the staggering number of children affected by war or, to lay specific blame, the madness of Axis power leaders Hitler, Mussolini, and Tojo. The film focuses on the lifestyles of children who had survived the war and were now languishing in peacetime. The corps footage was edited into a nineteen-minute documentary by Corporal David Miller, a Hollywood director before the war. Miller described the experience as "heart-rending" and claimed filming paused at times because the crew were too shaken to continue.[40] The black-and-white film features image after image of children whose appearance and behaviour challenged the ideals of a modern childhood favoured by most Canadians. Instead there are scenes of children missing limbs and eyes or staring blankly into the camera. In other scenes, dirt-smeared urchins dressed in rags scurry around like rats, stealing, begging, and even smoking. A narrator translated the shocking images for viewers, explaining how the baby seen lying in a crib was really a malnourished three-year-old. None of the children are portrayed living in homes or shown with families, instead they appear in public spaces or in institutional care. The film contrasted these experiences with the images of peaceful middle-class suburban homes and schoolyards in North America, and it placed the burden of responsibility for fixing this problem on "ourselves," those whose imaginations, "no matter how vivid, cannot convey the full meaning of what others have endured and still endure."[41]

Seeds of Destiny applauded UNRRA's accomplishments, yet its presentation of tragic images proved more support was needed. For example, the narrator argued, the annual UNRRA budget of $2 billion was equal to only 1 per cent of the participating countries' gross domestic product, which worked out to be less than the cost of five days of war. *Seeds of Destiny* concluded with a buoyant piece of hyperbole, suggesting that peace must be financed equally to war in order to "preserve the victories won by the fighting men of the United Nations, the hard way, and establish once and for all, that even stronger than the atomic bomb is the human heart."[42] Presumably the comparison between UNRRA and the atomic bomb was meant to suggest that the outpouring of transnational charity had the power to produce peace and stability, much as the Allies argued the bomb had done by ending the war. It did not acknowledge that the people behind UNRRA were the same people who invented such a destructive weapon and contributed to the very human consequences of war that UNRRA hoped to eradicate.

Seeds of Destiny premiered at the White House in the spring of 1946. UNRRA's director, Fiorello La Guardia, announced that the film must be shown everywhere; however, the National Association of Theater Owners deemed the shocking footage of emaciated and wild children too "gruesome" to be shown in public cinemas across North America, so Miller and La Guardia circulated the film among church groups, parent-teacher associations, unions, women's clubs, and other service groups.[43] Within two years, *Seeds of Destiny* was shown to eleven million Americans and Canadians whose private screenings generated $200 million in donations toward UNRRA, with donors giving on average $15 each.[44] As the recognition spread that much more needed to be done beyond the temporary framework of UNRRA, this film also inspired the founding of UNICEF, a UN agency specifically designed to look after children's bodies, minds, and spirits through educational, medical, and nutrition programs.[45] In Canada, public support for UN child welfare ventures and other aims were channelled through the UNA, a club founded in 1946 that was dedicated to celebrating and funding the UN.

THE UNA: A RESPECTABLE PEACEMAKER

As many parts of the world returned to a state of peace in 1945, hope was pinned on the UN as the foremost peacemaker, on one hand promising to intervene and avert war, and on the other, spreading internationalism, economic development, social justice, and human rights. As the Canadian UN delegation in New York and Geneva worked to shape the world Canada wanted, Canadian branches of the UNA did the same on the home front. They hoped Canadians would see themselves not only as citizens of their own nation but also as citizens of the world, taking an interest and responsibility in international affairs. UNA members pledged their support of these aims by developing programs to educate their fellow Canadians about the UN's goals and Canada's role in implementing them. As the Cold War progressed, the UNA supplemented its boosterism with constructive criticism, lobbying the Canadian government to propose structural and policy reforms that would make the UN a more effective world leader. This was not purely an altruistic venture; given the worry of a coming war fought with nuclear weapons, the UNA argued that Canadians had a vested interest in supporting the UN: it would make their nation and world safer. According to the UNA's first president, the postwar world was no time for apathy, isolationism, or defeatist talk: "The battle for peace has reached a critical stage ... This is surely the time for all who believe in international co-operation to speak out, insisting that a new world-conflict is madness that need not happen."[46]

Within a year of its founding, the Canadian UNA had grown to nineteen branches in seven provinces with more than 2,000 paid members, many of whom had previously belonged to the LON's Society.[47] Branch activities were initially devoted to introducing the new world body to the public by hosting mass meetings with big-name speakers such as Lester B. Pearson explaining Canada's position in the Korean War and Eleanor Roosevelt promoting the United Nations Education Science and Culture Organization.[48] The UNA also produced radio broadcasts about UN achievements, distributed free UN posters and literature, screened UN films, and raised money for UN agencies. Beginning in the mid-1950s, the UNA also promoted Canada's growing multiculturalism, spurred by postwar immigration, by hosting food, clothing, and music festivals and holding interdenominational religious services. These celebrations were meant to imply that, if Canada's diverse population could get along, so could the world. UNA programming was funded by membership fees ($2 for individuals, $10 for groups), donations, and an annual grant of $10,000 from the Department of External Affairs.

Initially the UNA was not very different from the real UN in terms of its male-dominated leadership. In the late 1940s the association's national executive was made up of what the UNA referred to as "opinion leaders ... [those] who could have direct influence on many other people."[49] This meant the executive was filled by men in leadership positions: businessmen, members of Parliament, journalists, professionals, clergymen, and former armed forces officers. Few women were considered to be opinion leaders in this era. One exception was Cora Taylor Watt Casselman, a former teacher from Kingston, who had been active all her life in women's organizations and had also been a member of the LON's Society. When her politician husband died, she ran and won his seat in Edmonton West and served in Parliament as an MP between 1941 and 1945, becoming the first female Speaker in the House of Commons and the only female in Canada's first delegation to the UN. After the war, Casselman did not seek reelection and returned to Edmonton, where she worked as the executive director of the YWCA and joined the UNA, becoming one of its most dedicated patrons and influential members. By the mid-1950s the gendered makeup of the UNA gradually began to include more women leaders. This can be attributed to two specific reasons, one of them being women's consistent dominance in membership numbers. The second reason was that more and more women were drawn to the UNA because of the association's new child welfare-focused agenda.

While men held most of the UNA's executive positions at the national and local level, women made up the majority of club's membership. As individual members and as representatives of women's associations, they joined the UNA in large numbers because it was a respectable outlet through which they could champion matters connected to peace, internationalism, and child welfare. In Edmonton, one of the most active UNA branches in Canada, membership was divided between 49 per cent women, 41 per cent men, and 10 per cent organizations in 1949. By 1962 women members made up 57 per cent of the membership, while men had dropped to 26 per cent. In 1971, 57 per cent of Edmonton members came from the new "family" category, followed by 31 per cent women members and 12 per cent men.[50] At the national level, the UNA had 479 women's groups (301 secular and 178 faith-based) as members in 1965, compared to participation from only forty-nine men's groups and forty-four mixed-gender organizations.[51] These groups sent representatives from their organizations to attend UNA meetings and report back, recommending initiatives they should support. Group membership came from all the major women's organizations, including the

National Council of Women of Canada (NCWC) and the Imperial Order Daughters of the Empire (IODE), which were also very active in civil defence work. These groups did not consider it hypocritical to have one subcommittee preparing for war while another one worked for world peace.

The NCWC was a great supporter of the UN and the UNA, as it was of emergency preparedness programs. In 1949 the Edmonton Local Council of Women, a branch already working with the Edmonton UNA, urged the NCWC to "work with and for the United Nations," but added that it was not enough to pledge their support, they needed to work alongside the international organization and "make big plans, which have the power to move men's souls," stating this type of action would "recapture the zeal of the foresighted women who founded the National Council of Women of Canada 55 years ago."[52] Although "big plans" was an exaggeration, in 1950 the NCWC passed a resolution urging all local councils to plan three-to-five-minute spots in their monthly programs on a topic related to the UN.[53] A year later, Mrs G.F.K. Kuhring, chair of the UN committee, proudly presented her report on how local councils incorporated support for the UN in 1951. Her examples included Halifax's fifteen radio broadcasts on the UN's work with refugees, Fredericton's competition for school children to design scrapbooks dedicated to a UN agency, and Brockville's series of UN library lectures. To Kuhring, this was proof that "women want, above everything else, a peaceful world, and they are beginning to recognize two facts; that to be lasting, peace must be worldwide; that peace does not come automatically after a world war."[54] Her comments came a month before the Korean War broke out, when there was a sense that the world was about to explode again. She warned the NCWC of the pressing need to continue this good work, reminding them, "these are dangerous days through which we are living. One crisis follows closely on the heels of another. One false step, a serious mistake in judgement, might precipitate a third world war at any moment."[55] Kuhring also claimed that their work played a critical role in helping Canada manage its foreign affairs. "By helping to inform public opinion," she stated, "we shall assist the Government in the difficult decisions it is called upon to make."[56] In this manner, the NCWC contextualized their efforts as making women voters knowledgeable about internationalism and Canada's foreign affairs.

The NCWC also frequently used the UN to frame their association's resolutions on national and international issues. For example, when lobbying the Canadian government, they found it was helpful to point out the differences between Canadian law and the sometimes more progressive UN policies. This occurred in 1949 when the Ontario Provincial Council of Women appealed to the federal government to end its discriminatory immigration policies toward China by arguing that Canada's quota and head tax were in direct opposition to the UN Charter.[57] During the Korean War, the NCWC sent the federal government their approval of the UN's Convention on the Prevention and Punishment of the Crime of Genocide and expressed hope that Canada would endorse the proposed convention, a matter they found greatly important considering the Korean crisis.[58] They also used the UN to advocate for women's rights internationally. Generally the NCWC was pleased with the UN's progress in this area, noting, "before 1945 in only 40 of the 80 sovereign states had women the vote. Since then, 75 countries have acceded to giving women political rights as well as in the educational, economic, and civil etc. fields."[59] But the NCWC also wanted the UN to do more to improve the status of women, such as when the British Columbia Provincial Council of Women petitioned Canadian representatives in the UN "in the name of 'National Womanhood'" (and in the name of thwarting communism) to allow Russian women married to nationals of other countries to leave Russia if they wished to be reunited with their foreign husbands.[60] In these ways, the UN became a useful tool to support the NCWC's indirect and direct efforts toward peace and gender equity. It raised the NCWC's stature if their resolutions reflected not only the humble efforts of Canadian women seeking change but the resolve of a respectable organization consisting of the world's leading intellectuals, diplomats, and service workers entrusted to guide and protect humanity's best interests.

In addition to stimulating interest in the UN within women's organizations, the UNA formed internal study groups to analyze specific problems and offer solutions. Although they firmly believed the UN was critical to achieving world peace, they did not see the UN in its current form as omnipotent. Each year UNA members proposed resolutions outlining policies they supported or wanted changed. These were voted on at the annual meetings and those that passed were forwarded to the Department of External Affairs. In 1948, before Pearson's work in the Suez solidified the idea, the UNA pledged support for a permanent peacekeeping force.[61] In the mid-1950s resolutions came forward that repeatedly asked the UN to be a leader in nuclear disarmament and place a ban on nuclear weapons testing.[62] One of the most controversial issues faced by the UNA was what to do with mainland China. While the organization did not condone Chinese policies, it believed shunning the communist state (and the world's largest importer of Canadian grain) would just add to the Cold War chaos.[63] In 1960, after years of internal debate among the membership and many failed resolutions, the UNA came out in favour of Canada and the UN recognizing the People's Republic of China, nine years before the UN did.

While the UNA were never as radical in their demands, they openly debated the same controversial issues other peace groups were condemned for promoting, and in all three of the examples mentioned above, the UNA approved reforms long before the Canadian government or the UN did. As a state-sanctioned body, the UNA was the only public forum to discuss matters of peace and security without being tainted with accusations of communist infiltration and suffering Red Scare harassment in the 1950s. This respectability also came from the organization's membership – a collection of leading and ordinary citizens, the majority of whom were women, whose gender, class, and faith in the UN helped ensure that their status and patriotism were rarely in question.[64] Even though the UNA at times criticized Canadian foreign policy and UN decisions, and advocated for controversial topics like disarmament, its faith in the UN as the solution meant that it was not ultimately challenging the Cold War consensus. Nor was the behaviour of UNA members threatening; there were no marches or protests – rather, they insisted problems could and should be worked out through debate and education. Embracing the UN became the most respectable way to advocate for peace during the early Cold War.

This respectability gave the UNA – unlike other peace groups – formal access to children and youth. In the 1950s and 1960s, the UNA had contacts in school boards, home and school associations, and parent-teacher federations across Canada, as well as in popular youth groups such as the Girl Guides and Boy Scouts. Through these connections the UNA distributed UN-focused social studies and history guides and ran UN clubs and pen pal programs that regularly became part of the academic and after-school curricula. One UNA branch even held an annual Miss UN pageant in the 1960s to increase and recognize the participation of young women in their association.[65] For many Canadian youth, the UN represented hope. Lorraine

Oak, Miss UN 1967, who was a youth volunteer for UNICEF, recalls how she "was acutely aware at a young age of the Bay of Pigs and world peace or we blow up, and of course we had the air raid practices and the sirens went off and we all went home, presumably to be annihilated. It was a time where serious kids were very aware about the dangers of the Cold War ... I had absolute faith. I truly believed in the United Nations and that would be our salvation."[66]

The UNA contextualized its education and service work with youth as a character-building exercise for Canadian children. As the future leaders of tomorrow, youth were seen to be critical players in achieving the UN dream, and the UNA's work ensured that children of the baby boom generation were familiar with and generally supportive of the UN.[67]

The focus on children and youth meant that in the 1950s and 1960s the UNA considered teachers to be critical opinion leaders, which opened more leadership positions to women. Bertha Lawrence, an unmarried high school teacher who had immigrated to Alberta from England as a child, held many positions within the UNA locally and nationally, including that of Edmonton's representative to the UN High Commission on Refugees. In 1955 Lawrence coauthored a new edition of the grade ten social studies textbook *Canada in the Modern World*, used in classrooms across Alberta between 1955 and 1966. In the post-1945 section, Lawrence devoted a lot of space to UN affairs. In this text she called the Cold War "the greatest problem confronting the world in its search for peace" and agreed that the UN "in spite of all its shortcomings ... was a meeting place where common aims could be formulated and common policies worked out by nations that were sincerely desirous of improving world conditions."[68] Lawrence credits her experience of returning to England to serve with the British Auxiliary Territorial Service in the Second World War as instrumental in shaping her desire for peace. To Lawrence, the UN seemed the only sane road to peace.

The UNA's most tangible success was seen in its work with youth. Reaching adults was much more difficult, and there was a constant fear that the UNA was only preaching to the converted. This is best illustrated by the organization's relatively small paid membership, which even in the organization's most active period (1945–65) hovered between 2,000 and 7,000. Membership was highest in Toronto and English Montreal and was solid across the West, but there were few members in French Canada or in the Maritimes. Compared with other countries' UNAS, Canada was viewed as not living up to its potential. In 1959 the UNA in Britain had a membership of 65,000; if support had been proportionally the same in Canada, the Canadian UNA should have had at least 22,000 members.[69] Theories abounded as to why more Canadians did not join: the cost, poor recruitment strategies, apathy, confidence in the government to manage foreign affairs, lack of awareness, and so on. Membership was an issue addressed at every annual meeting, branches constantly asked members to recruit among their friends and colleagues, and the national director went on speaking tours across the country to drum up support. Still, none of these strategies got the UNA close to its 10,000 membership target. Not only did the low numbers suggest a failure to reach their goals but, with membership fees accounting for most of all the branches' and approximately a third of the national office's revenue, the scope of what the group could realistically accomplish was hampered.

Most likely the disappointing membership numbers had to do with Canadians' inconsistent opinion about the UN throughout the early Cold War years. In 1950 *Maclean's* rated the organization's first five years by stating, "It has been fashionable, in public, to take for granted that UN is worth while [*sic*]. It is even more fashionable, in private, to sneer at UN as an empty futile debating society."[70] At the same time, the editorial concluded that while UN interventions in Kashmir, Palestine, and Indonesia were ultimately unsuccessful, they were effective and events in Korea proved the UN was necessary in wartime. Canadian support for the UN wavered during and after the Korean War, when it was unclear what had been achieved by sending and losing Canadian troops. Three years of fighting in Korea had ended in a stalemate, and the lack of power the UN had to intervene in civil conflicts in Greece and Hungary and the outbreaks of violence between the United States and China on the Taiwanese straits proved the organization's limitations. Events like these caused some Canadians to doubt the UN had the capacity to be a true beacon of hope for world peace. The UN's popularity rose in 1956 when Pearson's peacekeeping mission in the Suez brought Canada worldwide recognition. Pearson's approved recommendation for the creation of a UN peacekeeping force to monitor the ceasefire and withdrawal of the French, British, and Israeli forces from Egypt managed not only to cool the conflict over the Suez Canal but was a solution that kept the fragile British Commonwealth intact and restabilized the split Western Alliance. Although historians agree this was an example of Pearson's remarkable diplomatic skills, rather than something inherently Canadian, it is generally considered the moment when "Canada stood at the zenith of its prestige in the international community ... as an internationalist middle power, a mediator and a peacemaker."[71] Pearson's triumph was used as an example of the UN's legitimacy and Canada's leadership potential within the world organization, proving there were alternatives to militarism. Nevertheless, the financial crisis that followed the new and widespread need for peacekeepers brought uncertainty about the UN's ability to survive. Regardless of the funding crisis, even Pearson's version of peacekeeping could do nothing to temper the Cold War arms race. As original UNA members died and retired, Wilson Woodside, the UNA's national president in 1963, noted that younger Canadians were joining more radical peace organizations such as VOW, the Campaign for Nuclear Disarmament, or the World Federalists.[72] Despite a lack of faith in the UN's security plans and dwindling UNA memberships, however, Canadians continued to generously donate to UN programs, most notably UNICEF.

UNICEF: CHILDREN HELPING CHILDREN

Established in 1946, UNICEF represented the start of the UN's attentiveness to international child rights and child welfare, a commitment later cemented in the production of the UN Declaration on the Rights of the Child in 1959. This document expanded upon the LON's earlier recognition of international governance and responsibility for children's well-being written by Eglantyne Jebb, the founder of the British relief organization Save the Children. The 1959 declaration opens with the same preamble as that of the LON, stating that "mankind owes to the child the best that it has to give" and justifies this by explaining "the child, because of his physical and mental immaturity, needs special safeguards and care."[73] UNICEF was founded with these principles in mind, and its immediate focus was delivering care to young refugees across war-torn Europe and Asia. UNICEF, like UNRRA, was expected to fold after the immediate concern for children affected by the Second World War was met; however, the huge scope of the problem, combined with a seemingly never-ending line of new wars and nonwar-related development issues, forced the UN to reconsider their plan.

When debating the permanency of UNICEF in 1950, Canada, the agency's third largest contributor (behind the United States and Australia), initially withdrew its support.[74] The Canadian representatives explained that their decision was caused by the UN's impractical goal of saving all children and their reluctance to continue paying for the mistakes of irresponsible developing nations. This reaction illustrates the cost-benefit thinking behind the Canadian government's approach to foreign aid. It did not give money purely out of a sense of morality; it wanted clear results from its benevolence, ones that reflected Canadian interests.[75] The Canadian government was convinced to stick with UNICEF for three reasons. One was the persuasive argument from the American UN delegation about the necessity of specializing in children's needs rather than dividing UNICEF's responsibilities among other agencies. Secondly, the government was well aware of the Canadian public's unwavering support for UNICEF.[76] In a letter to the External Affairs Committee, the UNA's national secretary Kathleen Bowlby urged Canada to remain one of UNICEF key funders because "we Canadians can well afford all the assistance we are giving to the less favoured countries. Indeed, if we want to work toward a peaceful world, we cannot afford to ignore the needs that confront us. UNICEF has already built strong bonds of friendship. We trust that Canada will continue to play her part in the entirely commendable endeavour."[77] Finally, despite the Canadian representatives' concern about efficient spending, it was hard to deny the needs of suffering children and still consider Canada to be a compassionate nation. Therefore in 1952 the Canadian government confirmed it would continue to make an annual contribution of $500,000 to UNICEF, bringing its total contribution to date to $8 million, funds that by then had been distributed to sixty million children in more than seventy countries and territories.[78] Added to the government's annual contribution was $21 million raised for UNICEF between 1955 and 1975 through private donations by Canadians.[79] UNICEF's nongovernmental support in Canada was coordinated by a committee within the UNA. The committee eventually became even larger than the UNA itself, with thousands of volunteers and with subcommittees in every province, run mainly by women. The enthusiastic service shown by UNICEF volunteers reflected women's special interest in a project dedicated to aiding children, as well as the tendency for the UNA to direct interested female volunteers to UNICEF.[80]

124

Tarah BrookfieldTarah Brookfield

UNICEF's popularity among Canadians can be traced to two factors: an interest in helping improve the lives of children and UNICEF's low-cost and easy donation procedures. Unlike other foreign relief agencies, UNICEF's entire focus was on children, whose innocence and vulnerability made them the least controversial beneficiaries of aid. As seen in Freud and Burlingham's work, as well as in the ideologies present in civil defence and the peace movement, children's physical and psychological care in wartime required special attention. Not only did this appeal to the maternalistic energy of women's Cold War activism, it appealed to populations on both sides of the Iron Curtain. Making young people UNICEF's special mission allowed the new agency to avoid being a site of UN power struggles during the Cold War. This was helped by ensuring that funds were sent and received by nations on both sides of the Soviet and American alliances. Although the annual report for Canada's UNICEF Committee in 1961–62 mentioned a rumour circulating in the United States that most UNICEF money went to communist nations because most UNICEF volunteers were socialists, for the most part UNICEF avoided Red Scare controversy.[81] Ultimately, UNICEF came to be considered, in the words of Bowlby, the "United Nations organ for which everyone has the highest praise and which has a universal appeal. One of the world body's most cherished agencies."[82]

The organization's popularity can also be explained by how easy it made donating. It ran affordable and soon to be exceedingly familiar campaigns that only asked for a few dollars or even pennies. UNICEF's first national fundraising campaign involved the sale of greeting cards during the 1952 Christmas season. The Canadian UNA ordered 100,000 cards that depicted children greeting different kinds of animals used to transport UNICEF supplies around the world: an elephant in India, a water buffalo in Southeast Asia, a reindeer in Finland, a camel in the Middle East, and a donkey in Latin America. These cards were sold by volunteers, described by the Winnipeg UNA as "thirty women and some husbands."[83] The volunteers were advised to warn purchasers that "Because the United Nations represents all races and creeds the cards do not use special Christmas symbols. Appropriately, each carries season's greetings in the five official UN languages, English, French, Spanish, Russian and Chinese."[84] In the first year, Canadians bought 33,000 more cards than were originally ordered, raising $7,500 and making the country's per capita sales figure higher than that of any other participating nation. A press release for the UNA claimed the card sales were a coast-to-coast effort: "Anyone looking over the list of shipments would feel that there could hardly be a single community in Canada that was missed."[85] The cards became an annual fall project that by 1975 had raised more than $11 million.

UNICEF's second fundraising project, Trick-or-Treat for UNICEF, became the agency's most successful fundraiser and was responsible for raising almost half of the $21 million earned between 1955 and 1975. The program's success can be attributed to recruiting a relatively untapped group of volunteers and supporters, children, whose participation opened new avenues and labour for fundraising. UNICEF was not the first organization to use children to collect money to send overseas; this had long been a mainstay of Sunday school projects and children's clubs. For example, the French Catholic St Enfance Association in Quebec had been asking students to save their pennies to redeem and educate the children in "unfaithful" countries since 1843. Between 1930 and 1950 their alms went towards "buying" the souls of Chinese children, a project that raised almost $2 million before it was abandoned when all foreign missionaries had to leave China after the Communist takeover.[86] UNICEF's Trick-or-Treat scheme saw thousands – and later, hundreds of thousands – of children go door to door on Halloween asking for small donations to save children around the world. The idea was born in 1950 when a Sunday school class in Philadelphia decided to ask for coins instead of candy and raised $17 for UNICEF. In 1955 Canadian children joined the clamour for coins in addition to or in lieu of candy, raising $15,000 in their first year.[87] Four years later, 229,600 Canadian children were enrolled in the program.

There were organizational and ideological concerns to overcome before the Trick-or-Treat program became an entrenched feature of Canadian children's Halloween routine. Some parents questioned the suitability of turning a pagan or silly celebration into a charitable event, while others thought Halloween should be a lighthearted holiday. The adult workload appeared to be another roadblock. In preparation for making this an annual event, UNA members met with school boards, parent-teacher associations, youth groups, women's clubs, churches, and service groups, hoping to mobilize their support in launching this campaign every October. Although the collection took place on only one night per year, adult volunteers were needed to distribute UN literature in advance and educate the participating children and potential donors on the UNICEF cause throughout the autumn. Then on 1 November adults were needed to count, organize, and forward the collected coins to the local UNA. Since schools were the logical starting point, there were concerns over the increased labour bestowed upon teachers. The baby boom had put pressures on the school system, where the focus was on building new schools and hiring new staff not on new extracurricular activities.[88] Schools were reluctant to commit to the program, which left parents, women's clubs, and teenagers to pioneer the program with support from UNA branches. In many communities women's groups took the lead, making the milk-carton containers (in the years before the standard orange boxes became the norm) and holding roll-the-penny parties for the children after they came back from trick-or-treating.[89] One Ottawa mother, Mrs Phillion, attempted to run the campaign on her own when she had her four children collect coins one Halloween. Afterwards she wrote to the *Ottawa Citizen* explaining that the schools needed to take the project on because without large-scale awareness, Phillion found it difficult to raise much money in her neighbourhood.[90] In other locales, service-minded teens organized the collection with a little help from their moms and dads. High school student Oak recalls how she initiated the Halloween campaign in her Edmonton school district singlehandedly in the early 1960s:

> I contacted the UN association and they provided me with lots of little cardboard containers and my dear father ran around the schools with me where I went and gave talks about UNICEF and Brownie packs and whatever. I would then go and collect the little containers and count the money and turn it in to the UN association for UNICEF. I became very interested in the work of UNICEF ... I was always particularly moved by children in need and this was certainly a major organization that was focusing on children.[91]

It is possible that schools eventually came on board because they saw the value of supervising an effort that was producing global-citizen-minded students like Oak. Therefore the program could be seen as part of the social studies, health, history, or economics curriculum, rather than extra work.

Eventually UNICEF persuasively sold the campaign to schools and parents as a character-building exercise for Canadian children. One promotional flyer described the Halloween program as "a sharing project designed to benefit children everywhere, both at home and abroad."[92] Just as the UNICEF money went to help develop the minds and bodies of children in places like France, Egypt, and Malaysia, UNICEF was seen as developing the hearts of Canadian children by teaching them the value of money, charity, compassion, and gratitude for their own circumstances. From the "seeds of destiny" perspective, it was equally important to create the right kind of child in Canada and abroad; this would help preserve democracy. This message was viewed as empowering for many of the young participants. Being considered mini-UN ambassadors gave a different spin to the oft-heard message of do unto others. This time the so-called others were children just like themselves, an idea that was highly appealing and relatable to children. Oak explains she was drawn to participate in UNICEF because, "I remember [the UN] appealing to children to help other children ... we sort of expect adults to do everything and there are children in need. So we as children should be doing something. And I really felt that as a child, I felt that children should be doing something."[93] UNICEF insisted that children could make a difference; they did not have to wait to be adults to influence the world. To emphasize this, UNICEF showed how even the loose change collected by one child could help alter someone's life. Posters sent out to participants listed how just one penny could buy five large glasses of milk or enough vaccine to protect a child from tuberculosis, a nickel could buy enough penicillin to cure one child of yaws, and a quarter could buy enough DDT to protect two children for one year against malaria.[94] This aura of empowerment was illustrated in one UNICEF cartoon that showed two children dressed in costumes. The boy said, "SO far I've got three apples!" The girl, perhaps reflecting a gendered interest in UNICEF, looked into her UNICEF box and replied, "SO far I've saved three children."[95] When UNICEF won the Nobel Peace Prize in 1965, a newsletter recounted how one North American boy reportedly ran home to tell his mother that he won the Nobel because, since he had trick-or-treated for UNICEF, he was part of UNICEF.[96]

UNICEF attempted to mobilize everywhere in Canada, but their planning manual noted the difficulties this entailed. Children in rural areas and small towns were the first to get involved because it was easier to organize fewer people. It was more difficult to coordinate widespread support in urban centres where the prevalence of apartment buildings and dense neighbourhoods often made Halloween parties sponsored by schools or community centres the more popular and safer option than trick-or-treating.[97] This was the committee's reasoning behind regional variations in average participation and donations. For example, while children in Ontario and Quebec always brought in the most money, Prince Edward Island consistently had the highest per capita participation across the country.[98] Occasionally, Canada's climate also played a factor in geographic participation. Very often winter had arrived by late October, which made trick-or-treating times rushed – or even impossible – for children bundled into snowsuits over their costumes. In 1971 parts of Manitoba were hit by a major blizzard, an event that the national office expected would derail the province's UNICEF contributions. Surprisingly Manitoba managed to raise $9,500 that year, an increase of 78 per cent from the previous year, proof that UNICEF had become entrenched in Canadians' hearts as a duty not to be overlooked for lack of clear skies.[99]

By the late 1960s, UNICEF had even spread to northern Canada, where inclement weather was a minor inconvenience compared to the problems of regional underdevelopment and a small population. In 1965, eight schools in the Northwest Territories participated in UNICEF's Halloween program for the first time. Kate Aitken, one of UNICEF's national chairs, explicitly stated the background of the children in one Inuvik school in her annual report, proudly noting how "ten Eskimo, five white, and two Indian children" had collectively raised $2 for UNICEF.[100] This type of anecdote celebrates cross-cultural cooperation, a hallmark of internationalism. More importantly, it implied that all of Canada's peoples, even those presumed to be less fortunate, cared about UNICEF. This habit was not UNICEF's alone; other foreign relief agencies frequently used examples of the less affluent within Canada as propaganda to reinforce the diversity and inherent nobility of their donors.[101]

While donations came in from all sectors of society, the women who sat on the Canadian UNICEF committee leaned toward the elite. Many of the chairs and executive were well known and established in their communities – some were even nationally known, such as radio personality Kate Aitken and Senator Muriel Fergusson. Others were like Margaret Konantz, a long time club woman. Konantz had been active with the Junior League and the Red Cross and she volunteered with the Women's Voluntary Services in

England during the Second World War. After her children were grown and her husband dead, Konantz devoted more time to service work. In 1956 she was invited to London to work with the Women's Voluntary Service, which at the time was deeply involved in Cold War emergency preparedness. When she returned to Winnipeg she decided against helping organize a civil defence program; instead, she joined the UNA, explaining, "I chose an organization working for peace, rather than preparing for war."[102] Through the Winnipeg and National UNAs, Konantz became involved with UNICEF, chairing its National Committee between 1959 and 1965. As chair, she personally subsidized trips to Asia, the Middle East, and Africa, where she viewed UNICEF projects in progress in seventeen countries.

In Canada Konantz embarked on a national speaking tour to schools, women's clubs, and public meetings, hoping to enlighten Canadians about UNICEF's accomplishments and consequently raise more funds for the organization. Her speeches contained stories about the children she encountered and her strong desire to rescue them from their unfortunate situations. One story that frequently appeared in her talks was her observation of a little boy in Calcutta sitting in an alley. She described how the boy's eyes haunted her. He was too tired to even move them when she spoke to him. She did not have her camera with her but she "thought maybe if I could get a picture of this child, I would have proof how great this need was to help 600,000,000 in this world that lack adequate food, clothing, shelter and protection from disease."[103] Her example was similar to imagery found in UNRRA's film *Seeds of Destiny*, where the silent sad faces of a few spoke for millions, and the children's appearance, demeanour, and homelessness contrasted sharply with her audience's idea of the lives of most Canadian children. Through her travels and passion for UNICEF, Konantz concluded that internationalism was not something Canadians could choose but a reality that came from living in the modern world. In her speeches, like the one to the Junior League excerpted below, Konantz stressed the responsibilities that came with internationalism and warned how ignoring them would not only hurt children, like the little Indian boy in the alley, but also threaten Canada's security and commitment to freedom:

Our world today is very small. Whether we like it or not, we can look over the fences of our international neighbours all too

easily, and some of the things we see are not pleasant ... We of
the West believe that slums should not be tolerated. We know
that poverty, hunger, poor living conditions breed unrest, discontent, trouble, even rebellion. Surely in this constricting world of
ours we cannot sit idly by and not try to do something about
making basic improvements in health, education, production of
food, and trade where it is needed most.[104]

Konantz's speech concluded with an invitation to join an international organization, insisting that only through international understanding would peace occur.

Not happy with merely inspiring other individuals to carrying the
torch for peace, at age sixty-four Konantz entered national politics,
successfully running as the Liberal member for Winnipeg South. As
an MP, Konantz remained active with the UNA and UNICEF, becoming one of Canada's representatives to the UN in 1963. In 1965 she
was selected to represent Canada in Oslo when UNICEF received the
Nobel Peace Prize.[105] After meeting with Konantz in 1963, Prime
Minister Lester Pearson promised to increase the Canadian government's annual contribution to UNICEF to $1 million, explaining that
one of the factors in his decision was the "the nation-wide support
for the work of UNICEF as demonstrated in Halloween collections
and the greeting cards sales."[106]

Whether as an overseas employer, local community charity drive,
government lobbyist or simply a stimulus for world peace, the UN
welcomed women into its fold and served as space in which they
could combat global insecurity with expressions of internationalism
and maternalism. As the testimonies from UNRRA workers Brown
and McGeachy, UNA executive members Livingstone, Casselman and
Lawrence, and UNICEF volunteers Konantz and Oak attest – not to
mention the thousands of other women who worked behind the
scenes – Canadian women enthusiastically served as grassroots UN
ambassadors bolstering Canada's ideological and financial support
of the UN amid Cold War turmoil. While they engaged in the geopo-
litical issues debated at the Security Council, the women also valued
the simple yet promising premise behind many UN relief programs:
raising children to be healthy in mind, body, and spirit and free from
want would be a tremendous step forward in healing the wounds of
war and building a peaceful world.

NOTES

1 This work is adapted from chapter 4 of Tarah Brookfield's *Cold War Comforts: Canadian Women, Child Safety, and Global Insecurity* (Waterloo: Wilfrid Laurier University Press, 2012).

2 Robert Conley, "Faith Put in U.N., Not Shelters," *New York Times*, 1 December 1961, 1.

3 Doris Anderson, "Gesture of Sanity and Faith," *Chatelaine*, February 1962, 1.

4 Ibid.

5 Michael Carroll, "Canada and the Financing of the United Nations Emergency Force, 1957–1963," *Journal of the Canadian Historical Association* 13 (2002): 217–34.

6 Brenda Smith, "Paying for the UN," letter to the editor, *Globe and Mail*, 5 December 1961, 6.

7 This figure was calculated by adding each year's donations and returns from the various projects listed in the annual reports between 1955 and 1975 published by UNICEF Canada.

8 Library and Archives Canada (LAC), United Nations Association (UNA) fonds, MG28, I202, box 45, file 5, Annual Meetings 1962, Public Relations Study, Toronto UNA, July 1962, 1–2.

9 Archives of Ontario (AO), Local Council of Women fonds, F805-2-0-5, *The Councillor* 1962, 1963, "Report from UN Association in Canada–Women's Section," by Mrs G.E.M. Livingstone, *The Councillor: Official Bulletin of the Local Council of Women of Toronto*, March 1963.

10 For a broader analysis of women's Cold War activism, see Tarah Brookfield's *Cold War Comforts: Canadian Women, Child Safety, and Global Insecurity* (Waterloo: Wilfrid Laurier University Press, 2012).

11 Dominique Marshall, "The Cold War, Canada, and the United Nations Declaration of the Rights of the Child," in *Canada and the Early Cold War, 1943–1957*, ed. Greg Donaghy (Ottawa: Department of Foreign Affairs and International Trade, 1988), 185.

12 Dominique Marshall, "The Language of Children's Rights, the Formation of the Welfare State and the Democratic Experience of Poor Families in Quebec, 1940–1955," *Canadian Historical Review* 78, no. 3 (1997), 261–83.

13 *Seeds of Destiny* (Washington: Defense Department, United States Army War Department, 1946), film.

14 Ibid.

15 Laura Briggs, "Mother, Child, Race, Nation: The Visual Iconography of Rescue and the Politics of Transnational and Transracial Adoption," *Gender and History* 15, no. 2 (August 2003): 179.

16 Ibid., 182.

17 Sean Kennedy, *The Shock of War: Civilian Experiences, 1937–1945* (Toronto: University of Toronto Press, 2011), 10.

18 *Seeds of Destiny.*

19 Adam Chapnick, *The Middle Power Project: Canada and the Founding of the United Nations* (Vancouver: University of British Columbia Press, 2005), 3.

20 Grant Dexter, *Canada and the Building of Peace* (Toronto: Canadian Institute of International Affairs, 1944).

21 "Children Assisted: Campaign to Aid Europe's Destitute," *Toronto Telegram*, 10 January 1948.

22 No figures are given for the support for UNRRA; however, Jeff Keshen describes it as a "healthy majority" in "One for All or All for One: Government Controls, Black Marketing and the Limits of Patriotism, 1939–1947," *Journal of Canadian Studies* 29 (Winter 1994): 119.

23 Susan Armstrong-Reid and David Murray, *Armies of Peace: Canada and the UNRRA Years* (Toronto: University of Toronto Press, 2008), 9.

24 Ruth Compton Brouwer, *New Women for God: Canadian Presbyterian Women and India Missions, 1876–1914* (Toronto: University of Toronto Press, 1990), 3.

25 From *Toronto Star Weekly* 1944, quoted in Mary Kinnear, *Woman of the World: Mary McGeachy and International Cooperation* (Toronto: University of Toronto Press, 2004), 159.

26 Ibid., 174.

27 Ibid., 253, 260.

28 See Brown's letters to her brothers 13 October 1943 to 24 August 1944 in *The Army's Mister Brown: A Family Trilogy, 1941–1952*, ed. Harcourt Brown (Parry Sound, ON: Olympic Printing, 1982), 117–22.

29 Armstrong-Reid and Murray, *Armies of Peace*, 147.

30 Elizabeth Brown's personal account in Brown, *The Army's Mister Brown*, 136.

31 AO, Joshua Brown fonds, F1176, series C-3, box 5, file 17, draft of unpublished autobiography, 1950s.

32 LAC, Canadian Council on Social Development fonds, MG28, I10, vol. 106, file 785 Civil Defence, Advisory Committee 1951–57, Minutes from the Civil Defence Welfare Services Advisory Committee Meeting,

15 September 1956, 4; Advisory Civil Defence Welfare Committee Nominees, 13 October 1953.

33 LAC, Voice of Women (VOW) fonds, MG28, I218, vol. 2, file 10, Voice of Women International Co-operation Year Travel Mission, Personal Profiles, 1963. Ostry was also a key social worker in the migration of Jewish refugee children to Canada after the Second World War.

34 Everett M. Ressler, Neil Boothby, and Daniel J. Steinbock, *Unaccompanied Children: Care and Protection in Wars, Natural Disasters, and Refugee Movements* (New York: Oxford University Press, 1988), 12.

35 Armstrong-Reid and Murray, *Armies of Peace*, 197.

36 Ibid., 200, 220.

37 Hansi Kennedy, "Memories of Anna Freud," *American Imago* 53, no. 3 (1996): 205–9.

38 Anna Freud and Dorothy Tiffany Burlingham, *War and Children* (New York: Medical War Books, 1943), 11.

39 Ibid., 12.

40 Irene Kahn Atkins, "Seeds of Destiny: A Case History," *Film and History* 11, no. 2 (May 1981): 28.

41 *Seeds of Destiny.*

42 Ibid.

43 Atkins, "Seeds of Destiny," 31.

44 Ibid. When UNRRA folded in 1947, UNICEF inherited its remaining money.

45 Judith M. Spiegelman, *We Are the Children: A Celebration of UNICEF's First Forty Years* (Boston: Atlantic Monthly Press, 1986), 3–5.

46 LAC, UNA fonds, MG28, I202, UNA in Canada, box 54, file 8, Branch Officers, Correspondence 1946, memo to branch secretaries from National President James S. Thompson, 23 September 1946.

47 Lucille Marr, "'If You Want Peace, Prepare for Peace': Hanna Newcombe, Peace Researcher and Peace Activist," *Ontario History* 84, no. 4 (1992), 265.

48 These are a sample of talks hosted by the UNA in Toronto, advertised in the *Globe and Mail* on 15 November 1950 and 17 May 1955. Smaller branches had a more difficult time attracting such well-known speakers.

49 LAC, UNA fonds, MG28, I202, box 45, file 5, Annual Meetings 1962, Public Relations Study, Toronto UNA, July 1962, 1.

50 A sample of membership lists from the Edmonton branch in 1949, 1956, 1961–62, and 1971–72 is taken from various documents in the CEA, Bertha Lawrence fonds, MSS 688, boxes 1–4.

51 LAC, UNA fonds, MG28, I202, box 1, file 1, Affiliated Community Organi-
    zation, Correspondence, 1965.
52 City of Edmonton Archives (CEA), Edmonton Local Council of Women
    Clippings File, "Local Council Gives Annual Report," untitled newspaper
    clipping, 27 January 1949.
53 LAC, National Council of Women of Canada (NCWC) fonds, MG, I25,
    vol. 128, file 3, 1949–51, Annual Meeting Minutes, 1 June 1950.
54 LAC, NCWC fonds, MG I25, vol. 92, file 5, Standing Committees: Reports,
    Correspondence, "United Nations," Report, 1950–51.
55 Ibid.
56 Ibid.
57 LAC, NCWC fonds, MG I25, file 11, Resolutions 1947–1950, "Resolution,"
    Ontario Provincial Council of Women, 26 October 1949.
58 LAC, NCWC fonds, MG I25, Ibid. vol. 95, file 9, United Nations
    Convention: Correspondence 1950–53, Press Release, 14 September 1950.
59 AO, Local Council of Women fonds, F805-2-0-3, *The Councillor*, 1956–
    59, Mrs W.A. Riddell, "International," *The Councillor: Official Bulletin of
    the Local Council of Women of Toronto*, April 1958.
60 LAC, NCWC fonds, MG28, I25, vol. 128, file 3, 1949–51, NCWC Annual
    Meeting Minutes, 1 May 1949, 29.
61 LAC, UNA fonds, MG28, I202, box 45, file 1, Annual General Meeting,
    1958 Agenda, Minutes, Reports, Resolution from Montreal branch, 1958.
62 LAC, UNA fonds, MG28, I202, box 44, file 24 Annual Meeting Report
    1957, Report to Annual Meeting, 1957.
63 LAC, UNA fonds, MG28, I202, box 45, file 4, Annual Meetings 1961,
    Annual General Meeting, 20–21 May 1960.
64 LAC, UNA fonds, MG28, I202, box 54, file 8 Branch Officers,
    Correspondence 1946, Box List of Branch Presidents, 11 September 1946.
65 Tarah Brookfield, "Modeling the UN's Mission in Semi-formal Wear:
    Edmonton's Miss United Nations Pageants of the 1960s," in *Contesting
    Bodies and Nations in Canadian History*, ed. Jane Nichols and Patrizia
    Gentile (Toronto: University of Toronto Press, 2013).
66 Lorraine Oak, interview, 8 February 2010.
67 CEA, Bertha Lawrence fonds, MSS688, box 3, UNA in Canada,
    Hallowe'en for UNICEF for Children Everywhere, Planning Manual
    Produced by the National UNICEF Committee, Toronto, 1960.
68 Bertha Lawrence et al., *Canada in the Modern World* (Toronto: J.M. Dent
    & Sons, 1955), 223–4.
69 LAC, UNA fonds, MG28, I202, UNA in Canada, box 60, file 17, General
    Core, 1959, National Director, Willson Woodside.

70 "The UN Proves Its Worth with the Blue Chips Down," *Macleans*,
    1 August 1950, 2.

71 Reg Whitaker and Gary Marcuse. *Cold War Canada: The Making of a
    National Insecurity State, 1945–1957* (Toronto: University of Toronto
    Press, 1994), 113.

72 CEA, Bertha Lawrence fonds, MSS 688, Box 3, UNA in Canada, "National
    Directors Report" by Willson Woodside, 26 May 1963.

73 United Nations, "Declaration on the Rights of the Child," 1959.

74 CEA, Bertha Lawrence fonds, MSS 688, box 1, UNA in Canada, to External
    Affairs Committee of the House of Commons from Kathleen E. Bowlby,
    National secretary, 1952.

75 Ibid.

76 Marshall, "The Cold War," 196.

77 CEA, Bertha Lawrence fonds, MSS 688, box 1, UNA in Canada, to External
    Affairs Committee of the House of Commons from Kathleen E. Bowlby,
    National Secretary, 1952.

78 CEA, Bertha Lawrence fonds, MSS 688, box 1, UNA in Canada, press
    release, Department of Public Information, United Nations, New York,
    15 July 1952.

79 This figure was calculated by adding each year's donations and returns
    from the various projects listed in the annual reports between 1955 and
    1975 published by UNICEF Canada.

80 UNICEF Canada Office (UCO), UNICEF Canada Annual Reports 1955–75.

81 UCO, Annual Report, 1961–62, Report of Executive Director, Mrs Gordon
    Richards.

82 CEA, Bertha Lawrence fonds, MSS 688, Box 1, UNA in Canada, letter from
    Kathleen E. Bowlby, National Secretary, national office, to all branch pres-
    idents and secretaries, 8 May 1952.

83 UCO, UNICEF Canada Annual Report 1963–64, Report from Manitoba,
    41.

84 CEA, Bertha Lawrence fonds, MSS 688, box 1, UNA in Canada, UNICEF
    greeting cards press release, 17 October 1952.

85 CEA, Bertha Lawrence fonds, MSS 688, box 1, UNA in Canada, press
    release, 18 February 1953

86 Alain Larocque, "'Losing Our Chinese': The St Enfance Movement,"
    Working Paper 49, Joint Centre for Asia Pacific Studies (June 1987), 6.

87 CEA, Bertha Lawrence fonds, MSS 688, box 3, UNA in Canada, Report of
    the executive secretary for the UNA's National UNICEF Committee by
    Mary P. Carter, June 1960.

88 UCO, UNICEF Canada Annual Report 1966–67, Report from Calgary, 37.

89 CEA, Bertha Lawrence fonds, MSS688, box 3, UNA in Canada, Hallowe'en for UNICEF for Children Everywhere, Planning Manual Produced by the National UNICEF Committee, Toronto, 1960.

90 Mrs R. Phillion, letter to the editor, *Ottawa Citizen*, 16 November 1965.

91 Lorraine Oak, interview, 8 February 2010.

92 CEA, Bertha Lawrence fonds, MSS688, box 3, UNA in Canada, Hallowe'en for UNICEF for Children Everywhere, Planning Manual Produced by the National UNICEF Committee, Toronto, 1960.

93 Lorraine Oak, interview, 8 February 2010.

94 Ibid.

95 CEA, Bertha Lawrence fonds, MSS688, box 3, UNA in Canada, Hallowe'en for UNICEF for Children Everywhere, Planning Manual Produced by the National UNICEF Committee, Toronto, 1960.

96 CEA, Bertha Lawrence fonds, MSS688, box 2, UNICEF, *There May Be Tigers – Anecdotes about UNICEF from All over the World*, booklet, August 1966, 37.

97 UCO, UNICEF Canada Annual Report 1966–67, Report from Calgary, 37.

98 UCO, Annual Report 1971–72, PEI Committee Report.

99 UCO, Report of the Annual General Meeting, 1971–72, Report from Manitoba, 39.

100 UCO, Annual Report 1964–65, Kate Aitken's report, 33.

101 For more discussion on race and ethnicity see Tarah Brookfield, "Children as 'Seeds of Destiny': Nation, Race, and Citizenship in Postwar Foreign Relief Programs," in *The Difference That Kids Make: Bringing Children and Childhood into Canadian History*, eds. Tamara Myers and Mona Gleason (Oxford University Press, forthcoming 2016).

102 University of Manitoba Archives (UMA), Margaret Konantz fonds, MMI, box 4, file 5, Speeches, 1956–67, "The Moral Climate," speech by Konantz, panel discussion for 1967 Junior League Association Conference.

103 UMA, Margaret Konantz fonds, MMI, box 4, file 4, Notes and Speech fragments, undated, untitled speech fragment.

104 Margaret Konantz fonds, MMI, box 4, file 5, Speeches, 1956–67, "The Moral Climate," speech by Konantz, panel discussion for 1967 Junior League Association Conference.

105 "Manitoba's New Liberal Star Beaming Brightly: Konantz's Crew Raises Thunderous Applause," *Winnipeg Free Press*, 9 April 1963.

106 UCO, UNICEF Canada Annual Report 1964–65, 20.

5

In the Service of Peace

The Progressive Tenor
of Canadian Peacekeeping

Colin McCullough

A song by one of Canada's best-known folk singers, Stompin' Tom Connors, begins

> Yes we are the Blue Berets
> We're up and on our way
> With another UN flag to be unfurled
> Till the factions are at bay and peace is on its way
> We'll display our Blue Berets around the world[1]

Connors's song, "The Blue Berets," is an ode to Canadian participation in United Nations (UN) peacekeeping operations. The song was written in 1993, when more than 3,000 Canadians were involved in peacekeeping operations abroad in diverse locales, including Somalia, Cyprus, and the former Yugoslavia. Never one to chastise his home and native land, Connors's song extolled the virtues of Canadians for their service to the UN. A later stanza described how the Canadians were being sent to "bring some hope to an ugly world."[2] In many ways, Connors's song was a Canadian rejoinder to "The Ballad of the Green Berets," a promilitary song written by Robin Moore and Staff Sergeant Barry Sandler that became popular in the United States in 1966 and was also featured in the John Wayne film *The Green Berets*. In the Canadian version, the peacekeepers are sent to dangerous locales "where bullets fly and rockets madly hurl," but there is no reference to the peacekeepers dying for Canada, as there was in "The Ballad of the Green Berets."[3] Instead, the "Blue Berets" were said to soon be marching home to their orderly and peaceful neighbourhoods to say, "We love you all."[4] This altered conception of sacrifice enabled Connors to encourage Canadians to celebrate their national distinctiveness through their peacekeepers. The pronoun "we," employed throughout the song, further encouraged Canadians to see themselves in the deeds of their peacekeepers. Yet, the "we" Connors describes represents more than the peacekeepers themselves. It is this universality – the "we" who are "the Blue Berets" and the ones who can bring hope to the world – that is the primary focus of this study.

United Nations peacekeeping has been constructed as a progressive activity that was supposed to make Canada, and the broader world inhabited by Canadians, a better and more peaceful place from 1957 to 1997. Elsewhere, I argue that a progressive discourse of peacekeeping coexisted alongside nostalgic discussions of Canada's peacekeeping past and functional discussions of its peacekeeping present.[5] But given the recent strain in Canada's relationship with the UN, deftly discussed by Kim Nossal elsewhere in this collection, it seems instructive to emphasize several important ways Canadians expressed progressive ideas about their country and the larger world they sought to inhabit through constructing UN peacekeeping as a Canadian activity. Such expressions came through a myriad of formal and informal actions by the state, groups, and individuals. Three distinct, and instructive, means by which ideas about Canada's progressive peacekeeping identity can be gleaned are political speeches, which reached out to audiences across the country; letters to the government, which spoke about the need for Canada to help "increase the peace"; and high school history textbooks, which told Canadians to model their behaviour on peacekeeping. It is only through examining such cultural products that we can begin to understand why and how peacekeeping became entrenched in the national identity of many Canadians from 1957 to 1997 and how this motivating force for international action has been damaged by recent neglect on the part of the Canadian state. Given the limited space of this chapter, representative examples will be drawn from the political rhetoric of the Liberal Party between 1960 and 1970, while letters to the government from this era will also be examined. In the final section, history textbooks that were in use across English Canada between 1980 and 2000 will provide evidence of how persistent a progressive peacekeeping discourse was and how it affected countless Canadians in the past.

Peacekeeping's adoption into Canada's national symbology came from its employment in the litany of words, images, and objects about peacekeeping that could be found throughout Canadian society and culture after 1956. Any person who lived in Canada from 1956 to 1997 would have been exposed to a large amount of political speeches, news reports, and editorial cartoons about peacekeeping; would have also likely learned about peacekeeping in their high school history textbooks, perhaps watched some of the fourteen NFB films that had peacekeeping as either a major component or primary focus, visited a monument to peacekeeping located somewhere in the country, viewed one of three *Heritage Minutes* about peacekeeping, or used either the one-dollar coin (the loonie) or the ten-dollar bill, both of which have been emblazoned with a peacekeeper, to purchase something. There have also been public buildings and parklands named for peacekeeping and its key figures, a mention in the Molson's *Canadian* "Joe Canada" beer advertisement, dramatic plays, and national days of recognition for peacekeeping. The combined effect of these cultural products about peacekeeping was a saturation of Canadian life during these years.

The adoption of peacekeeping as a Canadian activity took place amidst considerable transmutations to Canada's national identity.[6] The last four decades have seen a scholarly reappraisal of the existence of national identities and the symbols that help sustain them.[7] Nations, according to Anthony D. Smith, constitute "a named human population which shares myths and memories, a mass public culture, a designated homeland, economic unity and equal rights and duties for all members."[8] Gerard Bouchard offers a similar ethno-cultural understanding of French Canada, and his work provides useful insights regarding the central narratives, or "myths," which a population tells itself to define its identity. Bouchard's approach stresses the hybridity of myths and their ability to flow between "reality and fiction, reason and emotion, truth and falsehood, consciousness and unconsciousness."[9] He emphasizes that we should investigate their origins, note the ebb and rise of their utility as markers of the nation, and examine their possible persistence in the future. This chapter shares Bouchard's methodology and seeks to better understand Canada's nationhood through its appropriation of an international activity, UN peacekeeping. Ultimately, it argues that the symbolic connotations of peace and hope for the future found throughout its use by actors across Canadian society from 1957 to 1997 facilitated its ready adoption into the nation's pantheon of symbols.[10]

Despite the presence of a progressive discourse across the entire country, language still bifurcated how peacekeeping was understood in Canada. As French Canada increasingly became associated with the borders of Quebec, conceptions of a French nation centred on Quebec's historical destiny and its beginnings apart from English Canada. Peacekeeping found favour in Quebec when it was presented as an internationalist policy that countered British imperial efforts, but it failed to find a more symbolic hold in French Canada as Quebec became more concerned with its own foreign affairs after the Quiet Revolution. Instead, Quebeckers tended to embrace peacekeeping as a functional policy that was far more desirable than war, but which needed to serve the interests of the host nation, rather than the broader cause of international peace.[11]

Peacekeeping's becoming interwoven with a Canadian national identity also represented a modification of a long-standing association between the nation and its military.[12] Canadians, as historians Jack Granatstein and David Bercuson remind readers, have been active supporters of military conflicts since well before there was a Canada as it currently exists.[13] Granatstein and Bercuson have also called peacekeeping's popularity an aberration for an otherwise strongly martial nation of volunteers and active servicepeople, who are credited with increasing Canada's international standing through their willingness to lay down their lives for causes as diverse as the imperial follies of Great Britain and the eminently justified struggle against Nazi Germany from 1939 to 1945.[14] Ian McKay and Jamie Swift's *Warrior Nation* deconstructs these associations and helps scholars understand that peacekeeping found an equal footing with other more militaristic notions of Canadian national identity for most of the latter half of the twentieth century.[15] In particular, many Canadians believed the Second World War, and the destructive power of atomic weapons, rendered international conflict too dangerous to be pursed as a foreign policy, even against international Communism, never highly regarded by most Canadians.[16] They put their support behind the UN and its peacekeeping apparatus, despite its considerable flaws, which were displayed regularly from 1956 to 1997, because it was perceived as being a better alternative to mutually assured destruction.

When combined, these years led to multiple generations, particularly in English Canada, learning about their country's peacekeeping acumen and adopting the blue beret of the UN peacekeeper as a symbol of their own. Proof of this support can be judged in an Environics poll from 1993, which asked respondents to name the most positive contribution that Canada was making to world affairs. Peacekeeping was by far the most popular response, with 40 per cent of those asked volunteering this answer. This would fall to 36 per cent in 2004 and 20 per cent in 2012, but it remained far above other answers such as contributing to the spread of democracy and helping through foreign aid.[17] The persistent belief in the possibility of peacekeeping affecting positive change does, however, indicate how influential it has been to Canada's history since 1956.

Thinking about peacekeeping in this manner required concerted actions by governmental and nongovernmental actors. As cultural theorists following Stuart Hall have noted, communication is a process and not simply a matter of messages being passively accepted by an audience. Rather, varied audiences must be willing to reconfigure a message into social practices – new ways of thinking about oneself as an individual or part of a group – if it is to be fully accepted into a culture, as peacekeeping was in the second half of the twentieth century in Canada.[18]

A progressive peacekeeping discourse was built upon a belief in a future without conflict. This progressivism sought a strong UN able to intervene anywhere in the world through the use of an international police force. Those who espoused progressive ideals based their ideas on "concrete utopias" and believed peacekeeping could encourage modestly "better" versions of the world in the future that also shared real elements from the present in Canada.[19] While the Left, either the Co-operative Commonwealth Federation or its offspring the NDP, is normally associated with the concept of progress, in the case of peacekeeping and Canadian foreign policy, as will be shown, progress was also crucial for the rhetoric of Canada's centre-left and centre-right political parties, the Liberals and the Progressive Conservatives (PCs). Within Canada's Department of External Affairs, there was considerable belief in the power of the UN after the Second World War, as David Mackenzie makes clear in his chapter in this collection.[20] Even the PC Party, traditionally preoccupied with Canada's relations with Britain, found cause to support peacekeeping as a major component of Canada's foreign policy.

SPEAKING ABOUT A BETTER FUTURE THROUGH
PEACEKEEPING

The successes or failures of specific peacekeeping operations and their impact on the host population were, as a by-product of this willingness to see peacekeeping as a symbol of progress for the future, regularly ignored in favour of larger discussions that centred on peacekeeping's value to *Canadians*. And while criticisms could be found in the political rhetoric of peacekeeping, or in outlets like newspaper columns and editorial cartoons, politicians' willingness to forecast Canada's role in achieving peacekeeping glories permitted them to tell their audiences that Canadians were a nation of "Blue Berets." These claims found widespread acceptance, particularly in English Canada.

The Liberal Party, more than any other organization, tried to strengthen the symbolic connections between Canadians and peacekeeping through its political rhetoric. Many Canadian foreign policy scholars suggest that one of the reasons Canadians came to share certain ideas about their country's external efforts during the years 1956 to 2005 was that a consistent set of principles was applied by successive governments.[21] Foregrounded in this thinking is the predominance of the Liberal Party in federal politics during this era. The Liberals were the party in power from 1945 to 1957, and they paid particular attention to enhancing the role of the UN in the fields of peacekeeping and aid distribution. The Diefenbaker years, 1957 to 1963, are recognized for a similar care for the UN and its peacekeeping activities despite inconsistencies in relations with the United States over the Cuban missile crisis and the stationing of nuclear weapons on Canadian soil.[22] Pearson's tenure as prime minister from 1963 to 1968 is similarly viewed as a having continued to promote Canadian engagement with the missions of the UN.

Prior to Pearson coming into office, the Liberals had included Pearson's actions during the Suez Crisis of November 1956 as a part of their long list of international successes. That crisis grew out of the long-standing influence of Britain and France in the operation of the Suez Canal and the decision by Egypt to nationalize the canal on 26 July 1956. On 29 October 1956, the Israelis sent an invasion force into Egypt. The French and British quickly issued an ultimatum calling for the withdrawal of Egyptian and Israeli forces around the canal. They then landed an Anglo-French force in the Canal Zone.

The actions of Britain and France infuriated the United States, among others, who they had conveniently not bothered to inform about their plans.[23]

In discussing the events of the Suez Crisis, the Liberals ran into considerable opposition from some Canadians, particularly those of British heritage, who were not ready to hear, as Prime Minister Louis St Laurent stated in November of 1956 in Parliament during the debate on emergency funding for Canadians who were going to take part in the United Nations Emergency Force (UNEF), that "the era when the supermen of Europe could govern the whole world is coming pretty close to an end."[24] But the Liberals persisted and used the international acclaim that had greeted Pearson's efforts (in support of the American proposal for a peace force), particularly his winning the Nobel Peace Prize, something no other Canadian then or since managed to replicate, as mud to throw in John Diefenbaker and the PCS' eyes for their "backsliding" with regards to international affairs while in office.[25]

Yet, the Liberals chose to discuss peacekeeping in symbolic terms far more often than they laid out the specifics of any operations. They spoke nostalgically of Canada's reputation under former prime ministers Mackenzie King and St Laurent and also forecast a return to such halcyon days if given another majority. Pearson wrote about his belief in the power of the UN to affect international change in an October 1961 article for the *United Church Examiner*. In this piece, Pearson advocated for Canada to not join the nuclear club, a position that he would reverse in the coming months, much to the consternation of the New Left and groups like the newly formed Voice of Women.[26] While Pearson reneged on this part of his platform on foreign policy, he also noted that Canada's most important international role likely came from its status as a middle power, which, he argued, gave its voice at the UN a greater reach than would otherwise be possible.[27] He felt that in this middle power role, Canada could be effective:

1. In pushing for a permanent United Nations Police Force and organizing and equipping Canadian forces for that purpose.
2. In strong and persistent advocacy of disarmament with inspection and control
3. In international economic assistance to new developing states
4. In taking a lead in UN initiatives that make for peace as crises develop.[28]

None of these four points would be fully realized in Pearson's life-
time, let alone his time in office, but he remained a strong advocate
for progressive ideas like a permanent UN police force and for the
developed countries of the world to devote a higher percentage of
their GDP to foreign aid. By making these four points central to how
his party discussed foreign policy in the 1960s, Pearson encouraged
Canadians to put their energy into the UN as well and envision it as
a vehicle for creating a better world.[29]

Pearson and the Liberals were ultimately successful in the 1963
elections, though they were only able to secure sufficient seats in
Parliament to form a minority government. Paul Martin Sr became
minister of external affairs under Pearson. Martin was an experienced politician who had unsuccessfully run for the leadership of the
Liberal Party against Pearson in 1958.[30] He took this loss in stride
and accepted the external affairs post, hoping to play a key role in
international affairs, as Pearson had done in the 1950s.

Martin was instrumental to the creation of the United Nations
Force in Cyprus (UNFICYP), which was formed in March of 1964
when majority Greek and minority Turkish Cypriots openly clashed
throughout the island, and especially in the capital of Nicosia, after
constitutional arrangements between the two sides stalled. Touring
around Canada in the spring and summer of 1964 to make sure that
support for the operation remained high, he noted at one stop that
peacekeeping represented a Canadian belief in "high international
ideals" that could not be defeated by those cynics who questioned its
value.[31] He spoke of the "obvious willingness of Canadians to contribute to the cause of international peace" through peacekeeping.[32]
Idealism was not a bad word, as far as Martin was concerned; he felt
that Canada's foreign policies needed a touch of idealism to comple-
ment their more practical bases. He also expressed his hope that
"Canadians [would] never be indifferent or insensitive to the suffer-
ings of peoples, no matter how remote geographically the situation
[might] be from Canada."[33] Support for UN peacekeeping was a
"sober and realistic" policy as well as a necessary policy if Canadians
were to be "true to ourselves, our country and to the international
community."[34] In this way, Martin was calling for Canada's international policies to really be an external projection of what the Liberals
considered to be where the country was headed domestically: a bilin-
gual country that sought to help those in need.

Martin's words, spoken to diverse audiences around the country, were not empty mutterings. Murray Edelman has described politics as a "passing parade of abstract symbols."[35] He argues that while any political act may speak directly to a particular issue, both the speaker and the audience recognize that the rhetoric used comes loaded with considerable symbolic baggage. The political rhetoric of peacekeeping that was used by Martin, and by Pearson and Diefenbaker in the 1950s and 1960s, symbolically condensed a considerable amount of meaning into the idea of peacekeeping. While many in Canada were no doubt unsure just what took place on an operation such as UNEF, or UNFICYP, audiences were implored to see peacekeeping as a Canadian action that suited the national character, while also benefitting the UN, the host nation, and perhaps stifling another site of Cold War conflict, as well.

Such views reflected those held by a significant portion of the Canadian population. By 1965, in fact, when asked about the likelihood of another world war, 67 per cent of Canadians surveyed believed it to be unlikely at any point in the future.[36] Gallup polls from 1960 onwards consistently demonstrated support for UN peacekeeping by at least 60 per cent of those polled, something that remained stable despite intermittent governmental support of peacekeeping and some notable setbacks on missions like Opération des Nations Unies au Congo, when Canadians were mistakenly attacked by Congolese forces for looking and sounding like their former colonists the Belgians, and UNEF, which was expelled by Egypt in 1967 prior to another round of Arab-Israeli conflict.[37]

WRITING ABOUT A BETTER FUTURE THROUGH PEACEKEEPING

While politicians like Martin and Pearson spoke to audiences about a brighter future through Canada's peacekeeping efforts, ordinary citizens communicated back to them through written letters. Letters to the government are filled with sometimes vivid and oftentimes banal descriptions of what people were experiencing, though they offer only interesting, if inconclusive, glimpses into public opinion. The historiography of letter writers in Canada has regularly noted the willingness of ordinary people to put pen to paper and send the government multipage correspondences regarding any and all matters, though economic hardships often caused concerned citizens to exhort themselves more frequently. In some cases, this was possible because Canadians did not need to pay for the postage of any letters sent to Parliament and its attendant offices. Lara Campbell, in her study of letter writers during the Great Depression, argues that by writing to the Ontario government in protest, men and women asserted a right to citizenship and all of the benefits that it entailed. She also highlights the affirmation of a Canadian identity from the letter writers during the crisis and upheaval of the Depression, saying that its appearance in popular discourse is "not surprising."[38] Both of these concepts, asserting citizenship through writing to government officials and affirming a Canadian identity in a time of crisis and upheaval, can be seen in the Library and Archives Canada (LAC) files which include letters to the government about peacekeeping.

Kevin Spooner, whose chapter in this work provides tangible proof that peacekeeping fell out of favour with the Canadian government in the 1990s, not solely under Stephen Harper's Conservatives, elsewhere looks at letters to the government to discuss the views Canadians held regarding their country's participation in the peacekeeping mission to the Congo. He uses these letters to show that Canadians were very concerned with the events that were transpiring in Central Africa. Yet, the Diefenbaker government chose to ignore such views in favour of a self-interested policy towards the Congo.[39] These cases demonstrate that letters to the government, while coming from a very specific portion of the population, allowed the views of some Canadians to find their way to politicians' offices, which was particularly important in an era before extensive polling was done.

After reading these letters, and the replies that various government officials sent back, it becomes possible to see how some Canadians viewed peacekeeping as part of a larger project to try and change the world for the better. That this occurred in the 1960s, an era that is nostalgically remembered as a time of hope and possibilities, makes these letters an interesting glimpse into how some Canadians understood the concept of peacekeeping as a progressive one and also how peacekeeping came to occupy a place of prominence as a symbol of a Canadian national identity.

With Canada's peacekeeping acumen being foregrounded by all of Canada's leaders from 1956 onwards, it is not surprising that by the 1960s many letter writers made reference to the missions on which Canadians were participating, but more frequently to the broader concept of keeping the peace, when discussing peace in the world. What is perhaps more surprising is that their appeals made reference to a global, and not exclusively Canadian, citizenship. The idea of global citizenship is one that has recently become more popular when discussing the 1960s. A collection that came out of a conference at Queen's University in 2007 made it the central theme of their book. The editors of that work explain the idea as follows: "One of the defining features of the political and cultural movements of the [1960s] was the feeling of acting simultaneously with others in a global sphere, the belief that people elsewhere were motivated by common purpose. No matter how "local" the activity, it was often conceptualized in tandem with a larger worldwide movement."[40] In the letters on peacekeeping, there is clear evidence of people understanding their actions as a part of a larger movement to try to advance the cause of peace throughout the globe.

At the same time, using a term that Ian McKay has recently put forward regarding the history of the Left in Canada, ideas surrounding global peace were *transposed* by those who lived in Canada into concepts that reflected a distinctly Canadian look at the problem of how to bring peace to the world.[41] That the solution so often involved the use of peacekeeping forces indicates not only that Canadians felt strongly about their armed forces but also that they saw peace as a global issue that Canadians had a duty to address in a specifically Canadian manner.

The letters which have been kept at LAC can be divided into two larger categories: those whose purpose was to seek out more information on peacekeeping and those whose authors sought to voice their approval for Canada's UN peacekeeping record and, often, to advocate for more peacekeeping to be undertaking in the future. In the former case, individuals acting on behalf of groups such as local chapters of the United Nations Association of Canada, the World Federalist Society of Canada, and the Imperial Order Daughters of the Empire all requested information during this time period for their members.[42] Teachers also asked for specific materials that they could use for their high school history courses, while students as well, on occasion, asked for materials to help with an upcoming essay.[43] Such groups and individuals took an active interest in Canada's activities in the world, particularly peacekeeping through the United Nations, and hoped to be better informed on any international developments in this field.

Having the federal government as the contact point for information on peacekeeping meant that literature which showed peacekeeping in a positive light and commended Canada's role internationally was disseminated to students and groups across the country. Those seeking more critical evaluations of peacekeeping would have had a difficult time finding any such literature, though most Canadians remained enamoured with peacekeeping in the mid-1960s, regardless of its shortcomings.[44]

More often, though, letter writers urged the Canadian government to engage more actively in UN peacekeeping. They also regularly pleaded for the government to use whatever means it could to promote such views elsewhere in the world. One such person who expressed these views was Mr William Larson of Cloverdale, British Columbia who, on 29 September 1964, wrote a three-page, handwritten letter to minister of defence, Paul Hellyer. Mr Larson's letter dealt with peacekeeping and Canada's role on such operations. He opened his letter by stating, "I am of the opinion that each and every one of us in the world who believes in the freedom and the cause of the United Nations should bear the burden of cost regardless of the country in which we are living."[45] He added, "I am a past member of UN forces Korea and now a Canadian civil servant. My wages are not high but I am willing to contribute $1.00 per month ($12.00 yearly) to such a fund. If we have to lead the world by contributions of means and money let us show the rest of the world."[46] Writing less than five months after UNFICYP commenced, he further averred, "The average Canadian would welcome the opportunity to invest in a peaceful future, and contribute in this way."[47] Hellyer wrote a response letter thanking Mr Larson for his ideas and his financial contribution. Through this act of simple charity, Mr Larson made what he felt was a meaningful contribution to a more progressive future. His assertion that more money would solve this issue, and that other Canadians would be happy to provide the remaining funds necessary to create this better world through peacekeeping, intimates that some Canadians believed that basic, tangible steps could have profound repercussions in the area of foreign policy. His views of how Canada was, and should continue to act in international affairs were quite similar to what Martin and Pearson were telling Canadians in 1964, suggesting that the government and citizens such as Larson were communicating with each other.

A concurrent statement about human agency, and how Canadians could affect positive change through the UN, was expressed in a letter written by a sixteen-year-old woman from Rimouski, Suzanne Archambault, to Martin. This is the only letter from a French Canadian living in Quebec, and written in French, to have been preserved in the LAC file on peacekeeping and popular opinion, once again highlighting the difference between French and English Canadian enthusiasm for peacekeeping as a progressive force. It opens with Ms Archambault's declaration that she was a French-speaking Canadian who "who may not mean much to your eyes, even less to those of the world. But I want to do something: I want to help end war."[48] This was a young person who believed that by thinking differently about international conflict and encouraging the Canadian government to be more proactive in its advocacy for more peacekeeping operations a better world would emerge.

Writing in 1966, Ms Archambault wanted Paul Martin to speak on behalf of all Canadians and particularly for young people at the UN. She also felt it necessary to state "But I think that if I were to speak, to speak in the name of the youth of the world, I would say their aspirations and desires are to see a better and happier world. I am not a zealot or a fanatic. I am sixteen and I will soon be a woman of the world."[49] Her conception of herself as a French speaker, a Canadian, and a global female citizen suggests that she had attachments that went beyond the borders of her province or country, though she chose to appeal directly to her national government for more peacekeeping to be undertaken. An official at the UN division of the Department of External Affairs, J.O. Barry, responded to this letter on behalf of Paul Martin and thanked her for her interest in peace, assuring her that Canada would do and was doing everything it could to help bring peace to the world through the UN.

Other letter writers called on Canada to take the lead in the creation of an international police force that would be unarmed and use moral persuasion to try to change the behaviours of belligerent nations. In so doing they actively used language that Pearson had been employing for more than a decade and which he repeated often, as he had in the *United Church Examiner* in 1961. Mrs M. Eryl Roytenberg of Toronto, an executive member of the Toronto Peace Center, asked whether it was feasible for peacekeepers to do their missions unarmed, like British "bobbie" policemen.[50] Another letter writer, Joseph Crowley, writing on behalf of a "committee of retired business men" which had three main objectives – "Avoid World War III; retrain persons displaced by automation; and reduce juvenile delinquency" – thought Canada should lead the way in advocating for an "International Foreign Legion" that could act as a world peacekeeper.[51] Sandy Slade, a lawyer from Edmonton, asked, "Would it be possible with the nucleus of the RCMP to build a strong and intelligent force for police duty anywhere it is needed?"[52] Slade felt that the RCMP would carry an international reputation for moral strength that would help the cause of peace considerably. In all of these cases, the letter writers regarded Canada's international position as being ideal for creating a new force which would be able to quell global conflicts using peaceful means and called on the government to exercise any and all influence it had to bring such a force into being.

These opinions came from men and women, the young and the retired, and from most regions of Canada. These different Canadians all saw peacekeeping as a progressive force that might aid the cause of world peace, in spite of the repeated challenges that the UN and its peacekeepers faced in Cyprus and later, in 1967, when the UNEF was removed from the Sinai Region and the Gaza Strip. This suggests that many Canadians internalized the symbolic elements of UN peacekeeping and the promise of a more peaceful world it heralded and preferred to emphasize this possibility while downplaying the results that occurred on the missions.

Such enthusiasm and hope for what Canada could possibly do did not disappear when Pierre Trudeau took over as prime minister in 1968. Pierre Trudeau's Liberal governments from 1968 to 1984 largely refrained rhetorically from descriptions of peacekeeping being a symbolically Canadian activity. Instead, they framed peacekeeping as a policy that could allow Canada to play a *useful* international role. And while Pierre Trudeau's government called for a full foreign policy review in 1968, as Granatstein and Robert Bothwell convincingly argue, they in fact found surprisingly little to change in Canada's external affairs, particularly with regards to its participation in UN peacekeeping.[53]

Despite the Trudeau government's desire to not be a "helpful fixer" in the world, letter writers felt that, as a man who cared about peace, Trudeau could make a significant difference. Canadian peacekeeping forces were called for in the Middle East, Biafra, Cambodia, and, above all, Vietnam. On this latter conflict, Lucien Moreau of Winnipeg wrote: "You [Trudeau], in my opinion, are the man to promote a United Nations with a real purpose. Why could you not address the UN and start the ball rolling?"[54] Another letter writer, John Soltis, of Oshawa Ontario felt that it was time for Trudeau and other world leaders to hold a Peace Day in 1970, which might, in his words, "develop into one peace week, which, in turn, will develop into one peace month, which, in turn, will develop into one peace year and so on!"[55] And while there was considerable naïveté in such a letter, Soltis knew the chances of success were slim. Yet, he ended his letter by stating the following: "I make this appeal to you world leaders because I believe you can make this simple idea work on our earth and in our present society."[56] Like other letter writers, Mr Soltis sought a more tranquil world through the use of peace forces led by Canadians, and he pleaded his case to the federal government, and other governments around the globe, to do so. His views, and those of dozens of other Canadians who chose to write to the government to exhort them to do all they could to use UN peacekeeping to bring about a better world, remain as reminders that some Canadians did believe that progressive change was not only possible but was necessary and that, more often than not, they shared a language of discussing peacekeeping with the Liberal government of the time.

LEARNING ABOUT A BETTER FUTURE THROUGH PEACEKEEPING

When Trudeau left office, all hesitations regarding Canadian participation in UN peacekeeping operations seemed to leave with him. Brian Mulroney, prime minister from 1984 to 1993, was perhaps more enamoured with peacekeeping and the UN than any Canadian leader, save Lester Pearson, and his time in office saw Canadians volunteer for numerous peacekeeping missions to Afghanistan, Cambodia, Iran/Iraq, as well as Somalia and the former Yugoslavia, reflecting, in part, a wider international trend.[57] In their approach to world affairs, Mulroney and his ministers saw a renewed UN with Canada playing a leading role in peacekeeping as a solution to both the superpower stalemate of the Cold War and the challenges of the post-Soviet New World Order. Stephen Lewis was named Canada's ambassador to the UN from 1984 to 1988, and he served as a key spokesman for Canada's renewed interest in the world organization.

The United Nations became a site where Canada focused a considerable amount of its international energy, and peacekeeping was central to this. The threat of nuclear war also made peacekeeping a
favourable alternative that Canada was proposing to the world.
More cynically, Jack Granatstein has argued that some Canadian
politicians did not want to break the uninterrupted streak of
Canadian participation in peacekeeping missions and that they also
suffered from "Nobel Prize Syndrome" and sought the same international acclaim that Pearson had garnered.[58] The federal government, therefore, actively sought to encourage peacekeeping to be
seen as a solution to global conflict and a way that Canadians could
help the world.

In expressing this enthusiasm for peacekeeping, Mulroney's government actually found allies among progressive educators across
Canada who had been calling for a more active peace curriculum
prior to the PCs' election.[59] While many of them likely objected to
Mulroney's support for Ronald Reagan and his bellicose rhetoric
about the need to leave the "evil empire" of the Soviet Union on
"the ash heap of history," many of the textbooks that were approved
for use in high school history classrooms in the 1980s contained
lengthy sections on how peacekeeping could become a part of every
Canadian's daily life.[60]

The adoption of peacekeeping as a national marker would not
have been possible without sites like the classroom reinforcing messages that were produced by politicians and newspaper authors. For
those who entered high schools in Canada any time after 1959, their
approved teaching materials often included discussions about peacekeeping and Canada's role in its creation. Until 1997, discussions of
peacekeeping in some high school textbooks and other audiovisual
materials increased from perhaps a paragraph to several chapters
while the actual amount of history that was taken by most students
in Canada shrank considerably.[61]

The textbooks that appeared in the early 1980s presented peacekeeping as a past Canadian success in foreign policy as well as a
contemporary policy that Canadians should embrace because of the
dangers of possible nuclear war. Peacekeeping had also merited inclusion in every approved textbook for the previous twenty years, and
this firmly entrenched peacekeeping in the overall narrative of most
Canadian history texts. Peacekeeping therefore became a large topic
of English Canadian high school history material in part because it

was difficult for textbook authors to drop any content from text-books, since they were under pressure from the Ministries of Education and the publishing companies to include more information in their works.[62] Teachers and principals had considerable choice in which texts they wanted to use at this time, so it is difficult to know how many students would have been exposed to the messages in one of these texts. The similarities between them, however, give a strong indication that messages about peacekeeping were shared across English Canada.

One of these texts was 1984's *Canada: History in the Making*, which was edited by Gillian Bartlett and Janice Gallivan. In chapter 9, students would have come across section sixty-four, which was titled "Canada as Peacemaker," written by jazz legend Oscar Peterson. It is not clear why Peterson was the author of a text on peacekeeping, other than his being a well-regarded Canadian personality. Regardless, Peterson's text began by asking, "How often do you see a soldier carrying a rifle? How often have you seen a tank driving down a street?"[63] The presumed answer to these questions was "never." Instead, this work posited that Canadians were a "peaceable nation" and far from what might be understood to be a "warlike people." No attempts were made to differentiate Canadians from one another, and this presumed peaceableness was ascribed to all regions and peoples. Such a statement also ignored the memory of the FLQ crisis of fifteen years prior, when the federal government invoked the War Measures Act in response to the kidnappings of James Cross and Pierre Laporte, and soldiers marched and tanks roared through the streets of Quebec. However, such memories would most likely have not figured into the pasts of the English Canadian high school students who would have been the audience for this work. Rather, in calling Canada a "peaceable nation," it sought to present all Canadians with a past that downplayed the significance of war and hopefully would convince students of the necessity of peace in the present and the future.

After calling all Canadians to remember their peaceful pasts, the text then discussed the Suez Crisis and Lester Pearson. Pearson is noted to have won the Nobel Peace Prize, and Peterson suggests, as other texts suggested as well, that "[t]his was a great honour for both him and for Canada. It showed that the world recognized Canada's important role in keeping the peace."[64] Students were to continue to celebrate the past achievements of peacekeepers in their history

classes, but textbooks such as this one began to use language that
stated or implied that Canadians were peaceful and all Canadians
were peacekeepers themselves.

In keeping with the newer textbook format that was supposed to
appeal to "visual learners," this book was also full of illustrations,
including one of Lester Pearson accepting his Nobel Peace Prize. It
also contained several discussion questions for students. In a long
preamble, the text noted that Canada had sent soldiers to countries
that "have nothing directly to do with Canada" and that some of
these soldiers had been wounded or killed.[65] This led to the question
"Do you think Canada should continue to send soldiers as part of UN
peacekeeping forces?"[66] The text failed to address reasons why
Canada should not continue to send soldiers abroad, beyond noting
that several of them had been wounded or killed. Peacekeeping was
therefore presented as something almost entirely positive and something that Canadians were suited to because of their peaceful natures.
The text also advised students to discuss their opinions with their
classmates, to share their experiences with peace.

Similar understandings of peacekeeping appeared in a textbook
written by Ian Hundey, a teacher at Newmarket High School in
Ontario, and Michael L. Magarrey. *Canada: Understanding Your
Past* was approved for use in 1990 and contained many similar activities for students. In discussing Pearson as an individual, this textbook stated, "Lester Pearson is seen as a great peacemaker. In your
class, make a list of other people who worked for peace. Some examples are Mohandas Gandhi and Martin Luther King. Choose one and
write a 'people in history' article on that person."[67] Pearson was
placed in very select company in this textbook, and his efforts were
applauded as being some of the most important ever undertaken by
a Canadian. Students were also told that they could express their
feelings on the topic of peacekeeping by collecting "pictures, poetry
and songs" into a "peace book" for their class.[68] Arts and crafts and
peacekeeping were linked in such an activity, as were themes of peace
and the topic of peacekeeping. The teacher's guide for this text made
these links explicitly and also emphasized that both Lester Pearson
and Pierre Trudeau actively sought to promote world peace.[69]

Such a textbook was not alone in calling Canadians peacemakers
or in espousing the need for Canada to actively promote peace in the
world in the 1980s, as it had in the past. *Canada in the World:
Choosing a Role* by Allan Campbell and Derald Fretts; *Our Canada:
A Social and Political History* by Daniel Francis and Sonia Riddoch;

Canada's Century by Allan S. Evans and I.L. Martinello; *Canada Today* by Angus L. Scully, Carl F. Smith, and Daniel J. McDevitt; and Ian Hundey and Michael L. Magarrey's *Canada: Understanding Your Past* all are good examples of the shift in English textbooks towards a heavier emphasis on peace education through extensive coverage of peacekeeping operations and the spirit behind them.

These textbooks all contained entire chapters on peacekeeping that stressed Canada's global responsibility to help to bring about peace. Canada's past efforts to promote world peace were valorized, and young Canadians were told to aspire to be peacekeepers and perhaps even young Lester Pearsons. The teacher's guide in *Canada in the World: Choosing a Role* recommended making a map of all the places that Canada had sent peacekeepers, inviting a guest speaker from the Canadian Forces, and having students write a short essay on whether Canada should continue to be a part of peacekeeping efforts. In all of these cases, students were encouraged to think about the issue of world peace, and peacekeeping was seen as being one possible, and a uniquely Canadian, solution to this issue.

While questions remain about the effect such textbooks had on what students learned about peacekeeping during these years, there is clear evidence that the teaching materials that were available in classrooms emphasized Canada's peacekeeping past and its applicability for future peace missions. Specifically, it is not possible to know which classrooms used these texts, whether what was written in these texts was taught to the letter or altered, and if students simply learned material for a test or actively integrated these ideas into their conceptions of themselves. However, in the 1980s and 1990s, teachers were increasingly encouraged by most provincial governments to incorporate textbooks into their classes, which would have made it more likely that students were exposed to this content. And, most importantly, the presence of this progressive content about Canada and peacekeeping demonstrates that it was seen to be an important part of the high school curricula, meaning that it had permeated the oftentimes contentious world of how to best educate young Canadians, something that many other topics failed to do altogether.

PROGRESS ABATED?

The cause of peace was one that motivated numerous Canadians throughout the second half of the twentieth century. Some wrote to the government as part of their attempts to bring about change in the world; others might have felt that the peacekeeping process was one that they could actively replicate in their everyday lives. While it is not fully evident what sort of impact these forms of expression had on governmental policy, they provide an interesting and very public account of the thoughts of some Canadians and how they understood Canada's place in the world and, as well, how these could be refracted back through the political rhetoric of the era. They also demonstrate that Canadians were very interested in the global issue of peace, specifically in bringing about a particular *Canadian* brand of world peace through the use of peacekeeping forces. This suggests that peacekeeping had already embedded itself as a part of a Canadian identity, and this would remain so into the twenty-first century.

Peacekeeping could constitute a fluid vision of Canada's future potential to be a more peaceful, tolerant, and internationally active nation. This potential blinded many Canadians to the drawbacks of sending their forces abroad in the world to places like Somalia in the 1990s, where immense cultural gaps and highly trained but racist soldiers would perform atrocious acts.[70] In some cases, people came to feel, as Stompin' Tom Connors wrote in his ode to UN service, that we were "the Blue Berets" and could do no wrong on a peacekeeping operation. For most of the second half of the twentieth century, though, many Canadians looked at peacekeeping as a progressive policy that could, and should, effect positive change through the UN. While this discourse has largely disappeared from Canada's political and cultural milieu, it is worth remembering that many Canadians have hoped to bring about a better world through constructive international engagement through peacekeeping and that they might do so again in the future, if given the opportunity.

NOTES

1 Stompin' Tom Connors, "The Blue Berets" (Crown-Vetch Music Ltd., 1993).
2 Ibid.
3 Ibid.
4 Ibid.
5 For more on this, see "Introduction" and passim, Colin McCullough, *Creating Canada's Peacekeeping Past* (Vancouver: UBC Press, 2016).

6 An excellent study of these changes is presented in Jose Igartua, *The Other Quiet Revolution: National Identities in English Canada, 1945–1971* (Vancouver: UBC Press, 2006).

7 Some examples of works on national identity are: Gayatri Chakravorty Spivak, *Nationalism and the Imagination* (London: Seagull Books, 2010); Geoffrey Hosking and George Schopflin, eds., *Myths and Nationhood* (New York: Routledge, 1997); Eric Hobsbawm, *Nations and Nationalism since 1780: Programme, Myth, Reality* (Cambridge: Cambridge University Press, 1990); Homi K. Bhabha, *Nation and Narration* (London and New York: Routledge, 1990); Raphael Samuel, ed. *Patriotism: The Making and Unmaking of British National Identity Volume III National Fictions* (London: Routledge, 1989); Eric Hobsbawm and Terrence Ranger, eds., *The Invention of Tradition* (Cambridge: Cambridge University Press, 1983); Ernest Gellner, *Nations and Nationalism* (Ithaca, NY: Cornell University Press, 1983).

8 Anthony D. Smith, *Nations and Nationalism in a Global Era* (Cambridge: Polity Press, 1995), 90.

9 Gerard Bouchard, ed., *National Myths: Constructed Pasts, Contested Presents* (London: Routledge, 2013), 3.

10 For more on Quebec's national myths, see chapter 1, "The Small Nation with a Big Dream: Quebec National Myths (Eighteenth-Twentieth Centuries)" in ibid.

11 I discuss this more fully in McCullough, *Creating Canada's Peacekeeping Past* (2016).

12 One of the best works on this topic is Jonathan Vance, *Death So Noble: Memory, Meaning, and the First World War*.

13 For two examples of this, see J.L. Granatstein, *Who Killed the Canadian Military?* (Toronto: Harper Collins, 2004), 23; and David Bercuson, *Significant Incident: Canada's Army, the Airborne, and the Murder in Somalia* (Toronto: McClelland and Stewart, 1996), vi.

14 For more on these endeavours, see Robert Teigrob, *Living with War: Twentieth-Century Conflict in Canadian and American History and Memory* (Toronto: University of Toronto Press, 2016).

15 Ian McKay and Jamie Swift, *Warrior Nation: Rebranding Canada in an Age of Anxiety* (Toronto: Between the Lines, 2012).

16 Robert Teigrob, *Warming Up to the Cold War: Canada and the United States' Coalition of the Willing, from Hiroshima to Korea* (Toronto: University of Toronto Press, 2009), 20.

17 The Environics Institute, "Focus Canada 2012: Public Opinion Research on the Record" (2012), 48.

18 This discussion can be found in chapter 10, "Encoding/Decoding," of
    Stuart Hall et al., eds., *Culture, Media, Language: Working Papers in
    Cultural Studies, 1972–79* (London: Routledge, 1980).

19 Ian McKay, *Rebels, Reds, Radicals: Rethinking Canada's Left History*
    (Toronto: Between the Lines, 2005), 8.

20 Teigrob, *Warming Up to the Cold War*; Doug Owram, *Born at the Right
    Time: A History of the Baby Boom Generation* (Toronto: University of
    Toronto Press, 1996).

21 Tom Keating, *Canada and World Order: The Multilateralist Tradition in
    Canadian Foreign Policy* (Toronto: Oxford University Press, 2002), 1;
    Costas Melakopides, *Pragmatic Idealism: Canadian Foreign Policy, 1945–
    1995* (Montreal and Kingston: McGill-Queen's University Press, 1998), 3.

22 Melakopides, *Pragmatic Idealism*, 52; John F. Hilliker, "The Politicians
    and the 'Pearsonalities': The Diefenbaker Government and the Conduct of
    Canadian External Relations," *Historical Papers* 19, no. 1 (1984): 166.

23 For a thorough examination of the Suez Crisis and Lester Pearson's role in
    negotiating the creation of the UNEF, see Antony Anderson, *The
    Diplomat: Lester Pearson and the Suez Crisis* (Fredericton, NB: Goose
    Lane Editions, 2015).

24 "Painful Departure," *Montreal Gazette*, 28 November 1956, 8.

25 Much of the discontent at Diefenbaker's time in office was detailed in
    Peter C. Newman's *Renegade in Power: The Diefenbaker Years* (Toronto:
    McClelland and Stewart, 1963).

26 See chapter 3, "In the Name of Children: The Disarmament Movement,"
    in Tarah Brookfield, *Cold War Comforts: Canadian Women, Child Safety,
    and Global Insecurity* (Waterloo: Wilfrid Laurier University Press, 2012).

27 LAC, Lester Pearson Fonds, MG26 N9 vol. 21, "My Hopes for Peace," 1961.

28 Ibid.

29 These audiences are described in more detail in the chapters of Tarah
    Brookfield and David Webster elsewhere in this collection.

30 An excellent examination of Martin's life and career can be found in Greg
    Donaghy, *Grit: The Life and Politics of Paul Martin Sr* (Vancouver: UBC
    Press, 2015).

31 LAC, Paul Martin Sr Fonds, "UN Peace-Keeping Operations in Cyprus,"
    1964.

32 LAC, Paul Martin Sr Fonds, MG32 B12, volume 306. "Speech to the
    Toronto Empire Club," 1964.

33 LAC, Paul Martin Sr Fonds, MG32 B12, volume 307. "Speech to Ottawa
    UN Association," 1964.

34 Ibid.

35 Murray Edelman, *The Symbolic Uses of Politics* (Urbana and Chicago: University of Illinois Press, 1985), 5.

36 Canadian Institute of Public Opinion, "Gallup Poll, January 1965 #310" (Canada 1965).

37 For more on the Congo incidents, see Colin McCullough, "No Axe to Grind in Africa: Violence, Racial Prejudice and Media Depictions of the Canadian Peacekeeping Mission to the Congo, 1960–1964," in Karen Dubinsky et al., eds., *New World Coming: The Sixties and the Shaping of a Global Consciousness* (Toronto: Between the Lines, 2009), 229–36.

38 Lara Campbell, *Respectable Citizens: Gender, Family and Unemployment in Ontario's Great Depression* (Toronto: University of Toronto Press, 2009), 177.

39 Kevin Spooner, *Canada, the Congo Crisis, and UN Peacekeeping, 1960–64* (Vancouver: UBC Press, 2009), 8.

40 Dubinsky et al., eds., *New World Coming*, 3.

41 See Ian McKay's "Sarnia in the Sixties (or the Peculiarities of the Canadians)" in *New World Coming*.

42 See, for instance, B.G. Whitmore's letter to Paul Martin, LAC RG 25 A-3-c, file 3, 2 November 1964.

43 An example of this is the letter written by Mrs R.A. Proulx to the Department of External Affairs, LAC RG 25 A-3-C, file 3, 1968.

44 A positive narrative about UN peacekeeping was predominant in high school history textbooks and in newspaper coverage. See McCullough, *Creating Canada's Peacekeeping Past.*

45 William Larson to Paul Hellyer, LAC RG 25 A-3-C, file 3, 1964.

46 Ibid.

47 Ibid.

48 "ne suis peut-être pas grand-chose, à vos yeux, encore moins à ceux du monde. Mais je veux faire quelque-chose, [...] je veux aider à arrêter la guerre." (My translation.) Suzanne Archambault to Paul Martin, LAC RG 25 A-3-C, file 3, 20 November 1966.

49 "Mais, je crois que si je parlais, simplement parler au nom de la jeunesse du monde entier; je traduirais ses aspirations et ses désirs de voir le monde meilleur et plus heureux. Je ne suis pas une exaltée, ni une fanatique. J'ai seize ans et je serais bientôt une femme du monde." (My translation.) Ibid.

50 Mrs Eryl Roytenberg to Paul Martin, LAC RG 25 A-3-C, file 3, 25 October 1965.

51 Joseph Crowder to Lester Pearson, LAC RG 25 A-3-C, file 3, 22 October 1964.

52 Sandy Slade to Paul Martin, LAC RG 25 A-3-C, file 3, 14 February 1964.

53 See Robert Bothwell and J.L. Granatstein, *Pirouette: Pierre Trudeau and Canadian Foreign Policy* (Toronto: University of Toronto Press, 1990).

54 Lucien Moreau to Pierre Trudeau, LAC RG 25 A-3-C, file 3, 21 January 1969.

55 John A. Soltis to Pierre Trudeau, RG 25 A-3-C, file 3, 31 August 1970.

56 Ibid.

57 Stuart Allan, "Challenging Canada's Nuclear Commitments: An Analysis of Defence discourse," *British Journal of Canadian Studies* 17, no. 1 (2004): 2; Melakopides, *Pragmatic Idealism*, 144.

58 Granatstein, *Who Killed the Canadian Military*, 22.

59 For more on this, see chapter 2, "Wasted Hours and Abject Boredom," in Colin McCullough, *Creating Canada's Peacekeeping Past*.

60 Reagan made this comment during a speech on 8 June 1982.

61 In Ontario, for example, the percentage of history classes taken out of the total for all high school classes in 1964 was 11.4% while in 1981 it had dropped to 6.6%. Bob Davis, *Whatever Happened to High School History?: Burying the Political Memory of Youth: Ontario, 1945–95* (Toronto: James Lorimer and Company Limited, 1995), 48. In Quebec, on the other hand, history became a regularly taught subject, but the emphasis of such classes was the history of Quebec.

62 Michael W. Apple, ed., *The Politics of the Textbook* (New York: Routledge, 1991), 10.

63 Janice Gallivan and Gillian Bartlett, eds., *Canada: History in the Making* (Toronto: John Wiley and Sons, 1984), 457.

64 Ibid, 460.

65 Ibid.

66 Ibid.

67 Ian M. Hundey and Michael L. Magarrey, *Canada: Understanding Your Past* (Toronto: Irwin Publishing, 1990), 193.

68 Ibid.

69 Ibid., Teacher's Guide, 54.

70 A detailed account of this can be found in Sherene Razack, *Dark Threats and White Knights: The Somalia Affair, Peacekeeping, and the New Imperialism* (Toronto: University of Toronto Press, 2004).

6

Canada and the General Assembly

A Global Bully Pulpit

Kim Richard Nossal[1]

The literature of Canada and the United Nations tends to focus on the often significant role that Canadian officials played in the formation and development of this international organization and in using the UN as an integral part of a strategy of middle-power internationalism during the Cold War. In this view, Canadian governments saw the UN in largely *Realpolitik* terms, seeing the UN as an instrumental means of advancing broad Canadian interests in systemic peace.[2] But, as Allan Gotlieb, a former deputy minister of foreign affairs and ambassador to the United States, reminds us, Canadian governments have tended to swing between the poles of realism and romanticism in their foreign policies. One pole, he wrote in 2004, "ties us to hard reality, *Realpolitik* if you will, and makes us want our governments to protect our national interests when it deals with other states." The other pole is idealism, "a visionary, at times almost romantic, approach to our position in the world." This "idealistic vocation" emphasizes the pursuit of justice globally, the promotion of freedom and democracy, and the improvement of the condition of the poor, the weak, and the oppressed.[3]

In this chapter, I argue that the UN as a global institution has played an important role in the pursuit of Canadian romanticism in foreign policy. For the annual plenary session of the General Assembly offers an unparalleled podium for the articulation of Canadian views about global politics, not only to a global audience but also to a Canadian audience. In this sense, the iconic black and green speaker's rostrum has been used by Canadian leaders as a "bully pulpit."

At first blush, it may seem inappropriate to apply such a parochial phrase to the global. After all, the term is deeply connected to American politics and the American presidency in particular. It originated with Theodore Roosevelt, president of the United States from 1901 to 1909, and his view of the opportunity that the office of the president afforded him to push his progressive political agenda. According to Lyman Abbott, who was a keen advocate of Roosevelt's progressive politics and one of the president's friends, Roosevelt was unapologetic about using his messages to Congress to talk indirectly to the American people about moral principles in government. "I am accused of preaching," Abbott recounts Roosevelt telling a group of friends during his presidency, "but I have such a bully pulpit."[4] It should be noted that in the early 1900s, "bully" had a much wider range of vernacular meanings than it does now, when its dominant meaning is someone who hurts or frightens someone who is weaker. In the early twentieth century, "bully" not only had a range of negative meanings (including a protector of prostitutes and a hired ruffian) but a number of positive meanings. It was a term of endearment, particularly between men; and one of its many meanings in early twentieth-century vernacular was "capital" or "first-rate" (still used today in the expression "bully for you"), and it was in this sense that Roosevelt was using the word.[5]

Thus, despite its American origins, "bully pulpit" is an appropriate descriptor for the General Assembly rostrum, given the Oxford English Dictionary definition of the phrase today: a "position of authority that provides its occupant with an outstanding opportunity to speak out on any issue." But it is also an appropriate term in this context because it underscores the degree to which Canadian governments have on occasion been inclined to engage in what Fen Osler Hampson and Dean F. Oliver called "pulpit diplomacy."[6] Although they used this term in the context of their discussion of Canadian foreign policy during the Liberal government of Jean Chrétien from 1993 to 2003, it in fact has wider application, as Gotlieb clearly shows: the "visionary" inclination in Canadian foreign policy was evident both before and after the Chrétien era.

As I will show, from the founding of the United Nations in 1945, all governments in Ottawa prior to the election of the Conservative government of Stephen Harper in 2006 were inexorably drawn to using the General Assembly rostrum as a bully pulpit. We can see this dynamic occurring on both sides of politics: both Liberal and

Progressive Conservative governments used appearances in the General Assembly to press Canadian foreign policy objectives. To be sure, the more visionary tendency identified by Gotlieb tended not to emerge until the late 1950s, when the Progressive Conservative government of John G. Diefenbaker clearly saw the General Assembly podium as an opportunity to deliver a very particular visionary and romantic political message. But the tendency started by the Diefenbaker government was carried on. The Liberal governments of Lester B. Pearson (1963–68), Pierre Elliott Trudeau (1968–79, 1980–84), Jean Chrétien (1993–2003), and Paul Martin (2003–2006) and the Progressive Conservative governments of Joe Clark (1979–80), Brian Mulroney (1984–93), and Kim Campbell (1993) all used the General Assembly as a global bully pulpit (though in this chapter I do not look at the brief Clark, Campbell, or Martin governments). And between 2006 and 2015, the Conservative government of Stephen Harper, which openly disdained the United Nations, could not resist the temptation to pursue its own brand of romanticism using the General Assembly.

THE PULPIT IN HISTORICAL PERSPECTIVE

From the very beginnings of the UN, Canadian government leaders used the podium of the General Assembly to press for changes in global practices. In the first two years of the operations of the new international organization, the Canadian government became increasingly concerned about the role of the Soviet Union in global politics, particularly the aggressive efforts of the government in Moscow to expand its power and influence. This policy was reflected in the Soviet approach to the United Nations, which Moscow regarded as a Western-dominated organization. But while the Liberal government of William Lyon Mackenzie King was concerned about Soviet behaviour at the UN, it was also concerned that the Soviet Union and its allies would pull out of the UN. While some governments were arguing in 1947 that the solution to the emerging conflict at the UN was the reform of the UN Charter, the Canadian government decided to make its concerns about the future of the UN public, using the General Assembly podium to do so.

On 18 September 1947, the secretary of state for external affairs, Louis St Laurent, spoke at the UN General Assembly expressing concern about the "veto privilege," and the hope – aimed at the Soviet

Union – that "no member of the Security Council will flout clearly-expressed world opinion by obstinately preventing change," thereby putting the very existence of the organization in danger.[7] But St Laurent also used the General Assembly to float an idea that grew out of Canadian concern over the incapacity of the new Security Council to work effectively. He noted that states concerned about the maintenance of peace "will not, and can not, accept indefinitely an unaltered council ... which, so many feel, has become frozen in futility and divided by dissension."[8] Those states, St Laurent noted, may seek safety and security by forming "an association of democratic and peace-loving states willing to accept more specific international obligations in return for a greater measure of national security."[9] While Canada hoped that such a development would not be necessary, St Laurent said, it would push for such an association under the self-defence provisions if it became necessary.

James Eayrs has described this as "the most important initiative by Canada in world affairs" since W.A. Riddell's intervention at the League of Nations in 1935.[10] It floated the idea of a mutual security pact that would be consistent with the UN Charter, would provide security for Western states, but, most importantly, would not push the Soviet Union and its allies to leave the UN, thus preserving it as a universal international organization. In John English's characterization, St Laurent's speech was an important catalyst for the creation of the North Atlantic alliance: while other Western states had been mooting the idea of a collective security arrangement in the face of Soviet expansionism, the Canadian articulation of the idea at the UN General Assembly moved the project forward.[11]

St Laurent's use of the General Assembly podium in 1947 was a good example of the realist pole in Canadian foreign policy: an attempt to shift the political strategic environment in Canadian interests. By contrast, the use of the General Assembly by the Progressive Conservative government of John G. Diefenbaker, prime minister from 1957 to 1963, was an example of the emergence of the "visionary" inclination identified by Gotlieb.

As Trevor Lloyd has noted, Diefenbaker was "clearly attracted by the United Nations and the opportunities it offered for taking up a position as a world statesman."[12] Shortly after taking office in June 1957, Diefenbaker took the opportunity to address the General Assembly. Because the 1957 election campaign had featured efforts by the Progressive Conservatives to criticize the United Nations for its role in the humiliation of Britain during Suez Crisis the previous year,[13] Diefenbaker's speech to the General Assembly on 23 September sought to provide reassurance to the global community that the new government was as committed to the UN as the Liberals had been: "So far as Canada is concerned, support of the United Nations is the cornerstone of its foreign policy."[14]

The following year, Canada's secretary of state for external affairs, Howard Green, delivered an address to the General Assembly focusing on the importance of nuclear disarmament and a reduction in tensions between East and West. That speech, propelled by the expansion of Soviet nuclear tests, laid the groundwork for a sustained push by the Canadian government in multilateral institutions for a new global regime in nuclear armaments.[15] While seeking to involve Canada in a new round of arms control negotiations might have been driven by hard-headed *Realpolitik* calculations of Canadian national interests, there is little doubt that the address to the General Assembly also reflected what has been called Green's "magnificent obsession" with arms control and nuclear disarmament.[16]

If Green's pursuit of disarmament initiatives had some romantic elements, Diefenbaker's address to the fifteenth session of the UN General Assembly on 26 September 1960 was an example of Canadian foreign policy romanticism in full bloom. The Canadian speech to the 1960 session of the General Assembly was supposed to have been given by Green. However, when he learned that a number of heads of government, including Nikita Khrushchev, leader of the Union of Soviet Socialist Republics (USSR), would be attending, Diefenbaker decided at the last minute that he would give the Canadian speech.[17] The speech that had been drafted by the Department of External Affairs for Green reflected the widely held view in the department – shared by the minister himself – that success on the disarmament file required a diplomatic approach to the Soviet Union that put an emphasis on accommodating Khrushchev.

Diefenbaker, by contrast, wanted to give a speech that strongly attacked Khrushchev and the Soviet Union, in particular for its domination of the "captive peoples" in Eastern Europe and incorporation of the Baltic states and Ukraine into the Soviet Union. The prime minister's memoirs indicate his frustration with the Department of External Affairs, whose various drafts "failed to contain the things I had told them I wanted to speak about." Finally, he told them, "I do not want any more of the pussyfooting or dilly-dallying that has characterized Canadian external affairs in recent years. You will prepare what I want."[18] The resulting speech to the General Assembly, according to Legault and Fortmann, "threw fuel on the fire."[19] It was a hard-hitting denunciation of the Soviet Union and of Nikita Khrushchev personally. Khrushchev had addressed the General Assembly three days earlier, delivering a long and strident speech that denounced the West, called for the ouster of the Secretary-General, Dag Hammarskjöld, the removal of the UN from New York, and the "complete and final elimination of colonial regimes."[20] In response, Diefenbaker outlined the processes of decolonization, noting that some 600 million people in more than thirty countries had been freed from the yoke of colonialism since the end of the Second World War. Then Diefenbaker asked, "How many human beings have been liberated by the USSR?"[21] He pointed to the Hungarian revolution of 1956, and to Estonia, Latvia, Lithuania, Ukraine, and other East European nations, and demanded that Khrushchev "give to those nations under his domination the right to free elections."[22] Diefenbaker regarded it as the most important speech he made on foreign policy in his six years in power, but its effects were primarily domestic, as Basil Robinson points out.[23] While Diefenbaker was widely applauded in Canada, particularly by the diasporas of those "captive peoples" on whose behalf he had spoken at the UN, the speech itself was a symbolic denunciation that did little to advance Canadian interests in securing Soviet support for other agenda items.

When Lester B. Pearson and the Liberals came to power after the April 1963 elections, the focus of Canadian diplomacy at the UN changed. But the new government was no less attracted by the idea of using the General Assembly as a pulpit for Canadian ideas. There is no better example than Pearson's first address to the General Assembly as prime minister. His speech on 19 September 1963 sought to put out for global consideration the favoured Canadian ideas about global governance of that era.[24] Pearson touched on a number of concerns, but most important were his proposals regarding peacekeeping. The speech was given in the shadow of the UN intervention in the Congo, and Pearson focused on the role of UN peacekeeping in contemporary interstate conflict. Dismissing the objections of those governments who saw UN peacekeeping as illegal and those governments who were "cynical, doubtful or indifferent," Pearson spoke out in defence of the creation of what in essence would be a standing UN peacekeeping force.[25] He noted that Canada maintained trained peacekeeping forces that could be "placed at the disposal of the United Nations on short notice anywhere in the world,"[26] and pointed to the creation by the Scandinavian states of a composite Nordic contingent that could be deployed for UN duties. Pearson also laid out a number of proposals for reform and change of the UN itself. Reflecting the considerable changes in the membership of the UN that had been brought about by the rapid decolonization of the late 1950s and early 1960s, Pearson was an early proponent of the reform of the Security Council, arguing that it was time to expand the council and change its functions so that it could more effectively pursue the overarching mission of the UN – the keeping of the peace. Finally, Pearson concluded with a call for an improvement in the "atmosphere" in which global problems were tackled, noting that while the UN was not the only means of fostering international collaboration, "the United Nations alone serves us all."[27]

Pearson's address to the 1963 Assembly was, in his own description, "a typical Canadian UN speech."[28] It reflected the overarching concern of governments of this era with systemic peace – a key component of the dominant idea of internationalism[29] – and an attempt to preserve the role of the UN as a key actor in the maintenance of systemic peace. But we can see in Pearson's efforts to push a UN standby force – a proposal that he had first bruited in 1957 – even in the face of considerable opposition at the UN,[30] an example of the romantic inclination at work.

Pearson's hopes for a more active UN peacekeeping role to which Canada could contribute was precisely the kind of foreign policy objective that Pierre Elliott Trudeau found problematic. When Trudeau succeeded Pearson as Liberal leader, and thus prime minister, in 1968, he embarked on a sustained critique of what he called the "helpful fixing" that was so associated with Canadian foreign policy during the Pearson era.[31] In time, however, Trudeau would embrace much of the middle-power approach to global politics that he had so robustly criticized in 1968. And while in the first ten years of his prime ministership he chose not to speak at the General Assembly plenary sessions,[32] he would eventually seek to use the General Assembly podium to articulate his proposals for global political change.

The issue that Trudeau chose to push at the UN was nuclear weapons. Trudeau had always been "horrified" by nuclear weapons. His memoirs note that he had consistently written of the "mindless horror of nuclear war" and that he had demonstrated against nuclear weapons as both a student and a professor.[33] Indeed, as Greg Donaghy reminds us, Trudeau deeply cherished his reputation as an antinuclear activist.[34] Indeed, he had been deeply critical of Pearson's 1963 decision to accept nuclear weapons for the Canadian Armed Forces.[35] As prime minister, he moved to reverse that decision (though it was not until 1984 that all nuclear weapons would be removed from Canadian soil[36]). India's decision in May 1974 to explode a nuclear device using plutonium widely believed to have been supplied by Canada as part of a program to assist Indian nuclear power generation "renewed" his concern about the spread of nuclear weapons.[37] At the 1975 Commonwealth Heads of Government Meeting in Kingston, Jamaica, Trudeau argued that nuclear weapons were "evil" and that every effort should be made to reduce and eliminate them.[38] President Jimmy Carter, who came to power in 1977, shared Trudeau's concerns about nuclear proliferation and encouraged him to speak out against nuclear weapons.[39] In the spring of 1978, Trudeau decided to give a major speech advocating a comprehensive set of measures that would reverse nuclear proliferation. The venue he chose for the speech was the General Assembly, which was holding a special session on disarmament.

The speech, delivered on 26 May 1978, put forward a comprehensive proposal for the overall reduction of nuclear weapons.[40] Boasting that Canada was "the first nuclear armed country to have chosen to divest itself of nuclear weapons," Trudeau outlined a comprehensive proposal for moving on the nuclear arms race, proposing to "lower our sights to the more practical aim of making progress toward a disarmed world by building it brick by brick."[41] His speech tackled both vertical and horizontal proliferation. Trudeau outlined the four steps he was proposing to "suffocate" the negative dynamic of the nuclear standoff – by "depriving the arms race of the oxygen on which it feeds."[42] First, he proposed a comprehensive ban on testing in order to halt the development of new nuclear explosive devices. Second, he argued for a complete ban on the flight-testing of all new strategic delivery systems. Third, he proposed a prohibition of all fissionable material for weapons systems. Finally, he suggested the negotiation of a multilateral agreement to limit – and then reduce – military spending on new nuclear weapons systems. While, as John English notes,[43] Trudeau's speech reflected the views of President Jimmy Carter and while Trudeau returned to some of the disarmament themes in his "peace mission" of 1983–84,[44] the disarmament proposals articulated in 1978 can be seen as visionary and highly idealistic. As Trudeau himself admitted later, at the end of his peace mission in February 1984, "Let it be said of Canada and of Canadians ... that we have lived up to our ideals; and that we have done what we could to lift the shadow of war."[45]

Brian Mulroney also used the General Assembly podium to push his concern about the deteriorating situation in South Africa. The response of Western countries to the outbreak of violence in apartheid South Africa in 1984–85 had fractured the West. On the one hand, the United States administration of Ronald Reagan and the Conservative government of Margaret Thatcher in the United Kingdom firmly opposed the use of sanctions as a means of bringing apartheid to an end. On the other hand, smaller Western countries such as Australia and Canada were pushing the large powers hard to reconsider their opposition to sanctions. Mulroney had decided that fighting apartheid would be one of his highest foreign policy priorities. At the Commonwealth Heads of Government Meeting in Nassau, 16–22 October 1985, Mulroney had a serious confrontation with Thatcher over Britain's opposition to sanctions.[46] A day later, on 23 October, Mulroney spoke at a special General Assembly session commemorating the 40th anniversary of the founding of the UN. It was his first address to the UN General Assembly, but he decided to "pull no punches" in laying out the Canadian position on the use of sanctions as a tool for bringing apartheid to an end. Not only did he indicate that Canada was ready to invoke total sanctions if there were no progress in the dismantling of apartheid but he also restored a sentence that officials in the Department of External Affairs had wanted removed from the prime minister's text: "If there is no progress in the dismantling of apartheid, relations with South Africa may have to be severed absolutely."[47] The effect on the General Assembly was electric, according to Stephen Lewis, Canada's ambassador to the UN: "You have to have been in the General Assembly to appreciate what happened when those words were uttered. I was at the UN for four glorious years. I had never seen anything like it before, and I never saw anything like it afterwards. It was an extraordinary moment. It was, for all the African delegations, a moment of hope."[48] Mulroney was mobbed by delegates eager to shake his hand and congratulate him for laying out a visionary position on apartheid.[49]

It should be noted that neither Trudeau nor Mulroney spoke often at
the United Nations. In his sixteen years in office, Trudeau appeared just
twice, in 1978 and in June 1982, when he continued to press his disarmament agenda.[50] Between 1984 and 1993, Mulroney spoke to the
General Assembly three times: in 1985, 1988, and 1990.[51] By contrast,
in his ten years in office, 1993–2003, Chrétien addressed the General
Assembly on five occasions: in 1995, 1997, 2000, 2002 and 2003, and
participated in a Security Council special debate on peacekeeping in
September 2000 during Canada's term as a nonpermanent member of
the Security Council in 1999–2000.[52] In addition, during the Chrétien
years, every foreign minister spoke to the General Assembly: André
Ouellet in 1994 and 1995, Lloyd Axworthy every year from 1996 to
2000, John Manley in 2001, and Bill Graham in 2002.

Such consistent participation reflected the strong support for the
United Nations of the Chrétien government. The Liberals came to
office in 1993 having promised during the election campaign that
Canada would be more active in seeking to improve the effectiveness
of the UN. "A Liberal government will bring the full weight and reputation of Canada to bear in gaining international support for a United
Nations Charter review," the Liberal Party's "Red Book" stated.
"Canada's strong legacy of support for the UN and the reputation we
have built there give us a unique opportunity to help lead this
effort."[53] In power, the Chrétien government sought to play an activist role. Chrétien's first foreign minister, André Ouellet, was a "UN
enthusiast."[54] His successor, Lloyd Axworthy, was also an enthusiast,
and saw the General Assembly as an important forum in world politics. The hall, he wrote in his memoirs, "always filled me with a mix-
ture of awe and reverence; it is as close as we have come to a world
forum for decisions affecting the grand sweep of peace, security and
well-being."[55]

It should not be surprising, therefore, that during this period, the
Chrétien government should regard the UN General Assembly as a
forum for pressing Canadian ideas about global politics. And indeed,
we can see a pattern of the ideas being articulated. True to the promises of the "Red Book," the Chrétien government pushed consistently
for the improvement of the UN and its operations, particularly the
Security Council. Part of this was a reminder to other countries to
pay their UN dues. This was stressed in Ouellet's first speech to the
General Assembly in 1994,[56] repeated in Chrétien's speech in 1995,[57]
and repeated regularly thereafter. And while Chrétien's first address

– given just days before the 30 October 1995 Quebec referendum – was directed primarily to a Canadian audience,[58] the tendency of Chrétien and his foreign ministers was to sound a number of consistent themes over the years that were directed at a global audience. Chrétien, Ouellet, and particularly Lloyd Axworthy used their appearances at the UN to urge global acceptance of key Canadian proposals. Ouellet first raised the issue of landmines in his 1994 address, foreshadowing the active pursuit of a global landmines ban by Axworthy in 1996. Chrétien invariably included those policy initiatives of his foreign ministers. For example, in his last speech before he retired in 2003, Chrétien pushed hard for the adoption of the recommendations of the International Commission on Intervention and State Sovereignty that his government had sponsored.[59]

Axworthy's activism in foreign policy – his championing of a landmines ban, support for the creation of the International Criminal Court, concern over those affected by war, and push for a rethinking of state sovereignty – is well reflected in the five addresses he delivered before the UN General Assembly.[60] The romantic nature of his quest is nicely revealed in the conclusion to his last address, delivered before his retirement from politics in 2000. In a speech that reiterated his encouragement that the members of the UN embrace a "people-centred approach to international relations," and pitched both the new International Criminal Court and the International Commission on Intervention and Sovereignty, Axworthy pleaded with his listeners to work "to ensure that this system we have built does not surrender to the cynics who offer no alternatives, or to the game players who paralyse the transcendent purposes of the United Nations for simple transitory diplomatic points."[61] Taken together, Axworthy's five speeches to the General Assembly from 1996 to 2000 have an exhortatory quality. One can readily see why Fen Hampson and Dean Oliver would characterize his approach as "pulpit diplomacy," but, confronted with the accusation that he was using the podium of the General Assembly to preach a different politics, it is not at all clear that Axworthy would have a different response to that of Theodore Roosevelt quoted above.

THE PULPIT IN CONTEMPORARY PERSPECTIVE

What is important about Canada's use of the General Assembly as a bully pulpit is that even a government that openly disdained the UN was ineluctably drawn to using it as a pulpit from which to pursue a romantic agenda in the sense that Gotlieb used it.

The Conservative government of Stephen Harper that was in power from February 2006 until November 2015 made no secret of its scepticism about the UN as an international institution.[62] That scepticism was on display from the outset, when Harper addressed the General Assembly in 2006 and spoke openly about the failings of the UN as an institution and his expectation that the UN needed to become more accountable and more effective.[63] Harper did not return to the General Assembly for another four years, and his absence was held up as indicative of his government's attitude towards the UN. For example, when he chose to miss Obama's address to the UN General Assembly in 2009 in order to attend an event at the research and development arm of Tim Hortons in Oakville, he was criticized for making a "donut run" rather than be at the UN.[64]

Following Canada's failure to secure election as a nonpermanent member of the Security Council in 2010 – the only time since 1946, when Canada lost to Australia in the elections for the very first Security Council, that a Canadian candidacy had been unsuccessful – Harper's attitude towards the United Nations clearly soured even further: for two years in a row, he decided to openly snub the UN. Unlike the "donut run" in 2009, when he chose to be in southern Ontario, in both 2012 and 2013 Harper purposely travelled to New York during the general debate, when heads of state and government normally address the General Assembly, but pointedly refused to go to the UN.[65]

And a new attack trope began to be used by Conservative ministers. At a Conservative convention in 2011, Harper claimed that his government had a purpose in global affairs: "And that purpose is no longer just to go along and get along with everybody else's agenda. It is no longer to please every dictator with a vote at the United Nations."[66] He pointedly added, "I confess that I don't know why past attempts to do so were ever thought to be in Canada's national interest."[67] The line "Canada no longer goes along just to get along" quickly became a mantra, repeated by both the prime minister and John Baird, his foreign minister from 2011 to 2015 (who, it might be noted, openly derided the UN as nothing more than a "gabfest for dictators"[68]). Indeed, it was repeated so often that Robert Fowler, a former Canadian ambassador to the UN, claimed that the mantra was tiresome and smug and that it was causing Canada's international reputation irreparable harm.[69] But behind the mantra lay a deeper disaffection. As Fen Osler Hampson put it in 2012, when Harper was in New York when the General Assembly was in session but chose not to attend: "Whatever lukewarm enthusiasm he had for the United Nations, I think he now views it as a cold tub of bath water and he's not about to jump into it."[70]

However, while the Conservative government clearly derided the UN, and while Harper may well have regarded it as a cold tub of bath water, both the prime minister and Baird were drawn to the UN General Assembly. Baird addressed the General Assembly in 2011, 2012, and 2013,[71] and Stephen Harper addressed the General Assembly in 2014.

Baird's speeches in 2011, 2012, and 2013 remain a telling reflection of the Harper government's romantic approach to Canadian foreign policy.[72] For its much-touted "principled foreign policy" was mainly rhetorical. Jeffrey Simpson decried it as "bullhorn diplomacy."[73] Joe Clark – Progressive Conservative prime minister in 1979–80, Mulroney's external affairs minister from 1984 to 1991, and a trenchant critic of the Harper Conservatives – liked to say that under Harper, Canada was the country that "lectures and leaves."[74] That is certainly a fitting characterization of Baird's addresses to the General Assembly. Baird used the podium to lay out the essence of Canadian foreign policy under the Conservatives: that the evil in the world had to be confronted (and that what the West did at Munich in 1938 remained an apposite reminder of that crucial truth); that Canada would no longer "go along just to get along," and certainly not to "please every dictator with a vote at the United Nations"; that Canada would actively work to protect the freedoms of religious minorities and the human rights of women and young girls; that Canada would work hard to battle extremism; that Canada supported Israel (which, for deeply partisan reasons, he invariably referred to as the "Jewish state"); and that Canada would work to bring the benefits of the market to the world through free trade. He openly called out countries where religious persecution was occurring, with the clear, though unspoken, implication that this was because of the lack of willingness of the state to halt it: Egypt, Nigeria, Iran, Iraq, Pakistan, Sri Lanka, Tanzania, and Syria. And because Baird himself divided the world into "white hats" and "black hats"

– Canada's friends and Canada's enemies – he was not at all hesitant to openly attack "black hats" by name – in particular Iran and North Korea.

But Baird also used the General Assembly podium to deliver sustained attacks on the UN itself. He liked to pointedly remind the delegates that the UN was about people, not states, and that in his view the UN spent far too much time and energy on itself and not enough on those it was supposed to serve. The billions who are hungry or lack potable water, he was fond of saying, do not care how many members sit on the Security Council. More fundamentally, Baird argued that the UN had lost sight of what he called the UN's "Founding Principles": maintaining international peace and security, preventing threats to peace, stopping aggression, respecting the equal rights and self-determination of peoples, strengthening universal peace, and promoting and encouraging respect for human rights and fundamental freedoms for all. But these purposes were being "debased" when Iran was given leadership positions in the UN, when blatant abusers of women's rights were welcomed to the Convention on the Elimination of All Forms of Discrimination against Women, and when a regime that illegally transferred weapons was made president of the disarmament conference.

In short, Baird appeared to take significant delight in calling out the hypocrisy of the United Nations, in naming the "dictators with votes," in blasting the institution for its self-serving and self-centred practices, and more generally in getting up the nose of the many "black hats" represented in the General Assembly. And if this took Canada "out of the game," to use Paul Heinbecker's characterization,[75] so be it. In this view, Canadian interests were not negatively affected.

By contrast, when Harper chose to return to address the General Assembly in 2014, there was no evidence at all of Baird's "lecture-and-leave" tendencies. There were no snarky references to dictators with votes or naming of "black hats." On the contrary: Harper gave what Lester Pearson might well have described as a "typical Canadian UN speech."[76] Harper was careful to acknowledge Canada's long history of support for the UN; he was careful and measured in outlining some of Canada's key objectives in global politics – noting in particular the importance of free trade for the generation of wealth and the benefits that this would bring to all peoples. But the main focus of his address was to generate support for the maternal, newborn, and child health initiative. He encouraged all states to reproduce the success of the 2010 G-20 summit, which raised $7.5 billion, and painted a vision of a set of new partnerships with the goal of preventing the deaths of thousands of children from readily preventable causes. He urged the Assembly to ensure that maternal, newborn, and child health remained a "clear and top priority" in the post-2015 development agenda. He ended by invoking the original 1942 declaration of the United Nations, noting that in such a world "there can be prosperity for the impoverished, justice for the weak and, for the desperate, that most precious of all things, hope."[77]

The contrast between Harper's – and Baird's – earlier treatment of the UN and the prime minister's 2014 address could not be more marked. But the different honey-and-vinegar approaches taken by the Conservative government at the General Assembly from 2011 to 2015 was a reminder that one does not have to be a strong supporter of the United Nations to be attracted by the opportunity to use the podium as a pulpit.

CONCLUSION

The sketches in this chapter are of necessity illustrative rather than comprehensive. But they are intended to demonstrate the degree to which Canadian leaders have been attracted by the General Assembly podium as a way to articulate and amplify the visionary inclinations that all Canadian governments have demonstrated in foreign policy. Some of the attraction lies in the domestic political payoff that an outing at the General Assembly podium can bring. Clearly this was a consideration in Diefenbaker's speech in 1960, Chrétien's speech in 1995, or Baird's speeches in 2011, 2012, and 2013. Baird's speeches in particular can be seen as little more than domestic politicking, since taking gratuitous shots at "black hats" and "dictators with votes" could serve no other useful purpose. Certainly Baird's hectoring had no effect on those in the hall. As Omer Aziz has noted archly, the Harper government's approach did not make "an inch of difference to the United Nations. But it … made Canada irrelevant in world affairs."[78] But what Aziz might have noted is that Baird's bluntness in fact resonated very well with many ordinary Canadians puzzled by the hypocrisy of global politics.

However, the survey in this chapter suggests that to dismiss these speeches as motivated purely by domestic politics would be to miss

the clear motivation that many Canadian leaders have had in trying
to effect political change at a systemic level. Certainly we could not
understand St Laurent's advocacy of a Western alliance in 1947 or
Pearson's advocacy of a UN standing force in 1963 or Trudeau's
"nuclear suffocation" speech in 1978 or Mulroney's dramatic speech
in 1985 or Axworthy's efforts to advance human security in the
1990s or Harper's advocacy on behalf of maternal, newborn, and
child health as anything other than an effort to change the behaviour
of other governments and perhaps the attitudes of other people. To
be sure, many of the policies being advocated were invariably at a
broad and indeed visionary level. But that is precisely the attraction
of the General Assembly podium – as a global bully pulpit.

NOTES

1 I am grateful to Jenna Adams for research assistance, and to Greg
   Donaghy and John English for helpful suggestions.
2 F.H. Soward and Edgar McInnis, *Canada and the United Nations* (New
   York: Manhattan Publishing, 1957); Garth Stevenson, "Canada in the
   United Nations," in *Foremost Nation: Canadian Foreign Policy in a
   Changing World*, eds. Norman Hillmer and Garth Stevenson (Toronto:
   McClelland & Stewart, 1977), 150–77; John W. Holmes, *The Shaping of
   Peace: Canada and the Search for World Order, 1943–1957* (Toronto:
   University of Toronto Press, 1979, 1982), vol. 1, chap. 8, vol. 2, chaps.
   12–13; Clyde Sanger, *Canadians and the United Nations* (Ottawa: External
   Affairs Canada, 1988); Keith Krause, W. Andy Knight, and David Dewitt,
   "Canada, the United Nations, and the Reform of International Institutions,"
   in *The United Nations System: The Policies of Member States*, eds. C.F.
   Alger, Gene M. Lyons, and John E. Trent (Tokyo: United Nations University
   Press, 1995), 132–85; Adam Chapnick, *The Middle Power Project: Canada
   and the Founding of the United Nations* (Vancouver: UBC Press, 2005);
   Tom Keating, *Canada and World Order: The Multilateralist Tradition in
   Canadian Foreign Policy*, 3rd ed. (Toronto: Oxford University Press, 2013).
3 Allan Gotlieb, "Romanticism and Realism in Canadian Foreign Policy,"
   Benefactors Lecture 2004, C.D. Howe Institute, Toronto, 3 November
   2004, esp. 28–31, https://www.cdhowe.org/sites/default/files/attachments/
   other-research/pdf/benefactors_lecture_2004.pdf. Accessed 15 February
   2016.

4 Lyman Abbott, "Theodore Roosevelt," *The Outlook*, 15 January 1919, 91, http://www.unz.org/Pub/Outlook-1919jan15-00091?View=PDF. Accessed 15 February 2016.

5 See Doris Kearns Goodwin, *The Bully Pulpit: Theodore Roosevelt, William Howard Taft, and the Golden Age of Journalism* (New York: Simon & Schuster, 2013), chap 1: when Roosevelt expressed delight, one of his favourite exclamations was "This is bully!" Likewise, crowds greeting Roosevelt in New York in 1910 on his return from Africa chanted "Teddy, Teddy, bully for you, Teddy!"

6 Fen Osler Hampson and Dean F. Oliver, "Pulpit Diplomacy: A Critical Assessment of the Axworthy Doctrine," *International Journal* 53, no. 3 (Summer 1998): 379–406.

7 UN General Assembly, 2nd Session, *Official Records, 83rd Plenary Meeting*, 18 September 1947, 63–66 (http://undocs.org/A/PV.83, accessed 15 February 2016); also Escott Reid, *Time of Fear and Hope: The Making of the North Atlantic Treaty, 1947–1949* (Toronto: University of Toronto Press, 1977), 32.

8 Ibid.

9 Ibid.

10 James Eayrs, *In Defence of Canada*, vol. 4: *Growing Up Allied* (Toronto: University of Toronto, 1980), 18.

11 John English, *The Worldly Years: Life of Lester Pearson, 1949–1972* (Toronto: Knopf Canada, 2011), chap. 1; Lester B. Pearson, *Mike: The Memoirs of the Rt. Hon. Lester B. Pearson*, vol. 2: *1948–1957* (Toronto: University of Toronto Press, 1973), 40–1.

12 Trevor Lloyd, *Canada in World Affairs*, vol. 10: *1957–1959* (Toronto: Oxford University Press, 1968), 132.

13 For example, John Meisel, *The Canadian General Election of 1957* (Toronto: University of Toronto Press, 1962), 58.

14 Quoted in Costas Melakopides, *Pragmatic Idealism: Canadian Foreign Policy, 1945–1995* (Montreal and Kingston: McGill-Queen's University Press, 1998), 58.

15 For a full account of Canada and the Ten-Nation Committee on Disarmament, see Albert Legault and Michel Fortmann, *A Diplomacy of Hope: Canada and Disarmament, 1945–1988* (Montreal and Kingston: McGill-Queen's University Press, 1992), 170–94.

16 Eric Bergbusch and Michael D. Stevenson, "Howard Green, Public Opinion and the Politics of Disarmament," in *Architects and Innovators: Building the Department of Foreign Affairs and International Trade*, eds.

Greg Donaghy and Kim Richard Nossal (Montreal and Kingston: McGill-Queen's University Press, 2009), 194.

17 Jamie Glazov, *Canadian Policy toward Khrushchev's Soviet Union* (Montreal and Kingston: McGill-Queen's University Press, 2003), 98–105.

18 John G. Diefenbaker, *One Canada: Memoirs of the Right Honourable John G. Diefenbaker*, vol. 2: *The Years of Achievement: 1956–1962* (Toronto: Signet, 1976), 107. His External Affairs liaison, H. Basil Robinson, notes that the department "gave him what we judged to be the best advice in the circumstances. At the time he did not reject that advice out of hand. He simply insisted on our helping him to find dramatic language in which to attack Khrushchev, with particular reference to Soviet domination of Ukraine and the Baltic states." H. Basil Robinson, *Diefenbaker's World: A Populist in Foreign Affairs* (Toronto: University of Toronto Press, 1989), 153.

19 Legault and Fortmann, *Diplomacy of Hope*, 191.

20 UN General Assembly, 15th Session, *Official Records, 869th Meeting*, 23 September 1960 (http://undocs.org/A/PV.869), paras 94–307. Accessed 15 February 2016.

21 UN General Assembly, 15th Session, *Official Records, 871st Meeting*, 26 September 1960 , paras. 194, 197 (http://undocs.org/A/PV.871, accessed 15 February 2016); also, Diefenbaker, *One Canada*, 110.

22 Ibid.

23 Robinson, *Diefenbaker's World*, 151, 155; for the reaction of other leaders to the speech, see Canada, Department of Foreign Affairs and International Trade, *Documents on Canadian External Relations*, vol. 27: *1960*, doc. 100.

24 UN General Assembly, 18th Session, *Official Records, 1208th Meeting*, 19 September 1963 (http://undocs.org/A/PV.1208, accessed 15 February 2016); the speech is reproduced in Lester B. Pearson, *Words and Occasions* (Toronto: University of Toronto Press, 1970), 212–19.

25 Ibid.

26 Ibid.

27 Ibid.

28 Ibid.

29 Kim Richard Nossal, Stéphane Roussel, and Stéphane Paquin, *The Politics of Canadian Foreign Policy*, 4th ed. (Montreal and Kingston: McGill-Queen's University Press, 2015), chap. 5; also Heather A. Smith and Claire Turenne Sjolander, eds., *Canada in the World: Internationalism in Canadian Foreign Policy* (Don Mills, ON: Oxford University Press, 2013).

30 Charlotte S.M. Girard, *Canada in World Affairs*, vol. 13: *1963–1965* (Toronto: Canadian Institute of International Affairs, 1980), 316–17.

31 J.L. Granatstein and Robert Bothwell, *Pirouette: Pierre Trudeau and Canadian Foreign Policy* (Toronto: University of Toronto Press, 1990), esp. chap. 1.

32 Stevenson, "Canada and the United Nations," 153; English, *Just Watch Me*, 380. Trudeau served as a member of the Canadian delegation to the 1966 UN General Assembly. As prime minister, he paid official visits to Secretary-General U Thant on 11 November 1969, and Secretary-General Kurt Waldheim on 21 March 1978.

33 Pierre Elliott Trudeau, *Memoirs* (Toronto: McClelland & Stewart, 1993), 332.

34 Greg Donaghy, "'The Ghost of Peace': Pierre Trudeau's Search for Peace, 1982–1984," *Peace Research* 39, nos. 1–2 (2007): 39.

35 Granatstein and Bothwell, *Pirouette*, 7: in *Cité Libre*, the political journal he edited, Trudeau called Pearson and his cabinet "idiots." Within two years, Trudeau would join the Liberal party, secure election, and be appointed Pearson's parliamentary secretary.

36 John Clearwater, *Canadian Nuclear Weapons: The Untold Story of Canada's Cold War Arsenal* (Toronto: Dundurn Press, 1998); Duane Bratt, *The Politics of CANDU Exports* (Toronto: University of Toronto Press, 2006), 58–9.

37 Trudeau, *Memoirs*, 333.

38 Ivan Head and Pierre Trudeau, *The Canadian Way: Shaping Canada's Foreign Policy, 1968–1984* (Toronto: McClelland & Stewart, 1995), 126.

39 John English, *Just Watch Me: The Life of Pierre Elliott Trudeau, 1968–2000* (Toronto: Alfred A. Knopf Canada, 2009), 376–7.

40 UN General Assembly, 10th Special Session, *Official Records, 9th Meeting,* 26 May 1978 (A/S-10/PV.27); the speech is reproduced in Pierre Elliott Trudeau, *Lifting the Shadow of War,* ed. C. David Crenna (Edmonton: Hurtig, 1987), 27–36.

41 Ibid.

42 Ibid.

43 English, *Just Watch Me*, 377.

44 Granatstein and Bothwell, *Pirouette*, 363–76; English, *Just Watch Me*, 593–602.

45 Trudeau, *Memoirs*, 341.

46 Brian Mulroney, *Memoirs* (Toronto: McClelland & Stewart, 2007), 402–4.

47 Ibid., 406.
48 Michael Valpy, "Brian Mulroney and Stephen Lewis on Principled
   Leadership in Foreign Affairs," *CIGI Online*, 15 April 2014.
49 Mulroney, *Memoirs*, 406–7; also Linda Freeman, *The Ambiguous
   Champion: Canada and South Africa in the Trudeau and Mulroney Years*
   (Toronto: University of Toronto Press, 1997), 133.
50 UN General Assembly, 12th Special Session, *Official Records, 18th
   Meeting*, 18 June 1982 (http://undocs.org/A/S-12/PV.18). Accessed
   15 February 2016.
51 UN General Assembly, 40th Session, *Official Records, 47th Meeting*,
   23 October 1985 (http://undocs.org/A/40/PV.47), accessed 15 February
   2016; 43rd Session, *Official Records, 11th Meeting*, 29 September 1988
   (http://undocs.org/A/43/PV.11), accessed 15 February 2016; 45th Session,
   Official Records, 14th Meeting, 1 October 1990 (http://undocs.org/A/45/
   PV.14), accessed 15 February 2016.
52 UN Security Council, 55th Year, 4,194th Meeting, *Provisional*, 7 September 2000 (http://undocs.org/S/PV.4194). Accessed 15 February 2016.
53 Liberal Party of Canada, *Creating Opportunity: The Liberal Plan for
   Canada* (Ottawa, 1993), 108–9, archived at http://www.poltext.org/sites/
   poltext.org/files/plateformes/can1993lib_plt_en_12072011_131100.pdf.
   Accessed 15 February 2016.
54 Michael Pearson, "Humanizing the UN Security Council," in *Canada
   among Nations 2001: The Axworthy Legacy*, eds. Fen Osler Hampson,
   Norman Hillmer, and Maureen Appel Molot (Toronto: Oxford University
   Press, 2001), 131.
55 Lloyd Axworthy, *Navigating a New World: Canada's Global Future*
   (Toronto: Vintage Canada, 2003), 241.
56 UN General Assembly, 49th Session, *Official Records, 10th Meeting*,
   29 September 1994 (http://undocs.org/A/49/PV.10). Accessed 15 February
   2016.
57 UN General Assembly, 50th Session, *Official Records, 36th Meeting*, 22 October 1995 (http://undocs.org/A/50/PV.36). Accessed 15 February 2016.
58 As Chrétien said, in French, "For although Canadians sometimes forget it,
   the highest hope of the global community is to achieve what we in Canada
   have achieved for ourselves. A means of living together in peace and
   understanding. Not an answer to every problem, but a means to pursue
   those answers together with respect, tolerance, accommodation and compromise." Ibid.
59 UN General Assembly, 58th Session, *Official Records, 8th Meeting*,
   23 September 2003 (http://undocs.org/A/58/PV.8), accessed 15 February

2016; video: http://www.un.org/webcast/ga/58/statements/canaengo30923.
htm. Accessed 15 February 2016.

60 UN General Assembly, 51st Session, *Official Records, 7th Meeting,*
24 September 1996 (http://undocs.org/A/51/PV.7), accessed 15 February
2016; 52nd Session, *Official Records, 12th Meeting,* 25 September 1997
(http://undocs.org/A/52/PV.12), accessed 15 February 2016; 53rd Session,
Official Records, 15th Meeting, 25 September 1998 (http://undocs.
org/A/53/PV.15), accessed 15 February 2016; 54th Session, *Official
Records, 10th Meeting,* 23 September 1999 (http://undocs.org/A/54/
PV.10), accessed 15 February 2016; 55th Session, *Official Records,
15th Meeting,* 14 September 2000 (http://undocs.org/A/55/PV.15),
accessed 15 February 2016. See also Canada, Department of Foreign
Affairs and International Trade, "Foreign Affairs Minister Lloyd
Axworthy at the 51st Session of the United Nations General Assembly,
September 24–26, 1996," http://dfait-aeci.canadiana.ca/view/ooe.
b2960886E/1. Accessed 15 February 2016.

61 UN General Assembly, 55th Session, *Official Records, 15th Meeting,*
14 September 2000 (http://undocs.org/A/55/PV.15). Accessed 15 February
2016.

62 For example, Louise Fréchette, "Canada at the United Nations: A Shadow
of Its Former Self," in *Canada among Nations,* eds. Hampson and
Heinbecker, 265–74.

63 UN General Assembly, 61st Session, *Official Records, 14th Meeting,*
21 September 2006 (http://undocs.org/A/61/PV.14), accessed 15 February
2016.

64 Steve Chase, "Harper Makes Donut Run," *Globe and Mail,* 22 September
2009.

65 Tom Parry, "Stephen Harper Accepts World Statesman of the Year Award,"
CBC News, 27 September 2012; Lee Berthiaume, "Despite Being in New
York, Harper Will Shun UN Podium Again," *National Post,* 20 September
2013.

66 Laura Payton, "Harper's Speech Fires Up Convention Crowd," *CBC News,*
10 June 2011; video at https://www.youtube.com/
watch?v=oovooPHDVxA, at 0:03:15. Accessed 15 February 2016.

67 Ibid, 0:03:54. Accessed 15 February 2016.

68 Brooke Jeffrey, *Dismantling Canada: Stephen Harper's New Conservative
Agenda* (Montreal and Kingston: McGill-Queen's University Press, 2015),
241.

69 Mike Blanchfield, "UN Official Praises Canada's Stand on Iran," *Canadian
Press,* 30 October 2014.

70 Bruce Cheadle, "Silence Speaks Volumes as Harper Snubs UN," *Canadian Press,* 27 September 2012, https://www.cigionline.org/articles/2012/09/silence-speaks-volumes-harper-snubs-un. Accessed 15 February 2016.

71 UN General Assembly, 66th Session, *Official Records, 26th Meeting,* 26 September 2011 (http://undocs.org/A/66/PV.26), accessed 15 February 2016; 67th Session, *Official Records, 19th Meeting,* 1 October 2012 (http://undocs.org/A/67/PV.19), accessed 15 February 2016; 68th Session, *Official Records, 21st Meeting,* 30 September 2013 (http://undocs.org/A/68/PV.21), accessed 15 February 2016.

72 Kim Richard Nossal, "Kicking It Old School: Romanticism with Conservative Characteristics," in *Seeking Order in Anarchy: Multilateralism as State Strategy,* ed. Robert W. Murray (Edmonton: University of Alberta Press, 2016).

73 Jeffrey Simpson, "The Trouble with Bullhorn Diplomacy," *Globe and Mail,* 2 August 2014.

74 Campbell Clark, "Joe Clark's New Book: Canada Is the Country That 'Lectures and Leaves,'" *Globe and Mail,* 1 November 2013.

75 Paul Heinbecker, *Getting Back in the Game: A Foreign Policy Playbook for Canada* (Toronto: Key Porter Books, 2010).

76 Ibid., 213.

77 UN General Assembly, 69th Session, *Official Records, 10th Meeting,* 25 September 2014 (http://undocs.org/A/69/PV.11), accessed 15 February 2016; video: http://webtv.un.org/search/canada-general-debate-69th-session/3807454776001, accessed 15 February 2016.

78 Omer Aziz, "Canada Is Missing in Action at the United Nations," *Globe and Mail,* 12 August 2015, http://www.theglobeandmail.com/globe-debate/canada-is-missing-in-action-at-the-united-nations/article25940757/. Accessed 15 February 2016.

7

A Wasted Opportunity

Canada and the New International Economic Order, 1974–82

Greg Donaghy[1]

Since the late 1940s, as the first of the former European colonies of Asia tottered towards independence, there has been an ongoing dialogue between the rich North and the impoverished South over the nature of their relationship. Initially, the North-South dialogue, a termed coined by a British diplomat in the late 1950s, revolved almost exclusively around the volume and terms of official development assistance (ODA). This shifted in the early 1960s when trade relations were added to the mix, an innovation signalled by the start of the first UN Conference on Trade and Development (UNCTAD) in 1964. It changed again in 1974, when the developing world, hard hit by a dramatic rise in oil prices and inspired by the success of the Organization of Petroleum Exporting Countries (OPEC), issued a ringing Declaration on the New International Economic Order (NIEO). Insisting that the rules regulating global trade, investment, and financial transactions favoured the industrialised North, the declaration demanded radical changes in the existing economic order, becoming the single most important issue in the North-South dialogue for the next eight years.

As the chapters in this collection by Tarah Brookfield and Suzanne Langlois demonstrate, postwar Canadians have shared a deep commitment to advancing UN goals across a broad front. Yet, despite the obvious importance that Prime Minister Pierre Trudeau placed on the North-South dialogue in the 1970s, students of his foreign policy have not paid sustained attention to Canada's role in UN sponsored negotiations over the NIEO. The contributions by

Kevin Spooner and Colin McCullough suggest one reason: when it comes to the UN, at least since the Suez Crisis of 1956, the attention of Canadians has settled unshakably on peacekeeping, and the high politics of crisis diplomacy and peace prizes. But there are other factors too.

Discussions of Trudeau's relations with what was then commonly called the Third World have been inclined to focus on aid – what Bothwell and Granatstein dismissively refer to as "the kindness of strangers" – with a passing reference to the NIEO tossed in as an aside.[2] Those who have looked more closely have focused on the yawning gap between Trudeau's rhetoric and his failure to adjust his government's economic policy, especially tariffs, to meet Third World expectations.[3] Depending on one's perspective, Trudeau is seen as an innocent, whose naive hopes are dashed by harsh economic realities,[4] or a cunning hypocrite, advancing a narrow national agenda behind a smokescreen of moral platitudes.

Neither view is entirely accurate, and both largely ignore the modest, consistent, and progressive set of diplomatic objectives that were at the heart of Trudeau's contribution to the North-South dialogue. Though the prime minister briefly tried to hammer out a coordinated approach to the Third World that fully reconciled national and international goals and objectives, he gave up in the face of sustained opposition from Ottawa's bureaucratic and political establishment, which favoured short-term notions of the national interest. Consequently, Trudeau and his allies adopted an incremental and ad hoc approach. Though this hardly resolved the tension between immediate Canadian and long-term global interests, it did ensure that Canadian attitudes remained advanced enough to allow Ottawa to act as a creditable interlocutor between North and South, pushing the more important players on both sides towards genuine dialogue and the prospect of long-term progress. To borrow from (and simultaneously challenge) Kim Nossal's critical analysis of prime ministerial UN diplomacy, this chapter contends that Trudeau followed a "realist" policy in pursuit of "romantic" objectives.

Though Trudeau had long been interested in relations with the Third World, which was the theme of his first speech as prime minister in April 1968, other, more nationalistic, concerns had dominated Canadian foreign policy during his first two terms in office. In the July 1974 election campaign that followed hard on the heels of the first UN General Assembly Special Session on the NIEO, however, he indicated his renewed desire to add a new dimension to his foreign policy. "If I were to identify any single criterion by which I hope Canada's presence in the world would be judged," Trudeau declared in the campaign's only foreign policy speech, "I hope it would be its humanism, its pursuit of social justice."[5] To tackle this new priority, the prime minister replaced the aging Mitchell Sharp as secretary of state for external affairs with the more progressive Allan MacEachen, who was told to take an active and leading role in the international struggle to solve "the basic issues of economic disparity."[6]

The minister soon struck a new interdepartmental Committee on Economic Relations with Developing Countries (ICERDC) to conduct a sweeping review of Canadian policies as they affected North-South issues. The committee got down to work in February 1975, when it began to discuss Trudeau's coming trip to Europe, the next Commonwealth heads of government meeting (CHOGM), and the UNGA's 7th Special Session, all occasions when the NIEO was expected to figure prominently. Michael Pitfield, the clerk of the privy council and Trudeau confidant, made it clear that the prime minister wanted to "extend Canadian policy" in this area and expected results in time for the Commonwealth gathering in April. Though he acknowledged the tensions that existed between departments with domestic interests and those more involved in international developments, he saw this as an opportunity for external affairs to develop coordinated "policy options that would take into account both national and international interests."

This was no easy assignment. The two major economic departments, represented by J.F. Grandy, the deputy minister of industry, trade, and commerce (ITC), and R.K. Joyce, the assistant deputy minister of finance, were deeply sceptical. They doubted the government's capacity to reduce tariffs to meet the expectations of less developed countries (LDCs), cautioned against adopting policies Canada was not prepared to implement, and cheekily demanded a clear sense of the cabinet's views. Though doubtful that sweeping change was possible or desirable, Michel Dupuy, an assistant under-secretary of state for external affairs, insisted that it was important to take the demands of the developing world seriously or there might be a complete breakdown in the North-South dialogue. He suggested setting up working groups to see if they could progress by concentrating on three specific areas: commodity prices, trade liberalization, and transnational corporations and the transfer of technology.[7]

Given the prime minister's clear views on the direction in which he wished Canadian policy to evolve, Pitfield was surprised and disappointed with the working groups' efforts. Bureaucratic infighting had made progress impossible and its papers contained no new initiatives or firm conclusions but merely identified areas where gains might be possible. This was still measurable progress in an exceptionally complex field. Concerned that Trudeau might demand speedier action, MacEachen urged the prime minister to treat the CHOGM as "a step in a continuing process ... [that] will be chiefly useful in identifying possible avenues for Canadian action looking toward the 7th Special Session of the General Assembly."[8] For the moment, Trudeau agreed. Thus, at the CHOGM in Kingston, Canada modestly set out to define with developing countries priority areas of shared concern, moving forward in a "pragmatic, step-by-step approach."[9]

ICERDC's next effort to reconcile the prime minister's foreign policy aspirations with Canadian economic and trade policy was no more successful. A revised memorandum tried to define principles that should guide policy, suggesting that Canada should encourage "appropriate adjustments in international economic relations as a means of reducing disparities between developed and developing countries." Rather than redistributing current wealth, the paper argued that Canada should promote a more equitable distribution of "the incremental product of economic growth." Again, however, this would best be achieved through a "pragmatic step-by-step approach" in contrast to "the integrated, comprehensive program espoused by the developing world."[10]

Briefed by Pitfield, who was growing sceptical of ICERDC's work, Trudeau was unimpressed. Characterizing the memorandum as "reasonable and pragmatic," he insisted it did not go far enough to avoid a confrontation with the developing world. He was concerned that Canada was lagging behind the Europeans and argued that it ought to take a leading role in the search for alternatives. It was necessary, the prime minister insisted, "to get down to the guts of the various issues involved." These views were reflected in the cabinet committee's final decision, which approved the memorandum's incremental approach but instructed officials to take a fresh look at the problem and develop specific proposals for action.[11]

Continuing opposition from ITC and finance made it impossible for external affairs to develop the kind of detailed policy the prime minister wanted in time for either the Commonwealth finance ministers' meeting in late August or the UNGA's 7th special session in September. Officials were given another opportunity, however, when negotiations on the NIEO shifted from the UN context to the more restricted Conference on International Economic Cooperation (CIEC). An expanded version of an earlier and abortive consumer-producer dialogue on energy, the CIEC was launched by US Secretary of State Henry Kissinger in the spring of 1975 and took shape over the summer and early fall. Although Canada was not involved in the preparatory discussions, external affairs had followed the matter closely, broadcast Ottawa's interest widely, and made sure Canada was invited. The CIEC was to begin in December with a ministerial meeting between nineteen developing states (G-19), representing the varied members of the Group of 77 (G-77) developing countries, and eight industrialised countries (G-8). Ministers would establish working commissions on energy, raw materials, development, and financial affairs, gathering in a year's time to review the results.[12]

Canadian preparations for the ministerial conference were handed over to ICERDC, which met in late October to draft a note to cabinet on the issues raised by the CIEC. The resulting paper was marginally more forthcoming on commodity questions than earlier efforts, but Canadian policy was still very cautious, disappointing the prime minister. Generally, the Canadian delegation, to be led by MacEachen and Alastair Gillispie, the minister of energy, mines, and resources (EMR), was expected to play an active part in the conference and ensure that it try to reduce disparities between rich and poor. Specifically, the delegation was to "protect and promote" Canadian interests in the commissions, especially Canada's ability to develop its energy sector, to preserve its mineral markets, and to safeguard the value of its outstanding loans to the developing world. At the same time, the delegation was to help transform the CIEC into a mechanism for strengthening international economic cooperation.[13] Typically, reflecting a hard truth about the dualistic nature of Canada's postwar approach to problems of world order, the draft paper was silent on how to reconcile the tensions between its two main objectives.

While officials completed the memorandum, Ottawa's stake in the conference increased markedly following a French suggestion that Canada might serve as a conference co-chair, representing the G-8. Although the role would place considerable demands on the minister's time and possibly force Canada to forgo its own interests to keep the conference moving, it offered the government a high profile opportunity to promote its foreign policy interests, particularly its relations with the developing world. After consulting Kissinger, who had hoped to secure the position himself, and checking with cabinet, MacEachen decided in late November that he would "reluctantly" accept the role if it was offered.[14]

As expected, when the CIEC opened in December, MacEachen was chosen co-chairman with Venezuela's foreign minister, Manuel Pérez Guerrero, representing the G-19. The co-chairs agreed that each would encourage his group to compromise and set the commissions to work defining the problems before them. Meanwhile, Dupuy, who had become MacEachen's principal economic advisor, turned his attention to the fourth UNCTAD slated for May in Nairobi. Retreating from the frustrating attempts to articulate a comprehensive policy towards the NEIO, Dupuy suggested developing concrete measures that Canada could use to stake out a position as one of the more progressive industrialised countries. Such a posture would enable Canada to press the more conservative states in the CIEC's G-8 to be flexible, allow Ottawa to maintain the trust of the developing world, and safeguard Canadian leadership of the CIEC.[15]

Dupuy's efforts to pursue this approach again encountered stiff resistance. Despite strong support from the prime minister, he found it impossible to persuade other departments to be very forthcoming. Repeatedly, external affairs was defeated on several key issues. Most important, it failed to persuade ITC to accept the principle of voluntary contributions to international commodity agreements, a policy Dupuy hoped to underline at UNCTAD by announcing a $6 million contribution to the international tin buffer stock. Finance also rejected proposals by external affairs to write down over $200 million worth of ODA loans to the least developed countries as likely to undermine Canada's case-by-case approach to debt relief and reduce Ottawa's standing with other western creditor countries. The department's suggestions for a series of measures designed to encourage developing country exports met similar opposition in the ICERDC Task Force.[16]

As a result, the draft memorandum to cabinet that ICERDC produced in late March outlined a position that put Canada among the least generous members of the industrialised world.[17] MacEachen himself fared just as poorly in the cabinet committee on priorities and planning, where he presented the agreed memorandum as well as a supplementary note outlining additional measures he wished included. Ministers endorsed the memorandum generally but referred MacEachen's key proposals for a financial contribution to the tin buffer stock, for a program of debt forgiveness, and for measures to liberalize trade to the full cabinet.[18] Opposed by the ministers of ITC and finance, who was wrestling with the government's new austerity measures, MacEachen made only limited progress. Canada would take no steps to ease Third World debt, would make a minimal contribution to the tin buffer stock, and introduce only a few very limited measures to encourage Third World exports to Canada.[19]

In May, MacEachen headed to Nairobi, where it was soon apparent that the discussions at UNCTAD had outrun Canadian policy. Buoyed by cash commitments from OPEC countries, developing states were campaigning hard for a common fund to finance commodity buffer stocks, an idea that Ottawa had long dismissed as impractical. As support for the fund gained momentum, it emerged as the symbol of the North's willingness to cooperate with the South in stabilizing commodity prices. In this context, Canada's posture seemed decidedly ungenerous and was criticized in Ottawa by a subcommittee of the House of Commons Standing Committee on External Affairs and Defence and denounced by Canadian nongovernmental organizations (NGOs), who were at the conference as CIDA-funded observers.[20]

The prime minister shared their concerns and indicated that he was prepared to see the matter returned to cabinet for review. MacEachen took the hint and asked his officials how Canada's posture might be improved so as to encourage a successful outcome in Nairobi. They had answers at hand: Canada should announce that it would be prepared to contribute to a common fund, if one was established, and that it was willing to examine the debt problems of the least developed countries with "particular sympathy."[21] Again, the department ran into opposition from finance, which insisted that Canada limit itself to indicating a willingness "to consider" a contribution to the common fund. This gesture was approved by cabinet on 27 May, allowing the Canadian delegation to support UNCTAD's final resolutions inviting members to continue discussing the creation of a common fund.[22]

Though MacEachen and Dupuy hoped that the consensus reached at UNCTAD might provide a basis for progress in the CIEC, they were soon disappointed. Looming elections in the US and Japan made it difficult for officials to develop new bargaining positions. The European Economic Community (EEC), with its cumbersome decision-making apparatus and internal divisions, also found it hard to start negotiating. The outlook was equally unpromising on the other side of the table. Burdened with a rigid consensus decision-making process and beset by accusations that some members of the G-77 were being inadequately represented, the G-19 placed considerable emphasis on its political unity, severely constraining its flexibility and making it impossible for LDCs to make the trade-offs necessary to respond to G-8 offers, however meagre.[23] Consequently, the two Canadians spent much of the next eight months shuttling back and forth across the Atlantic just to keep the talks alive.

Despite his own frustrations and the scepticism among some of his cabinet colleagues about the CIEC's value, MacEachen's support for the conference did not diminish. He continued to insist that the successful conclusion of the CIEC would provide a sound basis for improved political and economic relations with the LDCs. Indeed, the minister's success in keeping the group together had already greatly improved Canada's international standing on North-South issues. Since it had a more forthcoming policy than its Western partners, it seemed likely that the CIEC could be pushed towards its conclusion with little extra cost for Canadians. Ottawa's main contribution, Dupuy suggested in January, lay in encouraging the United States (as well as Japan and Germany) to concede more ground to the G-19.[24]

During the winter 1977, as President Jimmy Carter's newly elected Democratic administration settled in, Canada did just that. In early January, Jake Warren, Canada's ambassador in Washington, stressed the importance of a more forthcoming American posture in his first meetings with the US secretary of state designate, Cyrus Vance, the treasury secretary designate, Michael Blumenthal, and the incoming vice-president, Walter Mondale.[25] The following month, Dupuy headed to Washington to urge Richard Cooper, the under secretary of state for economic affairs, to come up with a positive US position in order to revive the CIEC.[26] Trudeau himself raised the subject at his first meeting with Carter, warning the president "that it would be unfortunate if the US were unable to make any real progress on this, its first opportunity to come to grips with North-South issues."[27]

Distressed by the painfully slow pace of American policy-making, Dupuy used a G-8 meeting in March to flush the US into the open. As chairman, he pressed Cooper for a frank assessment of the CIEC's prospects and US policy. The American was upbeat, for the first time unveiling Carter's plans to seek a substantial increase in bilateral ODA and to support a buffer stock mechanism to stabilize commodity prices that could be described as a common fund.[28] The EEC replied a week later with word that it would support a commodity price stabilization program and create a billion dollar Special Action Program (SAP) for multilateral aid through the International Development Association (IDA).[29]

Movement by the US and the EEC created two sets of problems for Canadian policy makers. In Paris, Dupuy was preoccupied with defending Canada's lead position in the G-8 as both the US and the EEC began to jostle for a higher public profile.[30] The forthcoming US and EEC postures also meant that changes were required in Canada's negotiating stance. These were essentially conditioned, Dupuy told ICERDC at the end of March, by the fact that Canada would have to move in tandem with the other members of the G-8.[31] In any event, MacEachen reminded his colleagues in April, there were good reasons for Canada to be as forthcoming as possible. The country had a strong interest in meeting the G-19 on commodities, debt relief, and ODA in order to secure an extended dialogue on energy. A successful conference would also bolster moderate opinion in the South and help maintain a constructive dialogue on North-South issues. Moreover, success would underscore Canada's capacity to manage a major international file.[32] He recommended that Canada endorse a common fund for commodities, contribute its share of $30–60 million to the SAP, and write off $229 million in outstanding debt to the least developed countries. Canada would also pledge to maintain its current ODA levels in real terms and renew its commitment to aim for the .7 per cent GDP target.[33]

With his recommendations heading for cabinet, MacEachen scooted back to Paris to assess the state of the talks with Pérez Guerrero. Early indications of G-8 thinking had not impressed the G-19, who worried about the lack of precision in the western offer and the G-8's political commitment.[34] The proposed US buffer stock mechanism had not met LDC demands for a common fund, and American opposition to the SAP spelled trouble over ODA levels. The

success of the conference, MacEachen wired Trudeau, who was about
to attend the London summit of Western leaders, the G-7, would
depend on wrestling a commitment from Carter to support the common fund.[35] At the Western summit in May, that commitment was
quickly forthcoming, and the G-7, adopting the strong language
drafted by Canada, promised, "to do all in our power to see the CIEC
conclude successfully."[36]

Buoyed by the G-7's communiqué and progress in the final round
of talks, Western ministers arrived in Paris confident of reaching an
agreement with the G-19 on energy and other North-South issues.
But Pérez-Guerrero dismissed the Western offer of more than a billion dollars in additional aid and the common fund as "below expectations."[37] The atmosphere deteriorated further when Pérez-Guerrero
manoeuvred the moderate majority in the G-19 into opposing an
agreement on energy consultations. Angry G-8 ministers wanted to
withdraw their offers, but Vance and MacEachen dissuaded them in
a dramatic midnight session. Even with the G-8 offers safely in his
pocket, Pérez-Guerrero resisted the efforts of western ministers to
draft an agreed communiqué that acknowledged their contribution.
Through the night and the next day, the talks continued, unbroken
for forty-three hours straight, until they produced a draft that papered
over their differences.

The collapse of the CIEC removed the most important source of
external pressure on Canada for a progressive response to LDC
demands. At the same time, new domestic pressures encouraged the
government to adopt a more self-interested policy toward the developing world. A slumping economy and rising imports from the more
advanced LDCs generated growing demands for tariff protection,
especially on footwear, textiles, and clothing. A series of high-profile
scandals at CIDA also eroded popular support for Canadian development assistance.[38] Finally, the burgeoning fiscal crisis and the election in November 1976 of a separatist government in Quebec, which
became Trudeau's main preoccupation, inevitably meant new foreign
policy priorities. Redefining these priorities, at least insofar as they
effected Canada's relations with the developing world, was left to
external affairs and its new under-secretary, Alan Gotlieb.

A hard-nosed realist, who was appointed in March 1977, Gotlieb
worried that Canada's prominent role in the CIEC was well beyond
its modest economic power and he wanted to reduce Ottawa's contribution to the North-South dialogue.[39] He was also anxious to

bring CIDA's aid program into closer alignment with his department's foreign policy objectives. Thus, in late July, he sought Pitfield's
support for a comprehensive review of Canada's relations with the
developing world.[40] Pitfield, who welcomed Gotlieb's proposal, had
his own ideas on North-South policy, notions that reflected recent
shifts in the balance of ministerial opinion. Most important, he
argued, relations with the South should serve Canadian interests by
promoting national unity, primarily through an effective aid program
with which all Canadians could identify. Equally important, Ottawa
should acknowledge the long-term commercial potential of selected
Third World countries and court those states whose support might
advance Canadian interests in various international fora.[41] An
ICERDC meeting in September indicated broad support among
senior officials for a policy that would more closely link Canada's
role in the North-South dialogue with defined Canadian interests.[42]

Gotlieb's review, which emerged in draft in late October, promised
a dramatic realignment in Canada's approach to North-South relations. Indeed, the very concept of the "South" was swept away, as the
developing world was "disaggregated" into its various components:
the least and the less developed, the oil-producers in OPEC, and the
newly industrializing countries. Though Canada would continue to
offer emergency aid for humanitarian reasons, the paper insisted
that the country's approach to the developing world should emphasis bilateral relationships with carefully selected countries.
Henceforth, Gotlieb insisted, Canadian partners should be chosen
on the basis of the following considerations: Canada's economic
interest; contributions to Canadian sovereignty and identity; the
humanitarian concerns of Canadians; geographic proximity; and
the promotion of human rights. When these considerations could
not all be met, the emphasis would be placed on the expansion of
economic relations with a limited number of the larger and wealth-
ier developing countries.[43]

Predictably, the economic departments were delighted with
Gotlieb's paper. Pitfield too was pleased, though PCO officials feared
"that the pendulum might swing too far."[44] Dupuy, now CIDA president, was quite concerned. He worried that the paper ignored the
multilateral dimension of the North-South problem and failed to
acknowledge that Canada's short-term economic interests might
conflict with its long-term political interests in incorporating LDCs
into a stable world order.[45] Dupuy's complaints forced Gotlieb to

recognize LDC demands for an NIEO. Dupuy also forced him to acknowledge that Canada had a stake in managing the evolution of the global economic order in ways that protected its interests and reflected its perceptions of how the system should evolve to accommodate the just requirements of the developing world.[46] However, the under-secretary resisted efforts to discuss precisely how to accommodate LDC demands or the tough choices ministers might have to make when Canada's immediate interests conflicted with its stake in managing international change and the redistribution of global power. Thus, Canada's approach to the NIEO remained ad hoc, a precarious balancing of limited national interests and loftier hopes for a more just world order, with individual issues addressed "on a case-by-case basis."[47]

That this was so was made especially apparent by Trudeau's behaviour during and after the next G-7 summit in late July 1978. At the Bonn meeting, he continued to insist strongly that the industrialized countries press ahead with the ongoing negotiations in UNCTAD for a common fund. But the prime minister also returned from Germany alarmed at the size of Canada's deficit and promptly rolled back the aid budget, which was projected to fall from .53 per cent of GDP in 1977–78 to .37 per cent of GDP by 1980–81.[48] The gulf between the prime minister's rhetoric and his actions sent officials scurrying for cover and reinforced the tendency already apparent in Gotlieb's paper to have Canada withdraw from the North-South dialogue. "It is difficult to speak firmly in the dialogue until we have a clear sense of what kind of economic relations ... with LDCs [that Canada's] evolving economic strategies will permit," observed Jacques Roy in October. The senior PCO official added, "we must seek a role of lower profile. This is already happening and we should not take action to resist it. We will maintain 'respectable' aid flows; we will take relatively progressive positions on commodity issues, including the Common Fund. We cannot, for the moment, do much more than this."[49]

The timing of Canada's retreat was unfortunate for North-South relations were again rising to the top of the international agenda. In the fall of 1979, the UN's underdeveloped majority, the G-77, proposed a new round of Global Negotiations on the NIEO. In contrast to the CIEC, whose representative nature often strained the G-77's political unity, every UN member was invited to participate. Each would help oversee integrated negotiations on commodities, energy, trade, development, and finance, giving individual states enormous disruptive power and rendering the G-77 hostage to its most radical outliers. As efforts to establish rules for the talks proceeded slowly in the spring of 1980, the former West German chancellor, Willy Brandt, released his report, *North-South: A Programme for Survival.* Brandt's Commission on International Development Issues emphasized "interdependence," urging a huge transfer of resources to the poor South to avoid the collapse of the international economy. Its emergency program repeated calls to increase ODA to .7 per cent of GDP by 1985, outlined possible agreements on energy and agricultural, and pressed for the reform of the world economic order. As a first step in this direction, the commission proposed a summit of twenty-five leaders from North and South to inject some political will into the proposed Global Negotiations.

The prospect of renewed global talks and the Brandt report attracted Trudeau's interest. Entering his final term in office after his reelection in March 1980, he was anxious to make some progress on these issues while he still had the power to act.[50] In May 1980, Mexican President Lopez Portillo offered Trudeau an appropriate platform when he informed the Canadian of his plans to host a North-South summit in Cancun, asking Canada to serve as a cosponsor. Trudeau quickly welcomed the Portillo initiative and agreed to attend the summit, though he refused to allow Canada to become a cosponsor until he had discussed the gathering with his G-7 colleagues at their July gathering in Venice. Though Western leaders were divided on the wisdom of the North-South summit and its timing, Trudeau was reassured to learn that several regarded it favourably. Indeed, the prime minister was able to secure his colleagues' agreement to make North-South issues the "major focus" of next year's meeting in Ottawa.[51]

By late summer, Trudeau's government began to position itself to play a leading role on North-South issues in the three summits – the G-7, the Melbourne CHOGM, and the Cancun summit – scheduled for 1981. The secretary of state for external affairs, Mark MacGuigan, was a long-time supporter of foreign aid and he quickly picked up on the prime minister's revived interest in relations with the developing world. Anxious to lend a hand, the rookie minister turned to his officials for advice. They were not encouraging. The minister, they explained, would clearly play a secondary role in the prime minister's summitry, though he did have two key domestic functions. First, he would be required to generate public interest in and support for

Trudeau's efforts. Second, and more important, as the minister in charge of CIDA, MacGuigan would have to convince his cabinet colleagues to be more generous during their forthcoming discussions on the future level of Canada's ODA, the ticket into the North-South dialogue.[52]

With the economy mired in recession and the deficit mounting, ministers proved tough to persuade. At a meeting of the cabinet's priorities and planning committee in late August, they rejected MacGuigan's plea for more aid, urging him to explore other, nonfinancial ways to signal Canadian support for the dialogue. Back in external affairs, officials reminded MacGuigan that the government could hardly reduce tariffs on LDC imports where it mattered – on textiles, clothing, and footwear – without paying a steep political price in Quebec and Ontario. International financial or monetary reforms were simply too large for Canada to have any impact. "[I]t is an undeniable truth," Gotlieb told his minister as he sent him back to cabinet for the dough, "that developed countries' performance on ODA is the standard against which all developing countries measure their commitment to progress on North-South issues."[53]

MacGuigan appealed directly to the minister of finance for help and got it. With MacEachen's support, MacGuigan persuaded his cabinet colleagues in mid-September to increase Canada's ODA from .37 per cent to .5 per cent of GDP by 1985, rising to .7 per cent of GDP by the end of the decade.[54] The good news was quickly proclaimed in New York, where MacGuigan encountered his Mexican counterpart and finally told him that Canada was ready to cosponsor the Cancun summit.[55]

The emerging commitment to North-South dialogue placed Gotlieb under pressure to develop specific initiatives for Trudeau. Indeed, the cabinet committee on foreign policy and defence had already asked for a review of Canada's approach to the developing world in July.[56] Pitfield too began to press the under-secretary for speedy progress. Gotlieb' s reaction was cautious.[57] Given its invigorated aid policy, its links to the Commonwealth and La Francophonie, and the reluctance of other G-7 countries to take the lead, Canada was well-placed to play "a leadership, or catalytic, role." It would be helpful, however, if the results of a recent series of policy papers with implications for the dialogue – on the IMF, aid eligibility, Petro-Canada's Third World program, the tariff and textile quotas, and domestic adjustment assistance – could be coordinated into a coherent whole, from which the government could pick the initiatives it wanted to pursue.⁵⁸

In mid-October, Trudeau met with MacGuigan, Gotlieb, and Larry Smith, the assistant under-secretary handling North-South relations in external affairs. The prime minister, MacGuigan later recalled, was "totally consumed" by the issue and "filled with youthful vigour and idealism."⁵⁹ Trudeau understood and welcomed the desire for policy coherence, though he was not particularly interested in short-term issues of aid and the transfer of resources. Instead, he wanted to use the upcoming summits, especially the Ottawa summit, to remind world leaders of their "responsibility to humanity and the future," encouraging them to adopt policies to change the international economic order over the long-term despite immediate political risks. "Power-sharing is the heart of the North-South dialogue," he explained, "and politicians should be able to understand this readily and recognize that it is better to share power now than in the future, even though it may be easier the other way round." What specifically, he asked, could he do to kick-start the process of North-South power-sharing?⁶⁰

MacGuigan thought two proposals merited close attention. First, he urged the prime minister to endorse the idea of a World Bank energy affiliate to help LDCs fund energy exploration and development. Partly capitalized by OPEC members, who would be appropriately represented on its board of directors, the energy affiliate represented one means of power sharing.⁶¹ Second, Trudeau should throw his weight solidly behind the UN effort to launch Global Negotiations. Despite discussions in the spring and a recent UNGA special session, these talks were stalled as the US, Britain, and Germany blocked passage of an enabling resolution, fearful that the negotiations would impinge on such specialized forums as the GATT and the IMF. Canadian officials shared these concerns and worried that the sprawling negotiations were likely to be unmanageable and unproductive. Nonetheless, there were good reasons for supporting them. The talks provided a venue for the LDCs to vent their frustrations and an "umbrella" under which more practical negotiations could occur. Moreover, Global Negotiations would allow each UN member a voice in determining the global economic order, an innovation that represented "a further move in power-sharing."⁶²

Armed with these two suggestions, Trudeau headed off on a series of visits to Africa, the Middle East, and Latin America to see for himself what the Third World wanted. He returned to Ottawa, he later told MacEachen, "reinforced in my view that the stability and order that Canada seeks in the international economy, financial and monetary systems will not be achieved unless there are some significant changes to ensure the equitable and productive participation of developing countries in the system."[63] Ominously, Washington was inclining sharply towards the opposite view. Determined to restore America's role in the world, President Ronald Reagan's Republican administration, elected in November 1980, wasted little time telling Ottawa that it wanted the G-7 leaders to focus on pressing East-West issues.[64] Moreover, the administration was distinctly hostile to the Third World and Global Negotiations, which Reagan privately derided as an example of "woolly-minded, impractical, Liberal thinking."[65] The president signalled his new priorities with a cut in US aid appropriations in January 1981, prompting the Washington embassy to warn headquarters that it might no longer be possible to discuss North-South issues at the Ottawa summit.[66]

Initially, the extent of these differences with the US was partly obscured by the mixed signals coming from Washington in early 1981. MacGuigan, who urged US Secretary of State Alexander Haig to restore American ODA levels, came away "encouraged by Mr. Haig's attitude on North-South questions."[67] At the February meeting of the personal representatives of the G-7 leaders – or sherpas – Gotlieb too found the US attitude reassuring. The American sherpa, Meyer Rashish, "was much less negative or dogmatic than many had feared." While Rashish warned that North-South issues would have to be considered in their proper context, he acknowledged that they would still figure prominently in Ottawa. A preliminary survey suggested that most participants shared Canada's view that the issue needed to be taken seriously and that the western approach needed to be "broadly political as well as economic." While differences remained – the US opposed Global Negotiations and the World Bank energy affiliate – Rashish assured Gotlieb that American policy had not yet been finalised. Asked to draft a discussion paper on the North-South dialogue, Gotlieb was cautiously hopeful that the US might be persuaded to come onside.[68] This seemed even more likely when Reagan indicated on the eve of his March visit to Ottawa that he would attend the North-South summit in Cancun.

When the Canadian draft was discussed by the sherpas in April, however, it brought the differences between the US and its allies sharply into focus. The Germans, Italians, Japanese, and the EEC expressed strong support for Canada's draft, which explicitly endorsed Global Negotiations and the World Bank energy affiliate. Even the British, despite Prime Minister Margaret Thatcher's generally hard-line views on Third World questions, adopted a "surprisingly supportive approach." The US, however, expressed a doctrinaire view that the West must get its own economy into shape before addressing LDC concerns. In addition, it insisted that the paper would have to be substantially rewritten to give pride of place to the private sector as the foremost means of development. Gotlieb was dismayed. The American conclusions could not be presented credibly as the G-7's position, raising the possibility that the Ottawa summit might fail to reach any consensus on North-South issues.[69]

Gotlieb maintained the pressure on the US during his next two meetings with the other sherpas. Indeed, in Vancouver, where the group met in early June, he stepped it up by circulating a paper with language for the final communiqué that committed the G-7 to work "actively" for an early launch of the Global Negotiations.[70] Rashish refused to yield and the US again found itself isolated on North-South issues (as well as macroeconomic policy). Anxious to make a success of Reagan's first foray into summitry, the US arrived at the final session of the personal representatives in a more flexible mood. The sherpas accordingly agreed to a compromise on North-South energy and included a vague reference to some kind of energy funding facility for LDCs in the draft communiqué. But on Global Negotiations, the US held firm, until just two days before the leaders began to gather in Ottawa, when Washington blinked. The US would join in "the process of global negotiations," Rashish told Gotlieb, cryptically adding that "global negotiations" should appear in lower case letters.[71]

Though Trudeau was forced to settle for this vague reference, he was not entirely disappointed with the results of the Ottawa gathering.[72] Nor were his officials, who characterised the reference as "significant forward progress," an assessment shared by much of the international community.[73] Even so, there were still questions about how far the US would actually go at Cancun to meet LDC expectations on Global Negotiations. Though Reagan was not expected to make a final decision until just before Cancun, the tide seemed to be running strongly against Global Negotiations. Anxious American officials, who were only now coming to realise how isolated the US had become, encouraged Western representatives to lobby the White House and belatedly tried to generate interest in a new North-South negotiating process.[74] The American plea touched a chord in external affairs, which warned that US isolation was in nobody's interest, especially Canada's. Perhaps, suggested the deputy under-secretary, Bill Jenkins, the time had come for Canada to tell the LDCs in New York and at the CHOGM in Melbourne that they would have to "trim their sails" and find some other way to engage the US in the dialogue.[75]

The reaction from Larry Smith, who was with the prime minister in Melbourne, was uncompromising. Doubtful that Reagan was ready to stand alone on this issue or that he would renege on his Ottawa commitment, Smith firmly opposed efforts to find a compromise with Washington. In any event, compromise was unlikely, since the LDCs could hardly back down from Global Negotiations at this late date without admitting defeat.[76] This was a view confirmed in spades at a restricted session of the CHOGM meeting. Even Thatcher agreed that success at Cancun would depend on progress towards the Global Negotiations, though the Commonwealth group proved flexible on the form and content of the talks. There was an equally pragmatic consensus in the group on how to approach Reagan, who, all agreed, should be gently persuaded over the course of the summit to see that a number of world problems could be tackled through Global Negotiations.[77] Confident of success, Smith declared that the "time for Canadian bridge-building will be after Cancun, not before."

He was wrong. Trudeau had been careful not to become closely identified with the Cancun summit lest it fail and planned on playing only a modest role in Mexico. However, the last-minute withdrawal of the Austrian cochair, who fell ill, thrust the Canadian prime minister, who was the obvious replacement, onto centre stage. Trudeau starred as a trilingual chairman and under his guidance the discussions, in which Reagan participated with surprising enthusiasm, were "frank, informal, pragmatic and non-ideological." The talks generated a consensus on food, agriculture, and Global Negotiations. Reagan, like most of the participants, tackled these directly in his opening remarks, indicating that the US would join the negotiations provided the jurisdiction of the specialized agencies would be protected to its satisfaction. Though the note on Global Negotiations in the "co-chairman's summary" did not go as far as either Canada or the US wanted – Algeria, Venezuela, and

Tanzania insisted on a crippling all-or-nothing formula – Canadian observers were encouraged by this evidence of Washington's new flexibility, which they felt would maintain the momentum toward Global Negotiations.[78]

Reagan's willingness to negotiate seriously was underscored in December when the US presented a resolution to the G-77 intended to finally launch Global Negotiations. The new resolution clearly met Canadian expectations but divided radical and moderate LDCs, who struggled through December and January to come up with a response. As the struggle over Global Negotiations entered its final phase, Ottawa mounted one final push to move the North-South dialogue out of the starting gate.[79] Building on a message he and Lopez Portillo had sent to encourage the Cancun participants in January, Trudeau decided in February 1982 to send Smith, now styled ambassador for North-South relations, on a tour to drive home the "importance of getting a process started without being too concerned about the fine print."[80]

Smith's reports on the lengthy endgame were discouraging. The US adopted a "constructive approach" to the talks but the G-77 did not. Algeria, Iraq, and Libya refused to support the emerging G-77 consensus, and flexing their veto powers, they rejected the US text and imposed their radical views on the moderate majority.[81] A counterdraft, on which Canada refused comment to avoid isolating the US, threatened to derail. In response to Canadian and French pleading, Reagan himself decided that the US would accept the G-77 text with only a handful of minor amendments, provided the new text was endorsed by the G-7.[82] This was forthcoming at the Versailles summit, where Canada, which had worked so hard to broker the deal, was asked to present the revised resolution to the G-77 in New York. For Smith, and Gérard Pelletier, Canadian ambassador to the UN and Trudeau's good friend, the next three weeks were a disappointing denouement. Despite overwhelming support among the G-77, its two most radical members, Algeria and Iraq, refused to accept the new text, finally killing the prospect of Global Negotiations.[83]

The end of the search for Global Negotiations had important consequences for both the world and Canada. Internationally, it put paid to the notion of a politically united South, and for most of the next two decades, its disparate elements would have to come to terms individually with an increasingly resurgent, conservative, and neo-liberal North. Closer to home, the collapse of the dialogue after

Cancun left Trudeau bitterly disappointed and he blamed the developing world for wasting a "golden opportunity."[84] Despite subsequent requests from his friends, Tanzanian President Julius Nyerere and Jamaican Prime Minister Edward Seega, Trudeau refused to bring North-South issues to the attention of his G-7 colleagues again.[85] Arguably, the South's claim to a greater share of redistributed global power remained on the margins of the international agenda until the Group of 20 (G-20) was created in 1999. Finally, the prime minister's North-South campaign had another, unpredictable consequence for Canadian foreign policy. Trudeau had watched the US compromise at Ottawa and Cancun, and concluded that Reagan, despite his stature as a conservative ideologue, was essentially a skilled politician, who would bend and yield to pressure.[86] And this was an insight that would animate Canadian diplomacy during Trudeau's final year in office and shape his next crusade, his 1983–84 peace initiative.

NOTES

1 The views in this chapter are Greg Donaghy's alone and do not reflect the policies of the government of Canada or his department.

2 J.L. Granatstein and Robert Bothwell, *Pirouette: Pierre Trudeau and Canadian Foreign Policy* (Toronto: University of Toronto Press, 1990), 286; David Morrison, *Aid and Ebb Tide: A History of CIDA and Canadian Development Assistance* (Waterloo: Wilfrid Laurier University Press, 1998), 110–12, 178–84.

3 Cranford Pratt, "Canada: An Eroding and Limited Internationalism," in his edited collection, *Internationalism under Strain: The North-South Policies of Canada, the Netherlands, Norway, and Sweden* (Toronto: University of Toronto Press, 1989), 24–69.

4 Michael Hart, *A Trading Nation: Canadian Trade Policy from Colonialism to Globalization* (Vancouver: UBC Press, 2002), 295–6.

5 "Notes for the Prime Minister's Remarks to the Canadian Jewish Congress, Toronto, June 16, 1974," RG 25, File 20-2-2-1, vol. 8821, Library and Archives of Canada [LAC].

6 Pierre Trudeau to A.J. MacEachen, 4 September 1974, Basil Robinson Papers, vol. 21, File 22, LAC.

7 "Record of Third Meeting of ICERDC, February 20," RG 25, vol. 14070, File 35-1-ICERDC, LAC.

8 Robinson, Memorandum for the Minister: PMO-PCO Working Group on the CHOGM, 7 April 1975 and Robinson (drafted with Dupuy), Memorandum for the Minister (Only), 7 April 1975, RG 25, vol. 10655, File 23-3-1975-3, LAC.

9 Guidance Memorandum: New Economic Order, RG 25, vol. 14133, File 35-4-NIEO, LAC.

10 MacEachen, Memorandum to the Cabinet, Cabinet Document 442-72, 17 June 1975, RG 25, vol. 14133, File 35-4-NEIO, LAC.

11 MacEachen, Memorandum to the Cabinet, 17 June 1975; Pam McDougall, Memorandum for Robinson, 28 July 1975, RG 25, vol. 14133, File 35-4-NIEO, LAC. See also Minutes of the Cabinet Committee on Priorities and Planning, 25 July 1975, PCO Files; Michael Pitfield, Briefing Note for the Prime Minister, [July 1975], PCO File F-2-26, Privy Council Office [PCO].

12 Robinson, Memorandum for Ministers, 16 October 1975, RG 25, vol. 13482, File 39-4-IEP/SPC-1, LAC.

13 MacEachen, Memorandum to the Cabinet, 27 November 1975, RG 25, vol. 13482, File 39-4-IEP/SPC-1, LAC.

14 Peter Towe, Memorandum for McDougall, 14 November 1975; Robinson, Memoranda for the Minister, 17 and 18 November 1975; McDougall to Michel Dupuy, 28 November 1975, RG 25, vol. 13842, File 39-4-IEP/SPC-1, LAC; Cabinet Minutes, 27 November 1975, PCO.

15 Dupuy, Memorandum for the Minister, 13 April 1976, RG 25, vol. 13842, File 39-4-IEP/SPC-1, LAC.

16 ECD to PDT, 29 March 1976, RG 25, vol. 13999, 37-9-UNCTAD-12-76, LAC.

17 Eric Berbusch to Towe, 29 March 1976, RG 25, vol. 13999, 37-9-UNCTAD-12-76, LAC.

18 Robinson, Memorandum for the Minister, 2 April 1976 and Dupuy, Memorandum for the Minister, 13 April 1976, RG 25, vol. 13999, File 37-9-UNCTAD-12-76, LAC; and Minutes of the CCEPD, 14 April 1976, PCO Files, PCO.

19 Robinson, Memorandum for the Minister, 27 April 1976, RG 25, File 37-9-UNCTAD-12-76, LAC; Cabinet Conclusions, 29 April 1976, PCO.

20 Bergbusch to Wilson, 16 May 1976, RG 25, vol. 13999, File 37-9-UNCTAD-12-76, LAC.

21 Bonn (from SSEA) to Ottawa, Tel 893, 23 May 1976 and Ottawa to Vienna (for SSEA), ECD-481, 25 May 1976, RG 25, vol. 13999, File 37-9-UNCTAD-12-76, LAC.

22 Robinson, Memorandum for the Acting Minister, 31 May 1976, RG 25, vol. 13999, File 37-9-UNCTAD-12-76, LAC.

23 Karl Sauvant, *The Group of 77: Evolution, Structure, Organization* (New
    York: Oceana Publications, 1981), 14–16.
24 Draft CIEC Strategy Paper: Final Phase [December/January 1976], RG 25,
    vol. 13484, File 39-4-IEP/SPC-I, LAC.
25 Ottawa to OECD Paris, tel ECD-153, 17 January 1977, RG 25, vol.
    13484, File 39-4-IEP/SPC-I, LAC.
26 Ottawa to Washington, tel ECD-214, 3 February 1977 and Dupuy,
    Memorandum for the President of the Privy Council, 4 February 1977,
    RG 25, vol. 13484, File 39-4-IEP/SPC-I, LAC.
27 Washington to Ottawa, tel 671, 24 February 1977; Dupuy, Memorandum
    for the President of the Privy Council, 25 February 1977; and Robinson,
    Memorandum for the Minister, 3 March 1977, RG 25, vol. 13484, File
    39-4-IEP/SPC-I, LAC.
28 OECD Paris to Ottawa, tels 467 and 509, 4 March 1977, RG 25,
    vol. 13484, File 39-4-IEP/SPC-I, LAC.
29 Dupuy, Memorandum for the President of the Privy Council, 29 March
    1977, RG 25, vol. 13484, File 39-4-IEP/SPC-I, LAC.
30 Ottawa to OECD Paris, tel ECD-397, 4 April 1977 and Ottawa to
    London, tel PDP-501, 14 April 1977, RG 25, vol. 13484, File 39-4-IEP/
    SPC-I, LAC.
31 Bergbusch to Dupuy, 31 March 1977, and attached Record of Meeting of
    ICER-DC of March 18/77, RG 25, vol. 14707, File 35-I-ICERDC, LAC.
32 Robinson, Memorandum for the Minister, 22 April 1977 and attached
    Discussion Paper: Canada's Interests in CIEC, 21 April 1977, RG 25,
    vol. 13484, File 39-4-IEP/SPC-I, LAC.
33 Bergbusch to W.J. Jenkins, 25 April 1977 and attached Memorandum to
    Ministers, 22 April 1977, RG 25, vol. 13484, File 39-4-IEP/SPC-I, LAC.
34 CIEC Paris to Ottawa, tel 1110, 5 May 1977, RG 25, vol. 13484, File
    39-4-IEP/SPC-I, LAC.
35 CIEC Paris to Ottawa, tel 1085, 28 April 1977, RG 25, vol. 14124,
    File 35-4-ESC-London-1977, LAC.
36 Ottawa to London, tel ECL-1071, 11 May 1977, RG 25, vol. 14124,
    File 33-4-ESC-London-1977, LAC.
37 The account of the final ministerial meeting is based on CIEC Paris to
    Ottawa, tel 1490, 3 June 1977; OECD Paris to Ottawa, tel 1371, 6 June
    1977; and David Wright, "CIEC: The Last Ten Days," 16 June 1977,
    RG 25, vol. 13484, File 39-4-IEP/SPC-I, LAC. See also MacEachen, "All
    Those Years: Practice and Purpose in Politics" in Tom Kent, ed., *In Pursuit
    of the Public Good* (Montreal and Kingston: McGill-Queen's University
    Press, 1997), 13–14.

38 Morrison, *Tide and Ebb Tide*, 136–7, 140.
39 A.E. Gotlieb, Memorandum for the Minister, 16 June 1977, RG 25, vol. 13483, File 39-4-IEP/PSC-I, LAC.
40 Gotlieb to Dupuy, 29 July 1977, RG 25, vol. 14070, File 35-I-ICERDC, LAC.
41 Confidential source.
42 Confidential source.
43 Confidential source.
44 Confidential source.
45 Confidential source.
46 Don Jamieson, "Canada's Relations with Developing Countries," 14 March 1978, RG 25, vol. 14070, File 35-I-ICERDC, LAC.
47 Confidential source.
48 Confidential source; Morrison, *Tide and Ebb Tide*, 151.
49 Confidential source.
50 Patrick Gossage, *Close to the Charisma: My Years between the Press and Pierre Elliot Trudeau* (Toronto: McClelland and Stewart, 1986), 202; Christina McCall and Stephen Clarkson, *Trudeau and Our Times*, Volume 2: *The Heroic Delusion* (Toronto: McClelland and Stewart, 1994), 342–3.
51 Trudeau to Lopez Portillo, 14 May 1980 and 16 July 1980 RG 25, vol. 14767, File 37-9-3-1, LAC.
52 J.K.B. Kinsman, Memorandum for the Under-Secretary, 11 August 1980 and Gotlieb, Memorandum for the Minister, POL-77, 15 August 1980, RG 25, vol. 13895, File 37-9-3, LAC.
53 Gotlieb, Memorandum for the Minister, EBD-1019, 26 August 1980, RG 25, vol. 15701, File 37-9-3, LAC.
54 Morrison, *Aid and Ebb Tide*, 181.
55 Mark MacGuigan, Memorandum for the Prime Minister, 3 October 1980, RG 25, vol. 15701, File 37-9-3, LAC.
56 ECR (John Paynter) to ECO/ECE, 24 September 1980, RG 25, vol. 13895, File 37-9-3, LAC.
57 Pitfield to Gotlieb, 16 September 1980, RG 25, vol. 14767, File 37-9-3-1; Gotlieb to Pitfield, 30 September 1980, RG 25, vol. 13895, File 37-9-3, LAC.
58 Ibid.
59 MacGuigan, Unpublished Memoirs, GAC Historical Section, 162.
60 [Larry Smith], "Memorandum to File: North/South Briefing Session with the Prime Minister," 28 October 1980, RG 25, vol. 13895, File 37-9-3, LAC.
61 [Smith/P.D. Lee], Draft Memorandum for the Prime Minister, 4 November 1980, RG 25, vol. 13895, File 37-9-3, LAC.

62 Ibid.

63 Confidential source. See also, Gossage, *Close to the Charisma*, 202–24.

64 Confidential source.

65 Quoted in R.B. Byers, ed., *Canadian Annual Review for 1981* (Toronto: University of Toronto Press, 1984), 323.

66 Washington to Ottawa, tels 368, 369 and 381, 26 January 1981, RG 25, vol. 13895, File 37-9-3, LAC.

67 Minister's Office to General Economic Relations Division, 11 February 1981, RG 25, vol. 13895, File 37-9-3, LAC; On Haig, see also MacGuigan, *An Inside Look at External Affairs*.

68 Gotlieb, Memorandum for the Prime Minister, 2 March 1981, RG 25, vol. 15494, File 35-4-ESC-Ottawa-1981, LAC.

69 Gotlieb, Memorandum for the Prime Minister, 4 May 1981, RG 25, vol. 15494, File 35-4-ESC-Ottawa-1981, LAC.

70 Paynter to Gotlieb, ECR-665, 1 June 1981, RG 25, vol. 15494, File 35-4-ESC-Ottawa-1981, LAC.

71 Washington to Ottawa, tel SPS-382, 16 June 1981, RG 25, vol. 15495, File 35-4-ESC-Ottawa-1981, LAC.

72 Byers (ed.), *CAR for 1981*, 323.

73 Ottawa to All Missions, tel SPS-386, 23 July 1981, RG 25, vol. 15495, File 35-4-ESC-1981-Ottawa; on the international assessment, see Ottawa to Rabat (for PM), 4 August 1981, RG 25, vol. 14768, File 37-9-3-3, LAC.

74 Paris OECD to Ottawa, tel 3219, 25 September 1981 and Washington to Ottawa, tel 4971, 28 September 1981, RG 25, vol. 14767, File 37-9-3-1; Washington to Ottawa, tel 5010, 30 September 1981, RG 25, vol. 13897, File 37-9-8-1, LAC.

75 Ottawa to Melbourne (PM's Delegation/Smith), tel WWJ-47, 28 September 1981, RG 25, vol. 14767, File 37-9-3-1, LAC.

76 PM's Delegation/Melbourne to Ottawa (Jenkins), tel PMDL-20, 30 September 1981, RG 25, vol. 14678, File 37-9-3-1, LAC.

77 Ottawa to Delhi, tel LHS-50, 13 October 1981, RG 25, vol. 14768, File 37-9-3-1, LAC.

78 Ottawa to Washington, tel 1342, 27 October 1981, RG 25, vol. 14769, File 37-9-3-1, LAC.

79 Smith to Robert Johnstone, 29 January 1982, RG 25, vol. 15701, File 37-9-3, LAC.

80 MacGuigan, Memorandum for the Prime Minister, RG 25, vol. 15705, File 37-9-3-1, LAC.

81 Smith, Memorandum for the Minister, ECR-372, 12 March 1982, RG 25, vol. 14767, File 37-9-8-1, LAC.

82 de Montigny Marchand, Memorandum for the Prime Minister, 27 April
    1981 and Washington to Ottawa, tel 2997, 29 May 1982, RG 25,
    vol. 15496, File 35-4-ESC-Versailles-1982, LAC.

83 MacGuigan, Memorandum for the Prime Minister, 6 July 1981, RG 25,
    vol. 15702, File 37-9-3-1, LAC.

84 Ottawa to Washington (and other G-7 capitals), tel ECR- 902, 6 July 1982,
    RG 25, vol. 14767, File 37-9-8-1, LAC.

85 Trudeau to Julius Nyerere, 23 August 1982; MacEachen, Memorandum to
    the Prime Minister, 18 March 1983, and ECD/Morantz to PTE, 18 March
    1983, ECD-449, RG 25, vol. 13895, File 37-9-3, LAC.

86 See Greg Donaghy, "The 'Ghost of Peace': Pierre Trudeau's Search for
    Peace, 1982–84," *Peace Research: The Canadian Journal of Peace and
    Conflict Studies* 39, nos 1–2 (2007), 36–57.

8

Legacies and Realities

UN Peacekeeping and Canada, Past and Present

Kevin Spooner

Popular conceptions of peacekeeping are deeply entrenched in the Canadian national identity. Indeed, in this volume, Colin McCullough has examined the very process by which peacekeeping became embedded in Canada's national symbology. From McCullough's contribution, we can see that explaining the origins, nature, and significance of these conceptions is a complex project. With the images and idea of peacekeeping so pervasively deployed on and within national monuments, currency, stamps, *Heritage Minutes*, books, Stompin' Tom Connors songs, and even beer commercials, it is perhaps not surprising that peacekeeping became a nationalist signifier of what political scientists Pierre Martin and Michel Fortmann have recognized as a Canadian core value: internationalism.[1] Canadians have imagined themselves to be good, moral citizens of the international community, and there is evidence to suggest this image has resonated with views of the nation also held by non-Canadians. Peacekeeping has been found to be a durable explanation for this image.[2]

Yet, the contemporary popularity of peacekeeping conceals a reality that views about Canadian peacekeeping were not always so universally positive. By the 1970s, not even fifteen years after the Suez Crisis had resulted in the deployment of the first large-scale United Nations (UN) peacekeeping efforts, critics of Canadian peacekeeping were already expressing concern over this role played by the Canadian Armed Forces. Lt Col James H. Allan argued that given "the perennial problems and frustrations which Canadian peacekeepers have encountered ... a more critical approach to participation in peace-keeping ventures [is] something long overdue." Allan suggested the armed forces were being stretched too thin in attempting to meet all their operational duties and in what would become a common refrain, he concluded, "In 1978, the government has re-discovered NATO and, with emphasis in equipping, manning, and training going to NATO forces, peacekeeping emphasis is bound to decline."[3] Allan left little doubt that the government needed to approach peacekeeping with circumspection; reequipping for NATO service to fight the Cold War needed to be Canada's key priority. Similarly, historian J.L. Granatstein was convinced peacekeeping was little more than a passing fad. In a 1974 *Canadian Forum* article, pointedly titled "Canada and Peacekeeping: Image and Reality," Granatstein suggested, "Canadians now recognized that peacekeeping was just a dirty thankless job." "As an exportable and Canadian-designed commodity," he argued, "peacekeeping had gone off the market almost completely, barely fifteen years after its introduction."[4] Peacekeeping's critics were not entirely unjustified in delivering such pessimistic projections. In the 1970s, the decade long stalemate on Cyprus stood as a ready example of how peacekeeping might just freeze rather than resolve an international conflict, and the Egyptian government's dramatic and sudden expulsion of the United Nations Emergency Force (UNEF) from the Middle East highlighted further still the limitations of international peacekeeping.

History, however, would prove the critics wrong – at least with respect to the continuing peacekeeping role played by the armed forces. More than 120,000 Canadians ultimately served in more than fifty UN peacekeeping operations.[5] In fact, 122 Canadians have died while in service as UN peacekeepers – the sixth-highest figure of all peacekeeping nations and the highest of nations in the west.[6] For decades, Canada continued to contribute personnel to each and every peacekeeping mission created by the United Nations. Through the late 1980s and early 1990s, peacekeeping continued to be seen as important to Canadian defence and foreign policies. In 1987, Brian Mulroney's Progressive Conservative government issued a defence white paper that reasserted the importance of peacekeeping.[7] And, in this case, policy was backed up with practice. With the end of the Cold War, more attention could be focused on regional conflicts considered too dangerous or destabilizing to address. Peacekeepers were in demand, helping to oversee settlements to conflicts like the Iran/

Iraq war. Under Mulroney, more Canadian soldiers were serving abroad than at any time since the Korean War.

Fast-forward to today, and Canada no longer contributes significant numbers of personnel to UN peacekeeping. In October 2014, the *Toronto Star* published an article typical of media commentary highlighting this reversal. National Security reporter Michelle Shephard, in a story titled "How Canada Has Abandoned Its Role as Peacekeeper," presented a graph that illustrated the dramatic decline in Canadian personnel.[8] Using data readily available from the United Nations, the illustration demonstrating Canada's departure from UN peacekeeping would surprise no one who was at all familiar with Canada's actual peacekeeping record, though it may well have been shocking to some unsuspecting Canadians who had remained convinced the nation was actively engaged in UN efforts at global peacekeeping. A version of this graph, augmented with additional notations for the purposes of this chapter, can be seen at figure 8.1. Perhaps Granatstein and Allan were correct in their predictions of peacekeeping's demise after all; was it just the timeline of their 1970s projections that was off? It is worth closely parsing this graph to gain a fuller understanding of the story it reveals about just how Canadian UN peacekeeping virtually came to an end. In fact, we might be inspired by historian J.L. Granatstein's incredible gift for coming up with great titles, by suggesting the rest of this chapter is devoted to the question: "Who killed Canadian peacekeeping?"[9]

The golden age, or at least high-water mark, of Canadian peacekeeping comes at the beginning of the graph (see figure 8.1). From late 1990 to March 1992, the international community was adjusting to the implications of a post Cold War world. At this time, the Canadian commitment and contribution to UN peacekeeping was significant. In March 1992, just before a tremendous surge in UN peacekeeping that continues for the remainder of that year and into early 1993, Canada was first among the fifty-eight nations providing personnel to the ten UN missions operating at the time.[10] Almost all were first generation, relatively passive operations; for instance, nearly 80 per cent of Canadian peacekeepers were serving with UNFICYP in Cyprus and UNDOF in the Middle East.

Over the following year, there was a tremendous surge in UN peacekeeping. Large and complex missions to Cambodia, Yugoslavia, Somalia, and Mozambique resulted in an increase in peacekeepers from a little more than 14,000 to beyond 78,000 (see figure 8.2).

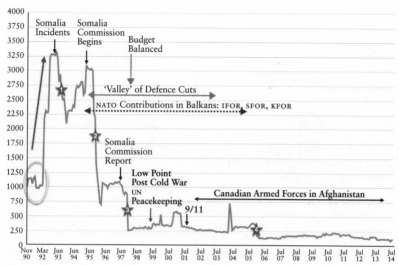

Figure 8.1 Canadian contribution to UN peacekeeping, 1990 to 2014

Canada's contribution kept pace and paralleled this rapid increase through to April 1993, when the number of Canadian peacekeepers serving with the UN reached an all time high of 3,336. At the time, Canada remained the third most important contributing nation to UN peacekeeping – even as the total number of nations now contributing to UN efforts to keep peace around the world had risen to seventy.[11]

Then, for the remainder of 1993, the first of four discernible and distinct periods of decline in Canadian peacekeeping occurs (see figure 8.1). In terms of contributions to specific operations, this decline is largely attributable to the almost complete withdrawal of Canadian peacekeepers from Cyprus and Cambodia, and a nearly 25 per cent reduction in the contribution to UNPROFOR in the Balkans. Notably, this period of decline does coincide with the transition in power from Prime Minister Brian Mulroney to his Progressive Conservative successor, Kim Campbell – and the subsequent transition again from Prime Minister Campbell to the new Liberal government under Prime Minister Jean Chrétien. Indeed, this decline may well be accounted for primarily by this instability in the federal government. That explanation appears all the more plausible when one considers that in the first six months of the new Liberal government, the number of Canadians serving as UN peacekeepers was again on the rise – though never quite reaching the April 1993 peak.[12]

Figure 8.2 Number of peacekeepers serving in United Nations operations, 1990 to 2014

The second and most precipitous period of decline occurs beginning August 1995 and continuing till March the following year (see
figure 8.1). Again, with reference to specific peacekeeping missions,
the decline is the result of the almost complete withdrawal of
Canadian peacekeepers serving with the UN in the Balkans and the
full withdrawal from Rwanda. By March 1996, the Canadian contribution to UNMIH in Haiti involved the largest contingent of personnel at 474, but even the number of peacekeepers here had been
declining. Overall, Canada was contributing to fewer missions than
it had in the previous period and the total number of peacekeepers
was well below the threshold of 1,000 seen at the end of the Cold
War. While this decrease is certainly dramatic, it also occurs within a
context of equally dramatic contraction in UN peacekeeping generally. In the same period, the overall number of UN peacekeepers fell
from nearly 70,000 to about 25,000 (see figure 8.2). So, in spite of
the sharp reductions in Canadian peacekeepers, Canada still ranked
sixth overall among nations contributing personnel to UN operations
(see figure 8.3).[13]

The third period of decline then occurred in November and
December 1997. With the end of the brief police training mission
(UNTMIH) in Haiti, the total number of Canadian personnel serving
with the UN fell to 254 (see figure 8.1). With the exception of brief
surges to provide personnel for UNTAET in East Timor, UNMEE in

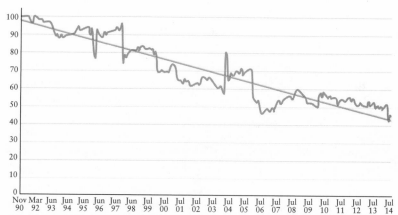

Figure 8.3 Relative rank of Canadian contributions to UN peacekeeping, compared to other contributing nations (as a %)

Ethiopia and Eritrea, and MINUSTAH in Haiti, the total number of Canadian peacekeepers serving the UN hovered between 250 and 500 for the remainder of the Liberal governments of Jean Chrétien and Paul Martin, through to 2006. Significantly, it is during this time that Canadian and UN trajectories of peacekeeping diverged. As Canada's contribution stagnated, the number of UN peacekeeping missions and personnel began once again to spiral upward in a trend that continues presently (see figure 8.2). As Prime Minister Martin prepared to leave office, Canada provided about 350 of the UN's 73,000 peacekeepers. The nation's relative rank in the list of contributing nations had fallen to 33rd (see figure 8.3).[14]

The fourth and final decline coincided with the arrival of the Conservative government under Prime Minister Stephen Harper (see figure 8.1). From February to March 2006, the number of Canadian peacekeepers fell from 352 to 169, as a consequence of the withdrawal of the Canadian contingent in UNDOF, the UN's mission in the Golan. Reflecting a trend that continues now, most of the Canadians who remained to serve the UN at this point were in fact police and not armed forces personnel. While a few dozen Canadian troops would continue to serve the UN, spread thinly across a number of peacekeeping missions, the Canadian armed forces had essentially ended any further significant contributions to the UN. Once again, this was reflected in Canada's overall rank as a contributor nation falling further to 49th (see figure 8.3).[15]

So, the end of Canadian peacekeeping with the UN was something of a process, drawn out over a decade, with four critical or key episodes of decline. But, if this explains and clarifies the timeline in finer detail, it still doesn't answer what is perhaps the more interesting (and difficult) question: who or what ultimately killed Canadian peacekeeping? Here, there are multiple suspects – and not necessarily the usual or likely suspects.

Given the Harper Conservative government's dismissive, even antagonistic approach towards the United Nations, one might expect that it would be a key suspect in the demise of Canadian peacekeeping. But, close attention to the timeline reveals that two of the key periods of decline fell clearly within the purview of Liberal governments and the other two happened at points of transition to or from Liberal governments. It is true that in each case there was typically something of a rebound in deployments that followed a period of decline – but each time a lower plateau was established and with each successive drop fewer and fewer Canadian personnel were left serving with the UN.

Often in scholarly literature and media reports, Canada's departure from UN peacekeeping is connected to the terrible events associated with the missions to Somalia – the murder of Somali teenager Shidane Arone in particular.[16] Interestingly, the first three periods of decline in peacekeeping do in fact fall respectively within months of the incidents in Somalia, the beginning of the Somalia Commission of Inquiry, and the release of that Commission's report (see figure 8.1).[17] To suggest, however, that the events in Somalia alone explain the overall decrease is too simplistic an explanation. There may be some degree of correlation, but this should not be seen as an exclusive factor.

Another explanation frequently offered for the decline is the significant cuts in defence spending undertaken during the Chrétien years, from 1993 to 2003 (see figure 8.4).[18] These cuts do begin just prior to the second period of decline and continue through and past the third period of decline, even as the federal budget was balanced just before the third decline occurred. Certainly, as resources became more limited, the capability of the armed forces to sustain all its defence activities, including UN peacekeeping, was compromised. Yet, it is important to recognize that other multilateral military activities involving the Canadian armed forces did continue throughout this period of fiscal restraint – just much less so under UN auspices.

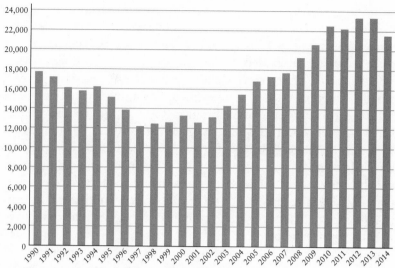

Figure 8.4 Defence expenditures in millions (2014$)

Budget cuts were a contributing factor to the demise of Canadian peacekeeping – but, again, not exclusively.

An important element of the explanation rests with the shift in Canada's multilateral military commitments from the UN to NATO – a process that is particularly evident from just before the second period of decline through to just before the fourth decline (see figure 8.1). At this time, Canada was actively contributing to NATO operations in the former Yugoslavia, with IFOR, SFOR, and KFOR.[19] Roughly 1,000 to 1,500 armed forces personnel were variously assigned to these operations.[20] Seen in the context of the defence cuts previously noted, contributions to NATO clearly came to be a competing and favoured military priority, relative to UN peacekeeping.

This shift from UN service to NATO missions also happens at a particular moment in time when the UN's inability to undertake and to manage effectively the newer, more complex *peacemaking* as opposed to *peacekeeping* operations was much in evidence. Critical attention centered on New York, and rightfully so given the disastrous failures of the international community in Somalia and Rwanda particularly. For UN Headquarters, the challenges posed by the Balkans also proved far too complex, not just politically but also operationally. Even the relatively successful efforts by the UN to assist with state building in Cambodia would later be scrutinized for the highly problematic and systemic social consequences that arose when peacekeepers engaged in corruption and gendered violence.[21] All these difficulties ultimately led to a period of introspection, perhaps best illustrated by Secretary-General Kofi Annan's decision to strike a panel to report on UN peacekeeping. For nearly five years before the August 2000 release of the Brahimi Report, the number of peacekeepers clearly declined while the organization attempted to grapple with the difficult lessons to be learned from the all too rapid surge of the early to mid-1990s (see figure 8.2).[22] Canada, it would appear, simply followed suit – though the Canadian armed forces were simultaneously being redeployed to NATO missions, a multilateral institution that seemed better able and equipped to deal with the challenges of robust peacemaking.

By the early 2000s, the UN began to reengage with international peacekeeping, in a more systematic and organized way. By then, however, potential Canadian contributions had already been redeployed to NATO led tasks. As the number of UN peacekeepers consistently increased practically every year, other nations became the key contributors of personnel. Arguably, this was a promising development. The appropriateness of White, western peacekeepers leading the efforts to restore or maintain peace in regions of the world where their cultural fluency sometimes proved sorely lacking was debatable.[23] In any case, Canada's relative rank as a peacekeeping contributor fell in a downward trajectory and never recovered (see figure 8.3). Another explanation for the demise of Canadian peacekeeping, then, clearly rests in the international context. The UN had significantly retreated from peacekeeping just at a time when a series of factors, particular to Canada, were also at play. The concurrence of this timing proved fatal.

The terrible events of 11 September 2001, and the subsequent "War on Terror," proved to be the *coup de grâce* for Canadian peacekeeping. Once again, it is worth noting that the Liberal governments of Jean Chrétien and Paul Martin made the initial commitments of Canadian forces to the war in Afghanistan – the earliest manifestation of the West's military commitment to combatting international terrorism abroad, after the 9/11 attacks. Then, however, the Conservative government of Prime Minister Stephen Harper enthusiastically rededicated the Canadian armed forces to service there once it gained power in 2006. Moreover, the Conservatives significantly increased defence spending over the following six years to equip and deploy the military for this mission (see figure 8.4).[24] The Harper government's unambiguous antipathy towards the UN all but ensured that the armed forces would continue in the trend, by then already well established, of service with NATO as the preferred multilateral instrument of the Canadian military.

In the end, we return to our earlier question: Who killed Canadian peacekeeping? The evidence suggests a complex explanation. There are multiple suspects that include more than one Canadian government and even a number of international events and trends that coincided at critical junctures to lessen and then virtually eliminate Canadian contributions to UN peacekeeping. Yet, the potency of Canadian peacekeeping mythology, the nationalistic sustenance of the image of Canada as international peacekeeper, has quite ironically managed to survive the more than two-decades-long death throes of Canadian peacekeeping. Image has yet to catch up with reality, which now might better be described as legacy. Perhaps the myth will be fundamentally challenged as Canadians digest and integrate more fully the experience of the Canadian Forces in Afghanistan into their collective, historical consciousness.

Given the potent criticism the myth has received in the past, much of it published even as Canadian peacekeeping with the UN was already substantively diminished if not dead,[25] the future will see renewed and vigorous debate over roles that might be played by the Canadian forces as they confront increased fiscal pressures while searching out and defining defence priorities in the years ahead.[26] With the defeat of the Conservatives in the 2015 federal election and the return to government of the Liberal Party, under the leadership of Prime Minister Justin Trudeau, the stage is set for a revived Canadian engagement with the United Nations. Within days of his victory, Trudeau issued a statement recognizing the need for "Canada to be an active and constructive member of the United Nations – not only for the help the UN provides to millions of people affected by conflicts and other humanitarian disasters, but also because it serves Canada's interests: a more peaceful world is a safer and more prosperous world for Canada, too."[27] While the record of previous Liberal governments offers no guarantee that a renewed commitment to the UN would include peacekeeping by the Canadian armed forces, subsequent discussions between prime minister Trudeau and

UN Secretary-General Ban Ki-moon addressed expanded collaboration between Canada and the UN, particularly in the field of peacekeeping operations.[28] At the same time, the Trudeau government decided to curtail Canada's contribution to the NATO bombing campaign against ISIS in the Middle East, fulfilling a key campaign promise made during the 2015 federal election. Only time will tell how this rebalancing between NATO and UN commitments will ultimately shape Canadian peacekeeping realities in future years.

NOTES

1 Pierre Martin and Michel Fortmann, "Public Opinion: Obstacle, Partner, or Scapegoat?," *Policy Options* 22, no. 1 (Jan/Feb 2001): 66–72.

2 A number of Canadian and international polls and studies have demonstrated global perceptions of Canadian foreign policy, some focusing particularly on the role of peacekeeping in shaping these perceptions. "16-Country Global Attitudes Report Released June 23, 2005: Canada," The Pew Global Attitudes Project; "The Canada's World Poll," Canada's World (January 2008), 13, 31; "Israel and Iran Share Most Negative Ratings in Global Poll," BBC World Service Poll, 2007; "World Likes Canada, China and Russia Last," Angus Reid Global Monitor, 15 June 2007; "World Sees Canada as Tolerant, Generous Nation," Angus Reid Global Monitor, 12 November 2006. As noted at the outset of Colin McCullough's chapter in this volume, more recent polls demonstrate the continuing resonance of the peacekeeping image also amongst Canadians.

3 Lt Col James. H. Allan, "The Future of Peacekeeping for Canada," *Canadian Defence Quarterly* 8, no.1 (Summer 1978): 30, 36.

4 J.L. Granatstein, "Canada and Peacekeeping: Image and Reality," reprinted in *Canadian Foreign Policy: Historical Readings*, rev. ed. (Toronto: Copp Clark Pitman Ltd., 1993), 285.

5 United Nations Association in Canada, "The Canadian Contribution to United Nations Peacekeeping," http://unac.org/wp-content/uploads/2013/07/CdnUNPkpgBooklet_e.pdf, accessed February 2016.

6 United Nations, "Fatalities by Nationality and Mission up to 31 January 2016," http://www.un.org/en/peacekeeping/fatalities/documents/stats_2.pdf, accessed February 2016. The five nations to have experienced a greater number of fatalities are India (161), Nigeria (146), Pakistan (137), Ghana (134), and Bangladesh (125).

7 National Defence, Canada, *Challenge and Commitment: A Defence Policy For Canada*, 1987, accessed at publications.gc.ca, February 2016.
8 Michelle Shephard, "How Canada Has Abandoned Its Role as Peacekeeper," *Toronto Star*, 31 October 2014.
9 For example, see J.L. Granatstein, *Who Killed Canadian History?* (Toronto: HarperCollins Publishers, 1998) and J.L. Granatstein, *Who Killed the Canadian Military?* (Toronto: HarperCollins Publishers, 2004). It's worth noting that the first chapter of the latter volume is entitled, "Fatal Distraction: Lester Pearson and the Unwarranted Primacy of Peacekeeping."
10 United Nations, "Troop and Police Contributors Archive, 1990–2014," http://www.un.org/en/peacekeeping/resources/statistics/contributors_archive.shtml, accessed February 2016.
11 Ibid.
12 Ibid.
13 Ibid.
14 Ibid.
15 Ibid.
16 Shephard, "How Canada Has Abandoned Its Role as Peacekeeper." This article, referred to at the outset of the chapter, is a typical example from media identifying Somalia as a factor in the Canadian decline in peacekeeping. Shephard suggests, "Canada's commitment had already started to drop dramatically in the late 1990s, in large part due to failures of UN missions in Rwanda and Bosnia and Canada's shameful role in Somalia that ended with the death of a Somali teenager."
17 Commission of Inquiry into the Deployment of Canadian Forces to Somalia, *Dishonoured Legacy: The Lessons of the Somalia Affair: Report of the Commission of Inquiry into the Deployment of Canadian Forces to Somalia*, 1997, http://publications.gc.ca/site/eng/9.646634/publication.html, accessed February 2016.
18 Department of Finance, Canada, *Fiscal Reference Tables*, October 2014, http://www.fin.gc.ca/frt-trf/2014/frt-trf-14-eng.asp, accessed February 2016. Historical figures adjusted to 2014 dollar values, using Bank of Canada Inflation Calculator, http://www.bankofcanada.ca/rates/related/inflation-calculator/, accessed February 2016.
19 IFOR: Implementation Force; SFOR: Stabilization Force; KFOR: Kosovo Force.
20 National Defence, Canada, *Operations Database*, http://www.cmp-cpm.forces.gc.ca/dhh-dhp/od-bdo/index-eng.asp, accessed February 2016.

21 See, for example, Olivera Simić, "Does the Presence of Women Really
    Matter? Towards Combating Male Sexual Violence in Peacekeeping
    Operations," *International Peacekeeping* 17, no. 2 (2010): 188–99; Sandra
    L. Whitworth, *Men, Militarism and UN Peacekeeping: A Gendered Analysis*
    (Boulder: Lynne Rienner Publishers, 2004); Sarah Martin, *Must Boys Be
    Boys? Ending Sexual Exploitation and Abuse in UN Peacekeeping Missions*,
    Refugees International, October 2005, http://www.childtrafficking.com/
    Docs/refugees_int_05_boys_0708.pdf, accessed February 2016.

22 United Nations, *Report of the Panel on United Nations Peace Operations*,
    2000, http://www.un.org/en/ga/search/view_doc.asp?symbol=A/55/305,
    accessed February 2016.

23 An important scholarly critique of Canadian peacekeeping for its racist
    orientation can be found in Sharene Razack, *Dark Threats and White
    Knights: The Somalia Affair, Peacekeeping, and the New Imperialism*
    (Toronto: University of Toronto Press, 2004).

24 Department of Finance, Canada, *Fiscal Reference Tables*. Historical figures
    adjusted to 2014 dollar values, using Bank of Canada Inflation Calculator.

25 Sean Maloney, "We're Not Peacekeepers," *Maclean's* 115, no. 42 (21
    October 2002): 51–2; Sean Maloney, "From Myth to Reality Check; From
    Peacekeeping to Stabilization," *Policy Options* (September 2005): 40–6;
    J.L. Granatstein, *Who Killed the Canadian Military* (Toronto:
    HarperCollins, 2004); J.L. Granatstein, *Whose War Is It? How Canada
    Can Survive in the Post-9/11 World* (Toronto: HarperCollins, 2007).

26 The parliamentary budget officer has recently raised questions as to the
    fiscal sustainability of the Canadian armed forces. Office of the
    Parliamentary Budget Officer, *Fiscal Sustainability of Canada's National
    Defence Program*, 26 March 2015, www.pbo-dpb.gc.ca/files/files/Defence_
    Analysis_EN.pdf, accessed February 2016.

27 "Statement by Prime Minister-designate Justin Trudeau on United
    Nations Day," 24 October 2015, https://www.liberal.ca/statement-by-
    prime-minister-designate-justin-trudeau-on-united-nations-day/, accessed
    February 2016.

28 "Prime Minister Justin Trudeau Meets with United Nations Secretary-
    General Ban Ki-moon," http://pm.gc.ca/eng/news/2016/02/11/prime-
    minister-justin-trudeau-meets-united-nations-secretary-general-ban-ki-
    moon, accessed February 2016.

The Importance of Civil Society to the Present and Future of the United Nations

Kathryn White

Would the world have a landmine agreement, an international criminal court, UN Women, without an active, engaged, disciplined, and organized civil society? Would the United Nations (UN) itself be investing in citizen-based outreach on the post-2015 development agenda; would the global community have heard about abuses of power, child soldiers, rape camps; would it be investigating the egregious child sex abuse by French peacekeepers or have framed the issue of climate change as a foundational threat if not for civil society?

Would Canada have pulled back from a former role as trusted broker in the Middle East, moved to a development focus on maternal, child, and newborn health while leaving out sexual and reproductive health, focused political attention and heft on early, child, and forced marriages but not on opportunities to see women as agents and actors in peace processes and in their own security if not for pressures from civil society? The role of civil society in the present and future of the UN is unique, essential, challenging, and here to stay. Civil society is also evolving in fleet, high-impact, and dynamic ways.

Civil society is recognized as encompassing more than a "sector." It includes an ever wider and more vibrant range of organized and unorganized groups, as new civil society actors blur the boundaries between sectors and experiment with new organizational forms both online and off. Roles are also changing: civil society actors are demonstrating their value as facilitators, conveners, and innovators as well as service providers and advocates. At the same time that globalization and technology have given rise to the strengthened civil society role, other actors' roles are also changing: the private sector is playing an increasingly visible role in the UN as nonstate actors on the development side – along with its more conventional role in the areas of trade treaties and business norms. It is understood in the opening litany of effects and impacts of civil society that the role of faith groups has always been a key, active and, often, well-funded part of this mix – key to development and service delivery and active on issues where it seeks to influence policy, in Canada, no less than in other countries. Since we are focused on Canada, we should point out that there are current challenges, too. The situation for civil society and the UN changed when the government of Stephen Harper altered traditional approaches toward development, global policy, and international engagements.

It seems to me that the most valuable example of a civil society with an impact on the UN that I can present is the United Nations Association in Canada. UNA-Canada (as we say in our global role, in order to differentiate us from UNA-China, UNA-Cuba, etc.) held its 69th Annual General Meeting, spring 2015. Let me tell you about an historic Canadian, nonpartisan charity with a mandate to educate and engage Canadians in the work of the United Nations and the global issues that impact us here in Canada. Our mandate, since our founding in early 1946, is to "grow global citizens." We do this both through a dedicated, passionate professional team based in Ottawa, with satellites in BC and Alberta, and through twenty imaginative, engaged, all-volunteer branches and contacts across the country.

By inspiring and elevating young scholars – from elementary school to postgrad – UNA-Canada works to change lives through our innovative programming. Our prestigious International Development & Diplomacy Internship Programme provides a bridge to employment for talented but un- or underemployed graduates through training and development, as well as six-month internship placements in vitally needed field agencies of the UN and international agencies. Sport-in-a-Box works with marginalized youth from ethno-cultural minorities and aboriginal communities to engage and showcase their strengths through the power of sport to forge positive diversity, healthy living, intergenerational learning, and peer-to-peer training – and fun. UNA-Canada is implementing Sport-in-a-Box during the Women's World Cup, with a singular focus on engaging aboriginal youth and their communities, supported by FIFA's Football for Hope, the government of Alberta, and private sector supporters.

With the support of the government of Canada, the Sport-in-a-Box program will also activate communities in seven cities outside of the GTA – especially among new Canadians from communities of the Pan American and Parapan American Games to bring the excitement and sustaining outcomes from the games around the social determinants of health more broadly to Canadians.

Our Model UNs are the foundation and launch of many an aspiring global citizen. UNA-Canada has stretched and reinvented this empathy-based global citizenship education to bridge communities – for example through a December 2015 Waterloo region high school Model UN, which will bring a delegation of young scholars from Toronto Community Housing to the Balsillie School of International Affairs – awakening, we know, the aspirations to inclusion and leadership. UNA-Canada has created The New Diplomacy of Natural Resources, a respectful conversation on natural resources engaging graduate students and new employees from aboriginal communities, environmental NGOs, various levels of government, and the energy and mining sectors to develop, through assuming the role of one of these sectors, resolutions on the forward development of our natural resources. UNA-Canada also created and hosted the first Model Arctic Council and a Model International Joint Commission, which we held to mark the 100th anniversary of the IJC.

Let me also describe how we are able to elevate these youth engagement strategies to the halls of decision-making. In collaboration with a number of national youth-serving agencies we organized a "Youth Day on the Hill" in May – an opportunity to speak across party lines about the need to engage youth and their issues in the upcoming election debates. It was a discussion of how to make it happen – the "what" will come from the youth themselves. And of course UNA-Canada leads and engages in creating made-at-home solutions to global challenges. We have hosted and briefed Secretary-General Ban Ki-moon, his officials, including heads of UN Agencies, both when they travel to Canada but also on an ongoing basis. We have brought Helen Clark, head of the UN Development Programme (UNDP), to government and civil society audiences in Ottawa and Calgary. Sha Zukung, then leading the Rio + 20 Conference, was the keynote speaker at a CANIMIN gathering in Edmonton, but he also met with Alberta government officials and toured the tar sands for a hands-on look at an environmental challenge.

At the same time, we also meet regularly, and often at their request, with elected leaders and government officials. We bring an all-party approach to engage house committees where helpful, including the Standing Committee on Foreign Affairs and International Development. As an organization, we very much value our access to ministers and their staff. At a different level, UNA-Canada will host a cross-country experts' forum on climate change in collaboration with the embassy of France – the hosts of the UN Conference of the Parties or COP 21 on climate change at the end of 2015. We will engage with city and provincial leaders, with the UN Secretary-General's special rapporteur on climate change, as well as his special rapporteur on cities and climate change, former NY mayor Michael Bloomberg, and with Ontario's lieutenant governor and her former agency, the UN Environment Programme (UNEP). While the UN is an organization whose key relationships are with sovereign states, they also have relationships with what they call subnational governments and what we call provinces and territories. This climate change series will allow us to elevate and showcase the leadership and action of subnational governments taking place at this level across Canada. This is UNA-Canada – civil society – seizing an opportunity to innovate and act, and to showcase innovation and action.

As we marked the seventieth anniversary of the UN in 2015, UNA-Canada engaged Canadians on the development of the new sustainable development goals. In the absence of leadership from the government of Canada to engage Canadians on the post-2015 development agenda, UNA-Canada invested in this engagement, including with our branches and with other civil society organizations. We also focused on the inclusion of youth voices in this consultation.

At the same time, we offered what positive encouragement we could to both large- and small-"g" governments to mobilize their exponentially larger muscle. Alas, what we had at the federal level, as citizens, was a month-long web survey posted long after meaningful exploration and input had occurred. Nevertheless, I believe that our work has had an impact.

In November of this year, UNA-Canada will host the World Federation of United Nations Associations (WFUNA) plenary assembly in Vancouver – showcasing the global reach and strength of critical but hopeful multilateralists in civil society in both the global south and north. In my role as chair of WFUNA, representing 115 UNAs globally, we frame ourselves as the "peoples' movement of the

UN." Together we aspire to keep the United Nations as the unique organization of enduring relevance in peoples' day-to-day lives and to urge Canada to bring the leadership we can and must show at the United Nations, living up to the expectations and hopes of all.

UNA-Canada is one of many civil society organizations – both Canadian and from all corners of the globe – that have ongoing connections with the UN system and interact in various ways to contribute to essential dialogues on the issues affecting our lives and our world. Collectively we add real value. At its best, civil society is the glue that binds public and private activity in such a way as to strengthen the common good. It represents service. In playing this role, civil society actors need to ensure they retain their core missions, integrity, purposefulness, and high levels of trust. The world will always need independent organizations to act as watchdogs, ethical guardians, and advocates of the marginalized or under-represented. Civil society, in all its forms, has an important role to play in holding all stakeholders, including itself, to the highest levels of accountability. In the interests of framing the stewardship belief and commitment at the core of civil society – and as we celebrate the UN at 70 – I share this quote from Rabindranath Tagore, a Nobel Literature laureate. He wrote: "I slept and dreamed that life was joy. I awoke and saw that life was service. I acted and behold, service was joy."

Contributors

LLOYD AXWORTHY is a former minister of foreign affairs and is currently the chair of CUSO and chancellor of St Paul's University College.

TARAH BROOKFIELD is an associate professor in the Departments of History, and Youth and Children's Studies, Wilfrid Laurier Brantford.

GREG DONAGHY is head of the Historical Section in Global Affairs Canada (GAC) and an adjunct professor at St Jerome's University.

SUZANNE LANGLOIS is an associate professor in the Department of History at Glendon College, York University.

DAVID MACKENZIE is a professor in the Department of History at Ryerson University.

COLIN MCCULLOUGH is an adjunct professor in the Departments of History at McMaster University and at Ryerson University.

KIM RICHARD NOSSAL is a professor at the Centre for International and Defence Policy at Queen's University.

KEVIN SPOONER is an associate professor in the Department of North American Studies, Wilfrid Laurier University.

ROBERT TEIGROB is a professor in the Department of History at Ryerson University.

DAVID WEBSTER is an associate professor in the Department of History at Bishop's University.

KATHRYN WHITE is the president of the United Nations Association of Canada.

Index

Our Canada: A Social and Political History (textbook), 154
Out of the Ruins (1945), 57, 62, 73, 80n83
Owen, David, 86
Owen, Robert, 88

pacifism, Canada, 28–9, 32, 149–51
Palestine, 4, 110, 121
Pan American Child Institute, 21
Pan American Institute of Geography and History, 21
Pan American League of Canada, 35
Pan American/Parapan American Games, 223
Pan American Sanitary Conference, 35
Pan American Security Bureau, 20–1
Pan American Union (PAU), 20, 31–3; American concerns of British influence over, 33, 36; American opposition to Canadian membership in, 36; Canadian participation in, 21–2, 32–6; French Canadian support for, 34
Paris Peace Conference (1919), 24, 26–7
Pathé, 57
peacekeeping, Canada, xiii, 137, 142–5, 152, 184; and Africa, 212–13, 219n16; and the Balkans, 7, 53, 67, 86, 92, 110, 137, 151, 210–12, 215, 219n16; and Blue Berets, 137; Canadian casualties during, 209; and Canadian national identity, xi, 6, 8, 14–15, 138–41, 145–7, 152,

156, 208, 216; Canadian public and, 12, 13, 142, 148–51, 218n2; and Cold War, 209–12; criticism of, 208–9; disengagement from, 13–14, 210; during Chrétien government, 170, 211, 213; during Diefenbaker government, 142, 145; during Harper government, 13–14, 210, 213–14; during Martin government, 13, 213; during Mulroney government, 152, 211; during Pearson government, 144–5; during Pierre Trudeau government, 9, 12–13; and education, 138, 152–5, 160n61; and English Canada, 138, 141, 152–3; and French Canada, 139–40, 149; and Haiti, 212–13; and Middle East, 209, 221; post–Cold War, 9, 209–17; and Rwanda, 212; and Somalia, 137, 151, 156, 210, 211, 214–15, 219n16; support for permanent peacekeeping force, 11, 118, 121, 141, 143–4, 149–50, 166–7, 176; and teachers, 147
peacekeeping, United Nations, xiii; 11, 121–2, 149
peacekeeping operations, UN (PKOS), xiv
Pearson, Lester B., xi, xiii, 12, 142–4, 166, 174, 179n35; address to UN General Assembly, 166–7; antinuclear position of, 143; and call for international peacekeeping force, 11, 121–2, 143, 166–7, 176; and Canada's commitment to UN, 130, 143–4; and Canada's role in UN, xi, 167, 176; elected chairman of UNRRA (1944), 54;

and foreign policy, 148; and
General Assembly, 163; and
Korean War, 115; and Nobel
Peace Prize, 143, 152, 153–4;
and nuclear weapons, 168; and
peacekeeping, 11, 121–2, 145,
151, 154–5, 166–7; and Security
Council reform, 167; and Suez
Crisis, 118, 121–2, 142–3, 153–
4, 208; and UNA-Canada, 115;
and UNICEF, 130
Pearson government, 163, 166
Pelletier, Gérard, 201
People's Republic of China. *See*
China
Pérez Guerrero, Manuel, 188, 191–2
Permanent Joint Board on Defence,
24, 35
Peru, 35
Peterson, Oscar, 153
Petro-Canada's Third World
Program, 196
Pickersgill, Jack, 94–5
Pickford, Mary, 108
Pitfield, Michael, 185–6, 193, 196
Portillo, Lopez, 195, 201
power politics. See *Realpolitick/*
realism
Prebisch, Raul, 89
*Productions of the National Film
Board of Canada from 1939 to
1989, The,* 70
Progressive Conservatives, 141,
163–5, 173, 211; and commit-
ment to UN, 163–5, 209, 211
public opinion, Canada: interna-
tional affairs, 13, 36, 148–51,
175; opposition to overseas
intervention, 13, 36; Pan

American Union, 34, 36; peacekeeping, 11, 148; UNRRA, 45

Queen's University, 147
Quiet Revolution, 140

Rashish, Meyer, 198–9
Read, Nicholas, 56, 62, 67, 72, 73
Reagan, Ronald, 152, 169,
198–202
Realpolitik/realism, 13–14, 161,
165
Red Cross, 19, 128
Rees, Louise, 74n11
refugees, 14–15, 56, 63, 122; and
Cold War, 122; post–Second
World War, 51–4, 66, 78n60,
107, 109–13, 133n33; UN and,
117, 120
Reinisch, Jessica, 74–5n11
Riddell, W.A., 164
Riddoch, Sonia, 154
Riefenstahl, Leni, 48
Robinson, H. Basil, 166, 178n18
Roosevelt, Eleanor, 115
Roosevelt, Franklin Delano, 66,
115; Four Freedoms Speech, 54
Roosevelt, Theodore, 162, 171,
177n5
Root, Elihu, 21
Rotary Clubs, 28
Roy, Jacques, 194
Royal Canadian Air Force, 3
Royal Canadian Mounted Police
(RCMP), 150
Russia, 4, 165

Saigon Foster Parents Plan
International (FPPI), 111–12

terrorism, xiii, 15, 40, 216
Thant, U, 104, 179n32
Thatcher, Margaret, 169, 199–200
Toronto Peace Center, 149
Toronto Star, 210
Torson, Patricia J., 47, 53, 55,
    74n7
Trade Union Circuits, 56
Treaty of Versailles, 24, 26
Triumph of the Will, 57
Trudeau, Justin, xii, 15, 217–8
Trudeau, Pierre Elliott, 9, 179n32,
    179n35, 192; and Brandt
    Report, 195; and Cancun
    Summit, 195–6, 198–202; and
    criticism of Pearson, 179n35;
    and General Assembly, 163,
    167–8, 170, 179n32, 185; and
    Global Negotiations, 197–202;
    and national unity, 39; and New
    International Economic Order,
    12–13, 183, 185–6; and North-
    South relations, 13, 184, 190–1,
    194–202; and nuclear weapons,
    167–9, 176; and peacekeeping,
    9, 150–1, 154, 167; respect for
    Reagan, 202; and social justice,
    185; and UN membership, 39
Trudeau government (1968–79,
    1980–84), 13, 188–90, 196
Truman, Harry S1, 83–4

Ukraine, 4, 67, 81n105, 165, 166,
    178n18
UN Assembly of Environmental
    Governance, xii
UN at 70: A Canadian Perspective
    (conference), 6
UN Charter, 10, 118, 163–4

UN Conference on Trade and
    Development (UNCTAD), 89,
    183, 188–9, 194
UN Convention on the Prevention
    and Punishment of the Crime of
    Genocide, 118
UN Declaration on the Rights of
    the Child, 122
UN High Commission on Refugees,
    120
United Artists, 62
United Church Examiner, 143, 149
United Nations (UN), 20, 121; and
    anticommunism, 87, 93; and
    arms control, 165; as "bully pul-
    pit," 12; and Cambodia, 215–16;
    Canadian criticism of, xi, 4–5, 7,
    12, 174, 208; Canadian influence
    in, 7, 40; Canadian support for,
    6, 104–7, 119; as check on US
    dominance, 6, 18, 38; and decol-
    onization, 83, 167; and
    Economic Council, 71; and eco-
    nomic development assistance,
    83, 88–9, 183; environmental
    policies of, xii, 6, 40; funding cri-
    sis of, 122; and global migration,
    xiii; and imperialism, 6; and
    international development goals,
    xii, 87; and ISIS, 218; and mem-
    ber states' national interests, 12;
    and natural disasters, xii; non-
    governmental organizations and,
    9; and official development assis-
    tance (ODA), 183, 188, 191,
    195–6, 198; paternalism of, 3,
    11, 216; and poverty, xii, 6,
    83–4, 88; and racism, 6; and
    Secretary General elections, xii;